Albert Roulier

The second book of French composition

Materials for translating English into French for advanced classes

Albert Roulier

The second book of French composition
Materials for translating English into French for advanced classes

ISBN/EAN: 9783337185442

Printed in Europe, USA, Canada, Australia, Japan

Cover: Foto ©Paul-Georg Meister /pixelio.de

More available books at **www.hansebooks.com**

THE SECOND BOOK

OF

FRENCH COMPOSITION.

THE SECOND BOOK

OF

FRENCH COMPOSITION

MATERIALS FOR TRANSLATING ENGLISH INTO FRENCH

FOR ADVANCED CLASSES.

BY

A. ROULIER,
Fellow Univ. Gallic.

FRENCH MASTER AT CHARTERHOUSE, PROFESSOR OF THE FRENCH
LANGUAGE AND LITERATURE AT BEDFORD COLLEGE, LONDON, AND
ASSISTANT-EXAMINER IN THE UNIVERSITY OF LONDON.

LIBRAIRIE HACHETTE & CIE.

LONDON: 18, KING WILLIAM STREET, CHARING CROSS.

PARIS: 79, BOULEVARD ST. GERMAIN.

1881.

TO

MARK PATTISON, B.D.

Rector of Lincoln College, Oxford,

Visitor of Bedford College,

THIS VOLUME

Is respectfully inscribed

BY THE AUTHOR.

PREFACE.

This volume is a *sequel* to my First Book of French Composition; it is based on the same principle, and the same plan has been pretty nearly followed throughout. Like the first, it is divided into two parts, one of them with, the other without Rules. The Rules have been arranged in Chapters, in order to make references to them more easy, and are followed by appropriate exercises of Translation. The book *is not itself a grammar*, but has, on the contrary, been made *so as to be used as a companion to any French grammar*. At the end of each principal division will be found exercises of recapitulation.

In the second part, the exercises at the beginning are intended to serve for a general revision of the Rules and difficulties contained in the first portion of the book, and have copious Notes and References added to them; but gradually the pupil is brought to pieces entirely without Notes. The latter pieces have themselves been graduated so as to become more and more difficult towards the end of the volume.

At the beginning of this volume has been added a Synopsis of the Rules contained in my first book, for those who have not used it, or who, having used it, want to refer to some of its Rules.

I hope this book will be found of great service, particularly to *such as prepare themselves for public examinations*. Papers set at such examinations have been inserted at the end, in order to enable the student to test his powers of translation.

The encouragements I have received since the appearance of the first volume have induced me to spare no trouble in order to make the present volume as complete as possible. Any hints or criticisms will be gratefully received.

I take this opportunity to thank Mr. H. E. HALL, M.A., for the kind assistance he has rendered me by perusing this volume, and the useful suggestions he has given to me.

CONTENTS.

	PAGE
SYNOPSIS OF RULES CONTAINED IN THE FIRST VOLUME	1

FIRST PART.

ARTICLE	8
SUBSTANTIVE	23
ADJECTIVE	26
PERSONAL PRONOUNS	31
RELATIVE PRONOUNS	38
DEMONSTRATIVE PRONOUNS	61
INDEFINITE PRONOUNS	70
VERB	75
,, PASSIVE VOICE	78
,, TENSES	86
,, MOODS	106
,, INFINITIVE AND PARTICIPLES	129
AUXILIARIES AND OTHER VERBS	142
INVARIABLE WORDS	174
ELLIPSIS AND EMPHASIS	209

SECOND PART.
RECAPITULATORY PIECES AND EXAMINATION PAPERS.

	PAGE
I.—OF TRANSLATION	221
II.—	222
III.—DEATH OF HENRY VIII.	223
IV.—THE GOAT, THE LION, AND THE FOX.	224
V.—BUFFON'S SON	225
VI.—THE BEAR	226
VII.—THE TWO RIVULETS	226
VIII.—THE COMPARISON OF WATCHES.	227
IX.—LITTLE EPPIE'S MISCHIEF	228
X.—LITTLE EPPIE'S MISCHIEF (*continued*)	229
XI.—FROM THE "LETTER TO THE EARL OF CHESTERFIELD".	231
XII.—INTERVIEW WITH A MALAY	232
XIII.—THE SHEPHERD'S DOG	233
XIV.—INGRATITUDE.	234
XV.—FIGHTING AT SCHOOL	235
XVI.—FRANCE.	235
XVII.—WILLIAM PITT, THE YOUNGER.	236
XVIII.—NICHOLAS NICKLEBY AND SMIKE	237
XIX.—HAMLET'S SOLILOQUY ON LIFE AND DEATH	239
XX.—FROM "THE SCHOOL FOR SCANDAL"	240
XXI.—FROM "THE SCHOOL FOR SCANDAL" (*cont.*)	241
XXII.—THE BOY AND THE CAKE.	242
XXIII.—THE IMPOSTOR AND THE MANDARIN.	243
XXIV.—FRENCH, ENGLISH, AND GERMAN	244

CONTENTS.

	PAGE
XXV.—THE LOVE OF OUR COUNTRY	244
XXVI.—THE DEAD WARRIOR	245
XXVII.—THE PEDLAR AND THE MONKEYS	246
XXVIII.—A CLEVER TERRIER	246
XXIX.—DEATH OF CHARLES II.	247
XXX.—HOME FOR THE HOLIDAYS	248
XXXI.—DRYDEN AND POPE	249
XXXII.—FROM "ALEXANDER'S FEAST"	250
XXXIII.—THE BATTLE OF IVRY	251
XXXIV.—MADAME DE SÉVIGNÉ TO MR. DE POMPONE	252
XXXV.—FROM ANTONY'S ORATION	252
XXXVI.—GULLIVER AND THE DWARF	253
XXXVII.—THE HARE AND THE TORTOISE	254
XXXVIII.—THE SHIPWRECK	255
XXXIX.—THE VICAR OF WAKEFIELD AND HIS WIFE	256
XL.—OF FRIENDSHIP	257
XLI.—ROBINSON CRUSOE'S FIRST ALARM	257
XLII.—PLEASURES OF A WINTER EVENING	258
XLIII.—DIRGE AT SEA (UNIVERSITY OF LONDON)	259
XLIV.— do.	260
XLV.—NIAGARA IN WINTER do.	261
XLVI.—CHARLES DICKENS'S READINGS do.	262
XLVII.—SELF-MADE MEN do.	263
XLVIII.—JAMES WATT do.	264
XLIX.—THE RAGGED SCHOOLS do.	265
L.—WHAT A BOOK REALLY IS do.	266
LI.—THE GLADIATOR'S DEATH do.	267
LII.—(THE ROYAL MILITARY COLLEGE, 1877)	268
LIII.—(THE ROYAL MILITARY ACADEMY AND COLLEGE 1879)	269

CONTENTS.

	PAGE
LIV.—(THE ROYAL MILITARY ACADEMY AND COLLEGE, 1879)	270
LV.—(THE ROYAL MILITARY COLLEGE, 1880)	270
LVI.—(CIVIL SERVICE OF INDIA, 1879)	271
LVII.—(do. do. 1879)	272
LVIII.—LAST YEARS OF GEORGE III. (STUDENT INTERPRETER AT CONSTANTINOPLE)	273
LIX.—(HOME CIVIL SERVICE, 1879)	274
LX.—(do. do. 1879)	274
LXI.—A WINTER EVENING IN THE COUNTRY (AGRÉGATION DE LA LANGUE ANGLAISE)	275
LXII.—ELEGY TO THE MEMORY OF AN UNFORTUNATE LADY (AGRÉGATION DE LA LANGUE ANGLAISE)	277

ROULIER'S

SECOND BOOK OF FRENCH COMPOSITION.

SYNOPSIS OF RULES

CONTAINED IN THE FIRST VOLUME.

I.—When a noun is used in a general sense, **the** is required in French.

Ex.—Iron is a metal, le fer est un métal.

II.—**The** should be put in French before the names of *countries*, except when they are preceded by **in**, *en*, or **from**, *de*, and when they are used adjectively.

Ex.—France is a large country, la France est un grand pays.
He is *in* France, il est **en** France.
This silk comes *from* France, cette soie vient **de** France.
The Queen of England, *i.e.* the English Queen, la Reine *d*'Angleterre.

III.—When a noun is used in a *partitive sense*, that is to say, when it expresses only a part, a certain quantity of the thing which it represents, the partitive article **some**, *du, de la, de l', des*, often understood in English, should be expressed in French. If there are several nouns, put it before each.

Ex.—Bring me turnips and potatoes, *i.e. some* turnips and *some* potatoes, apportez-moi **des** navets et **des** pommes de terre.

IV.—**Any**, coming *immediately* before a noun, is also rendered by **du, de la, de l', des**.

Ex.—Have you *any* horses? Avez-vous **des** chevaux?

V.—When the noun used in a partitive sense is preceded by an adjective in French, **de** is put for **some** or **any** instead of *du, de la, de l', des*. If there are several nouns, it should be repeated before each of them.

Ex.—Have you *any* good horses? Avez-vous **de** bons chevaux?

VI.—**Any** is **de** when the verb preceding it is negative.

No before a noun is to be translated like *not any*; if repeated, it is **ni...ni**, with *ne* before the verb.

Ex.—I have *no* butter or *not any* butter, je n'ai pas **de** beurre.

VII.—The preposition **de**, the **articles**, the **possessive** and **demonstrative adjectives** should be repeated in French before *each* noun.

VIII.—The articles **a** or **the**, though used in English, must be *omitted* in French before a noun in apposition, *i.e.* placed immediately after a noun and qualifying it, explaining what that other noun is.

Ex.—London, *the* capital of England, Londres, capitale de l'Angleterre.

IX.—**A** is also omitted in French before a noun expressing a *title, trade,* or *nationality* preceded by *to be*, unless the pronoun "ce" is prefixed to that verb, or the noun is attended by an adjective or some explanatory expression.

Ex.—His father is **an** Englishman, son père est anglais.
 It is **an** Englishman, c'est *un* Anglais.
 Shakspeare was **a** great poet, Shakspeare était *un grand poëte.*
 Corneille is **a** writer of the seventeenth century, Corneille est *un* poëte du dix-septième siècle.

X.—There is **no possessive case** in French; so, instead of saying, " Your brother's book," say, " The book of your brother."

XI.—The names of the **days, months, seasons, metals, colours** are *masculine* in French; those of **countries** are *feminine* when they end in *e* mute, and *masculine* when they do not.

XII.—In French, the adjective is generally placed *after* the noun it qualifies. Adjectives of **colour, nationality, shape, temperature**, as well as **past participles**, *always* come *after* the noun.

However, the following come *before* the noun : **beau, joli, bon, meilleur, gros, grand, haut, petit, jeune, vieux, long, sot.**

XIII.—In French, with the names of **sovereigns**, the numerals II., III., IV., etc., are used instead of the ordinal numbers 2nd, 3rd, 4th, etc. **Premier**, *the first*, is the only exception.

The same rule applies to **dates, chapters, paragraphs**, etc.

In dates, **le** is required before the numeral, which must always come *before* the name of the month. **On** and **of** should be omitted.

Ex.—*On* the first or the second *of* June, le premier ou le deux juin.

XIV.—Personal pronouns governed by a verb must be placed in French *immediately* before the verb, or the auxiliary, if the verb is in a compound tense. They are then called **conjunctive personal pronouns**. (See for exceptions Rules XV. and XVI.).

If there are several verbs, the pronoun should be repeated before each of them; however, if the verbs are in compound tenses, the pronoun may either be repeated, or not; only, if repeated, the auxiliary should be repeated also.

Ex.—They have caught and killed it: $\begin{cases} \text{Ils l'ont pris et tué,} \\ \quad \text{or} \\ \text{Ils l'ont pris et l'ont tué.} \end{cases}$

Rem.—The student should always see carefully if **him** is put for *to him*, **her** for *to her*, **them** for *to them*, **it** for *to it*, or not, and translate these pronouns accordingly.

XV.—When the verb is in the *imperative affirmative*, *i.e.* used without a negative, the pronouns must be placed *after* the verb; **moi** and **toi** are then used instead of *me* and *te*, and joined to the verb by a hyphen.

But if the imperative is *negative*, the pronouns must be placed *before* the verb, and **me** and **te** used.

XVI.—Personal pronouns, preceded by any other preposition but "to," must be placed *after* the verb. They are then called "disjunctive personal pronouns."

XVII.—The disjunctive form of the pronouns is also used:

1. When the pronoun, either subject or object, is *disjoined* from the verb.

Ex.—He alone was there, **lui** seul était là.

2. When there are several subjects or objects.

Ex.—Your brother and *I* wrote yesterday *to him* and *to her,* votre frère et **moi** avons (*or* **nous** avons) écrit hier à **lui** et à **elle.**

3. After " c'est, ce sont," or a reflexive verb.

Ex.—It is *I*, c'est **moi**. It is *they*, ce sont **eux.**
You must not trust him, il ne faut pas vous fier à **lui.**

4. When the verb is understood.

Ex.—Who is there? *I.* Qui est là? **Moi.**

5. For the sake of emphasis or contrast, and then, when a subject, it is generally followed by the conjunctive form of the pronoun employed, thus:

Ex.—*I* am English, but *he* is French; **moi, je** suis Anglais, mais
lui, **il** est Français.
Are you speaking to *me?* Est-ce à **moi** que vous parlez?

XVIII.—When we quote our own or some other person's words, the subject in such expressions as "I said, he replied," etc., is generally placed after the verb.

Ex.—"Good morning," *he said.* "Bonjour," **dit-il.**

XIX.—**That**, either a relative pronoun or a conjunction, **whom**, and **which**, are often understood in English, but must *always* be *expressed* in French.

Ex.—I hope you are well, j'espère **que** vous allez bien.

XX.—The **past participle** conjugated with **être**, *to be*, agrees in gender and number with the subject of "être."

If there is neither "être, to be," nor "avoir, to have," before the past participle, it is a mere adjective, and agrees in gender and number with the noun it qualifies. It is *always* put *after* the noun.

XXI.—After **combien**, *how much, how many*, either the noun or the verb may come first. In either case **de** must precede the noun.

XXII.—**En** is used for *in* in *dates*, or before a *noun* which is *not determined*; but before a noun which is determined, *i.e.* preceded by an article, or a possessive adjective, or a demonstrative adjective, **dans** should be used.

Reciprocally, if you know that *en* is to be used, do not put an article before the noun.

In after a superlative is **de**.

XXIII.—**In** or **to** must be translated by **en** before names of *countries*. **In, to**, or **at** are to be translated by **à** before names of *towns*.

XXIV.—**To**, placed before an infinitive, and meaning *in order to*, is to be rendered by **pour**.

XXV.—In French, a **preposition** cannot be the last word of a sentence ; it must be placed *before* the word which it governs. If there is no word, either expressed or understood, before which to put the preposition, it is generally left out.

XXVI.—In sentences referring to **weather**, *it is* must be rendered by **il fait**.

But if the sentence begins with " the weather," as in " **the weather** is cold," *is* must be translated by **est**.

FIRST PART.

ARTICLE.

(*See* Synopsis, Rule I. to X.)

RULE I.

The article **le, la, les** must appear in French before adjectives and nouns of **title, dignity, profession**, etc., preceding proper names.

Ex.—**Queen** Victoria, **La** reine Victoria.
Old Gregory, **Le** vieux Grégoire.

But the article is *omitted:*

1. Before **Lord** and **Sir**, these words being the same in French.

2. When the noun of title, dignity, etc., comes *after* the proper name, or is preceded by a passive or intransitive verb, as *was made, was created, became,* etc.

Translate.

I.—1. At the battle of Poitiers, King John made the utmost efforts **to** retrieve by his valour **what** his imprudence had **betrayed**; but at last spent **with** fatigue, and overwhelmed **with numbers, he** and his sons yielded themselves prisoners. 2. Young Edward received the captive king with all the marks **of** regard and sympathy, and paid **him** the tribute of praise due to his valour.— (*The Student's Hume.*)

NOTES.

1. To (*see* Invariable words, Rule XXXI.); what (*see* Pron., Rule XXIV.); betrayed, *compromis*; with (*see* Invariable words, Rule II.); numbers, put "the number;" he (*see* Synopsis, Rule XVII.)

2. Of (*see* Synopsis, Rule VII.); him (*see* Synopsis, Rule XIV., *Rem.*)

II.—1. Lord Palmerston became Premier **on** February 8, 1855, and popular enthusiasm demanded the vigorous prosecution of the Crimean war. 2. The Anglo-French alliance **was joined by** Victor-Emmanuel II., King **of Sardinia**, who was afterwards created King **of Italy**. 3. The Sardinians, under General La Marmora, bore the chief part **in** the victory of the Tchernaya (August 16, 1855). 4. A successful assault was made upon the southern defences on the 8th of September; and on the following night, Prince Gortschakoff withdrew in good order to the north side of the harbour, and the allies **entered** the city of Sebastopol. ... 5. The operations of the Black Sea fleet, commanded by Sir David Douglas Dundas, and the naval campaigns of 1854 and 1855 in the Baltic, under Admirals Napier and Richard Saunders Dundas, showed that British seamen **were** the same as **ever.**—(Dr. Smith's *Smaller History of England.*)

NOTES.

1. On (*see* Synopsis, Rule XIII.)
2. Was joined by, *à l'alliance Anglo-Française se joignit;* of Sardinia, of Italy (*see* Synopsis, Rule II.)
3. In (*see* Synopsis, Rule XXII.)
4. To enter, *entrer* **dans.**
5. Were (imperf.); ever, *autrefois.*

RULE II.

The definite article **le, la, les** often appears in French before a **part of the body** or a **faculty**

of the mind, preceded by *to have,* and *not followed* by a relative pronoun.

Ex.—The hare has **a** short and bushy tail, parted and very hairy lips.
Le lièvre a **la** queue courte et touffue, **les** lèvres fendues et très poilues.

Johnson had **a** quick wit, and **a** ready answer.
Johnson avait **l'**esprit vif et **la** repartie prompte.

Rem.—When the verb **to be** is joined to such nouns, the sentence generally admits of two translations.

Ex.—The face of Charles **was** regular and handsome, his body strong and healthy.
Les traits de Charles **étaient** réguliers et beaux, son corps robuste et sain; *or,*
Charles **avait** les traits réguliers et beaux, le corps robuste et sain.

Translate.

I.—1. The white, or Circassian race has a white skin, oval face, arched nose, high forehead, and teeth **in** the upper jaw perpendicular to **the lower.** 2. The tawny, or **Malay** race has for the most part brown skin; hair black and thick, and disposed to curl. 3. The yellow, or Mongolian race has the skin of an olive brown; long, coarse, thin hair; face flat and depressed, and the features running into each other. 4. The copper coloured, or Indian race **a good deal** resembles the Mongolian variety, but it has the skin of a **deeper brown,** with a red tinge, and the features more distinctly marked; the forehead is also very low and receding.

NOTES.

1. In, *de*; the lower, put "to those in the lower jaw."
2. Malay, *Malaise.*
4. A good deal (*see* Invar. words, Rule I.); deep brown, *brun foncé.*

II.—1. "Byron," says Macaulay, "**had** naturally a generous and feeling heart, but his temper **was** wayward and irritable. 2. He had a head which statuaries loved **to** copy, and a foot **the deformity of which** the beggars in the street mimicked."

NOTES.

1. Had, was (*see* Verb, Rule X.)
2. To, *à*; the deformity of which (*see* Pron., Rule XVIII. and *Rem.*)

RULE III.

The **possessive adjective**, used in English before a part of the body, is translated by **le, la, les,** when the sense clearly shows the possessor.

Ex.—He opened **his** mouth.

As it is obvious that he did not open any other mouth but his own, the definite article should be employed.

Il ouvrit **la** bouche.

Should there exist the least doubt about the possessor, add **me, te, se, lui, nous, vous, leur,** before the verb.

Ex.—You hurt **my** arm.

If we were simply to replace " my " by " the," and say,

Vous faites mal *au* bras,

it would not be evident whose arm is hurt; a personal pronoun must then be added before the verb, clearly to show the possessor. The sentence will thus literally become :

You hurt *the* arm *to me*;
Vous **me** faites mal **au** bras.
He has broken **his** (own) arm ;
Il **s'est** cassé **le** bras.

Rem.—Observe the use of the reflexive verb, when the action is done by the subject upon himself.

RULE IV.

The **possessive adjective** is, however, retained, when the part of the body is preceded by an adjective.

Ex.—"He cut his beard," is, " Il *se* coupa *la* barbe ; " but, "he cut **his long** beard," will be, " Il coupa **sa longue** barbe."

Translate.

I.—1. **Men** are drowned **by** raising their arms above water. 2. When a man falls into **deep water** he **will rise** to the surface, and will remain there if he does not elevate his hands. 3. If he moves his hands under water in any manner he pleases, his head will rise **so high as to** allow him **free liberty to breathe** ; and if he moves his legs **as in the act of walking**, or rather of walking up stairs, his shoulders will rise above the waters, so that he **may use** less exertion with his hands, or apply them to **oth**er purposes.

NOTES.

1. Men (*see* Synopsis, Rule I.) ; by (*see* Invar. words, Rule XII.)
2. Deep water, put " *a* deep water ; " will rise (*see* Verb, Rule XIX.)
3. So...as to, *assez...pour* ; free liberty to breathe, put " to breathe freely," and mind what sort of an object and what preposition before the verb are required after " to allow ; " as in the act of walking, put " as in walking; " he may use, put " he will be able to make ; " other, *i.e. some* other, *d'autres.*

II.—The Duchess of Marlborough, having been offended by her husband, **immediately** cut off her **beautiful and long** hair, **to** vex him.

NOTES.

Immediately (*see* Invar. words, Rule I.) ; beautiful and long (*see* Synopsis, Rule XII.) ; to (*see* Invar. words, Rule XXXI.)

ARTICLE. 13

RULE V.

When **its** and **their** relate to **inanimate** objects, see if you can turn them into "of it, of them;" if so, use **le, la, les** before the noun, and "**en**" before the verb; if not, use **son, sa, ses, leur, leurs.**

Ex.—I like Paris and admire **its** monuments, *i.e.* the monuments of it.
J'aime Paris et **j'en** admire **les** monuments.

The trees have lost **their** leaves,—as you cannot say "the leaves of them," translate: Les arbres ont perdu **leurs** feuilles.

Exception.—If "its, their" are preceded by a preposition, or if the noun before which they appear is the subject of a *transitive* verb, use **son, sa, ses, leur, leurs,** even if you can turn them into "of it, of them."

Ex.—I like Paris and admire the beauty **of its** monuments.
J'aime Paris et j'admire la beauté **de ses** monuments.

I like Paris, **its** monuments have charmed me.
J'aime Paris, **ses** monuments m'ont charmé.

Translate.

1. **It was** the unfortunate ambition of the next generation of authors **to** improve and perfect the new style, rather than to return to the old **one**; and **it cannot be denied** that they **did** improve it. 2. They corrected its gross indecency, increased its precision and correctness, made its pleasantry and sarcasm **more** polished and elegant, and spread through **the whole** of its irony, its narration, and its reflection, a tone of clear and condensed good sense, which recommended itself to **all who had**, and all who had not any relish for higher beauties.—(F. Jeffrey.)

NOTES.

1. It was (*see* Pron., Rule III.); to, *de*; one (*see* Pron., Rule XXXV.); it cannot be denied (*see* Verb, Rule IV.); did (*see* Verb, Rule LVII.)
2. More, must be repeated before each adjective; the whole, *l'ensemble*; all who (*see* Pron., Rule XXX.); had, (imperf.)

RULE VI.

Its, his, their, etc., following "whose," should be translated by **le, la, les**; when coming after a demonstrative adjective, "that, those," they should be turned into **which is his, theirs..., which belongs to them**, etc.

Translate.

I.—1. The eye is the first circle, the horizon which it forms is the second; and throughout nature this primary figure is repeated without end. 2. St. Augustine himself **described** the nature of God as a circle **whose** centre **was** everywhere and its circumference nowhere.

NOTES.

1. Described, put "*has* described;" whose (*see* Pron., Rule XVIII.); was (imperf.)

II.—Those whose minds are purified, and their thoughts habituated to **divine** things, with **what** constant and ardent wishes **do they breathe** after that their blessed immortality!—(Leighton.)

NOTES.

Divine, put "*the* Divine;" what (*see* Pron., Rule XXII.); do they breathe, put simply "they breathe."

RULE VII.

The must always be expressed before a comparative, when that comparative is meant for a superlative, as may be the case in English when speaking of two only.

Ex.—Of these two boxes, which is **heavier**;
De ces deux malles, laquelle est **la plus** lourde ?

ARTICLE. 15

RULE VIII.

Use **le, la, les** before a superlative relative, if in English it is preceded by **the**; and use the unchangeable article **le**, if in English there is no article prefixed to it.

Ex.—This girl is **the prettiest** of all;
Cette fille est **la** plus jolie de toutes.
It is in the evening that she is **prettiest**;
C'est le soir qu'elle est **le** plus jolie.

Translate.

I.—Let us compare the pains of the **sensual** with **those** of the **virtuous**, and see which are heavier in the balance.

NOTES.

Sensual, virtuous, add "men" to those adjectives; those (*see* Pron., Rule XXVI.)

II.—1. **The air** is heaviest and most dense near the earth; **the higher** we rise, **the rarer** and lighter **does** the air become. 2. **This is** because the air in the higher region presses on the air below it, and the **lower** air has thus a great weight **to** sustain.

NOTES.

1. The air...etc., put "it is near the earth that the air...etc." does (*see* Verb, Rule LIX.); the higher—the rarer and lighter (*see* Rule XI.)
2. This is (*see* Pron., Rule, XXVIII., Rem.); lower, *inférieur*; to (*see* Invar. words, Rule XXXII.)

RULE IX.

The more, the less, modifying a verb, are **plus, moins**; *the* is left out.

Ex.—**The more** I know him, **the less** I esteem him;
Plus je le connais, **moins** je l'estime.

RULE X.

If **the more, the less** modify a noun, *the* is also left out; besides, both the subject and the verb must come between "plus *or* moins" and the noun. Should the verb be understood in English, express it in French.

Ex.—**The less** money you will spend, the better;
 Moins vous dépenserez **d'argent, mieux** cela **vaudra.**

RULE XI.

The is likewise left out before adjectives or adverbs in the comparative degree, when antithesis or contrast is marked. Here also both the subject and the verb must be placed between "plus *or* moins" and the adjective or adverb, and the verb should always be expressed.

Ex.—**The more** enlightened men, the **freeer** they are;
 Plus les hommes **sont éclairés, plus** ils sont **libres.**

Rem.—"**More of a**" before a noun is simply rendered by **plus.**

 Ex.—He is **more of a** prose-writer than **of a poet;**
  Il est **plus** prosateur que poëte.

Translate.

I.—The memory is sometimes so capricious, that the more we attempt to recall a fact or a circumstance, the less chance we have **of** succeeding.

NOTES.

Of (*see* Invar. words, Rule XVII.)

II.—1. One day, the bear meeting the fox carrying some fish, asked the latter to teach him **how** to fish. 2. "Oh ! **it is** easy," answered the fox. 3. "You have only to cut a hole in the ice, stick your tail **into it**, and hold it there as long as you **can**; in fact, the longer you **hold** it, the better, for the more fish you will get."

NOTES.

1. How (*see* Invar. words, Rule XVI.)
2. It is (*see* Pron., Rule IV.)
3. Into it, *y* (before the verb); can, hold (*see* Verb, Rule XX.)

III.—1. "As long as you **have** the wisdom **to** keep the sovereign authority of this country as the sanctuary of **liberty**," says Burke in one of his speeches, " wherever the chosen race and sons of England worship **freedom**, they will turn their faces towards you. 2. The more they multiply, the more friends you will have; the more ardently they love liberty, the more perfect will be their obedience."

NOTES.

1. Have (*see* Verb, Rule XX.); liberty, freedom (*see* Synopsis, Rule I.)

IV.—The more command a man has over himself, and the more powerfully he rules his various faculties, the more of a man and the less of a thing he is; the more too his natural capabilities are **his own**, and deserve the name of faculties.

NOTES.

His own, *à lui.*

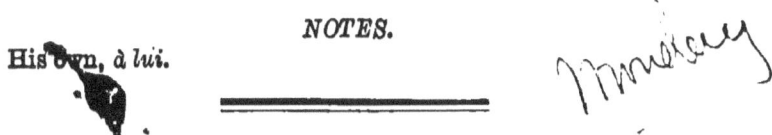

RULE XII.

The more, the less, when followed by " because," are **d'autant plus, d'autant moins**; **because** is translated by **que**.

Rem.—The same expressions are used in the case of an adjective or an adverb in the comparative degree preceded by " the " and followed by " because."

Ex.—He is **the more** timid, **because** he is poor;
Il est **d'autant plus** craintif, **qu'il** est pauvre.

So much the better is **tant mieux;**
So much the worse is **tant pis.**

Translate.

1. If you, **ladies, are** much handsomer than we, **it** is **but just** you should acknowledge **that** we have helped you, **by voluntarily** making ourselves ugly. 2. Your long, pliant, wavy tresses are the more beautiful, because we cut our **hair** short; your hands are all the whiter, smaller and more delicate, because we reserve to ourselves **those** toils and exercises which **make** the hands large and hard.

NOTES.

1. Ladies, *mesdames*; are, *vous êtes*; it (*see* Pron., Rule IV.); but (meaning *only*), *ne*...(verb)...*que*; just, you should... (*see* Verb, Rule XXIX. and Rule XXVI. Rem.); that (*see* Verb, Rule XXVI.); by, voluntarily (*see* Invar. words, Rule I. and Rule XII.)

2. Hair, put it in the plural; those (*see* Pron., Rule XXXII.); make (*see* Verb, Rule LXXIX.)

RULE XIII.

Prefix **un, une**, to a singular *abstract* noun preceded by an adjective of quality.

Ex.—He has shown great courage;
Il a montré **un** grand courage.

Rem.—"A love for, a passion for, a taste for, etc.," should be rendered by "**l'amour, la** passion, **le** goût, **du, de la, des**, etc."

Translate.

I.—The town of Calais was defended with remarkable vigilance, constancy, and bravery by the townsmen, during a siege of unusual length; at last John de Vienne, the governor, surrendered unconditionally.

II.—In his last unfortunate battle of Zama, Annibal displayed admirable foresight, daring coolness, consummate skill, but all these qualities could not supply the want of cavalry.

III.—A taste for gaming can captivate **but** an empty head or an empty heart.

NOTES.

But (*see* Invar. words, Rule X.)

IV.—**Pope Sixtus V.**, **whose** family name **was** Peretti, was at first a swine keeper; a Franciscan friar having met him, took him to his convent, where **young** Peretti **soon** manifested a love for learning, and afterwards acquired great reputation by his sermons.

NOTES.

Pope (*see* Article, Rule I.); Sixtus V., *Sixte-Quint*; whose (*see* Pron., Rule XVIII.; was (imperf.); young (*see* Art., Rule I.); soon (*see* Invar. words, Rule I.)

RULE XIV.

The article **a** preceded by **as** is omitted in French, when no verb follows the noun.

As may be rendered in two ways:

1. By **comme**, if it means *in quality of*, *in the character of*.

2. By **en**, if it means *with the feelings of*.

Ex.—" Je juge Bacon **comme** philosophe," will mean : " I judge Bacon *as a* philosopher, *i.e. in the character of* a philosopher."

" Je juge Bacon **en** philosophe," will mean : " I juge Bacon *as a* philosopher, *i.e. with the feelings of* a philosopher."

Translate.

I.—1. Louis XVI. being detected at Varennes and stopped in his flight, exclaimed to the crowd which surrounded him : " Yes, I am your king, and in your hand I place my destiny, and **that** of my wife, of my sister, and of my children. 2. I conjure you as a father, as a husband, as a man, as a citizen, leave the road free **to us**; and if you guard in your hearts that fidelity your words profess for **him** who was your master, I order you as your king."

NOTES.

1. That (*see* Pron., Rule XXVI.)
2. To us (*see* Synopsis, Rule XIV.) ; him, (*see* Pron., Rule I.)

II.—" His private deportment," says Hume, in his judgment on Oliver Cromwell, " as a son, a husband, a father, a friend, merits the highest praise."

III.—*Macd.* What, all my pretty chickens and their dam
At one fell swoop ?
Malc. Dispute it like a man.
Macd.   I shall do so ;
But I must also feel it as a man.

RULE XV.

A in English follows the words **so**, **such**, **too**, **half**, but in French it should *precede* them.

Such, such a, before an adjective in the singular, are **un si, une si**; **such,** before an adjective in the plural, is **de si** *or* **des** (noun) **si.**

Ex.—I never saw **such** unhappy people;
Je n'ai jamais vu **des** gens **si** malheureux,
or
Je n'ai jamais vu **de si** malheureuses gens.

Such, such a, coming *immediately* before a noun in the singular, are **un tel, une telle**; **such,** placed *immediately* before a plural noun, is **de tels, de telles.**

Ex.—I never saw **such** people;
Je n'ai jamais vu **de telles** gens.

Translate.

I.—1. Edward III., after the surrender of Calais, **only** consented to spare the lives of the defenders on the condition that six of the most considerable citizens should be sent to him **to be disposed of** as he **thought** proper. 2. When this **intelligence** was conveyed to Calais it struck the inhabitants **with** consternation, and they found themselves incapable **of** coming to any resolution in so cruel and distressful a situation. 3. **It** is surprising that so generous a prince **should** ever **have** entertained such a barbarous purpose against such men; but the entreaties of his queen saved his memory from that infamy.

NOTES.

1. Only (*see* Invar. words, Rule I.); to be disposed of, put "to dispose of them," and (*see* Invar. words, Rule XXXI.); thought (*see* Verb, Rule XX.), and translate as if it were "as he thought *it* proper."

2. Intelligence, *nouvelle* (fem.); with (*see* Invar. words, Rule II.); of (*see* Invar. words, Rule XVII.)

3. It (*see* Pron., Rule IV.); should have (*see* Verb, Rule XXIX.)

II.—Half an hour is a very short space of time ; yet, in half an hour, how much anguish **could** be crowded!

NOTES.

Could (*see* Verb, Rule LXX.)

III.—**Indolent** as Johnson **was**, says Macaulay, he **acquired knowledge** with such ease and rapidity, that at every school to which he was sent, he was soon the best **scholar.**

NOTES.

Indolent as, *tout indolent que* ; was (*see* Verb, Rule X.) ; to acquire knowledge, *apprendre*; scholar, *élève.*

SUBSTANTIVE.

RULE I.

Some English nouns ending in **er** have no direct equivalents in French, or if they have any, it may happen that such equivalents cannot be construed with an object. Some other expression should then be substituted, which, while rendering the meaning of the English word, would at the same time satisfy the requirements of the French language.

Ex.—His widow was long a **mourner** for his death.

You will find for " mourner " in a dictionary :

1. Personne en deuil, *i.e.*, *a person in mourning*.
2. Pleureur, pleureuse, *i.e.*, *a hired mourner*.
3. Qui pleure la perte.

Neither of these expressions can be employed, as the first two do not render at all the meaning of the English word, and the third can only qualify a noun. Here we must use a verb, as is often done in such cases, and say :

His widow **long mourned** for his death ;
Sa veuve **pleura longtemps** sa mort.

In the third sentence of the next exercise we find the expression "bad **speakers** of their language." The word *parleur* cannot be used with an object ; then some equivalent expression should be substituted, such, for instance, as " those who speak their language badly."

It may even happen that, only for the sake of elegance, a noun may be better rendered by a verb, or a verb by a noun.

Ex.—Hazlitt was a poor **painter**, but he **wrote** admirably.

It is advisable here to use either two nouns for " painter " and " wrote," or two verbs, in order to render the contrast more striking, and say:

Hazlitt **peignait** mal, mais **écrivait** admirablement,
or,
Hazlitt était un **mauvais peintre**, mais **un excellent écrivain.**

Translate.

1. God is the giver of **all good**.

2. **Man** was at first a wanderer, a keeper of cattle, and a dweller in tents; then a tiller of the ground, and a builder of houses.

3. Foreigners, says Hunt, are very **kind to** bad speakers of their language, and ought to shame us **Englishmen** in that matter.

4. The poet Keats, who died at Rome on the 27th of December, 1820, was interred in the English burying ground, near the monument of Caius Catius, where his friend and poetical mourner Shelley **was** shortly to join him.

5. God is the only rewarder and punisher of secret actions, although not of such actions only, but of all those whereby the Law of Nature **is broken**, whereof Himself is author; **for which cause** the Roman laws,

called the Laws of the Twelve Tables, requiring offices of inward affection which the eye of man cannot reach unto, threaten the neglecters of them **with** divine punishment.

NOTES.

1. All good, put " all the goods."
2. Man, (*see* Synopsis, Rule I.)
3. Kind to, *bons pour ;* Englishmen, *nous autres Anglais.*
4. Was (imperf.)
5. Is broken, (*see* Verb, Rule IV. *Rem.*) ; for which cause, (*see* Pron., Rule XV.) ; with, put "with *a*" (and *see* Invar. words, Rule II.)

ADJECTIVE.

RULE I.

There are three ways of expressing dimensions in French.

Ex.—This tower is 60 metres high.

    1st way: Cette tour **est haute de** soixante mètres.

    2nd way: Cette tour **a** soixante mètres **de hauteur** (*i.e.* has 60 metres in height).

    3rd way: Cette tour **a** soixante mètres **de haut**.

Prefix **de** to the numeral, if the object measured is preceded by the verb, or if there is no verb at all.

Ex.—I have seen a tower } A tower } 60 metres high.

    1st way: J'ai vu une tour } Une tour } **haute de** 60 mètres.

    2nd way: J'ai vu une tour } Une tour } **de** 60 mètres **de hauteur**.

    3rd way: J'ai vu une tour } Une tour } **de** 60 mètres **de haut**.

    So "high" may be either "de haut" or "de hauteur."
    "long"   ,,   "de long" or "de longueur."
    "wide"   ,,   "de large" or "de largeur."
but
    "thick" may only be rendered by "d'épaisseur."
    "deep"   ,,   "de profondeur."

Rem.—**In** before the noun of dimension is **de**. **By** is **sur**.

Ex.—This well is fifteen feet deep **by** four **in** circumference;
    Ce puits a quinze pieds de profondeur **sur** quatre de circonférence.

ADJECTIVE.

Translate.

(The expressions of dimensions in this exercise should be rendered in the three ways).

I.—1. The **largest** oak **in** England is the Calthorpe Oak, Yorkshire; it measures 78 feet in circumference **at the ground**. 2. In the mansion of Tredegar Park, Monmouthshire, **there is said to be** a room, 42 feet long and 27 feet broad, the floor and wainscot **of which were** the production of a single tree grown on the estate.

II.—Ham is a small town on the Somme. Its citadel has been much strengthened, and **serves as a** state prison. The central tower or donjon is 100 feet high by 100 feet wide, and the walls **are of** masonry, 36 feet high.

III.—The great Chinese wall is more **than** 450 leagues long. It generally stands 25 feet high, is about 24 feet thick at its base, and some 15½ towards the top, which is crowned **with** a parapet five feet in height.

NOTES.

I.—1. "Large," bear in mind that this adjective should not be translated by the French homonym *large*, which means *wide, broad*, but by " grand " if speaking of the capacity of some object (as une *grande* chambre), and by " gros," if you speak of the size of an object having a thickness, a body, as in the present instance; in (*see* Synopsis, Rule XXII.); at the ground, *à la base*.

2. There is said to be (*see* Verb, Rule IV.); of which (*see* Pron. Rule X.); were, put " are," as the fact still exists, is, so to say, *present*.

II. To serve as a, servir *de*; are of, put " are a."

III. Than (*see* Invar. words, Rule XXVI.); with (*see* Invar. words, Rule II.)

RULE II.

When a noun has two qualificatives without a comma between them, place one of them before, and the other after the noun, going by the rules given in grammars to know which should precede the substantives. (*See* Synopsis, Rule XII.)

Ex.—**Large blue** eyes.

"Blue," being an adjective of colour, *must* be placed after the noun, so "large" will be put before.

De **grands** yeux **bleus.**

Rem.—In some exceptional cases **both** adjectives will remain before the noun, as in:

A **good old** woman, une **bonne vieille** femme.

But here again the grammar teaches that those two adjectives are amongst those which generally remain before the noun.

RULE III.

If two or more qualificatives are divided by commas, or joined by "and," place them after the noun.

Of course there may be also exceptions to this rule, but it will be found to answer generally.

Translate.

I.—**In** our days every one sees himself a member of one vast civilised society which covers the face of the earth, and no part of the world is indifferent to him.

NOTES.

In, *de.*

II.—Queen Mab's whip is made of a cricket's bone; the lash, of film;

ADJECTIVE. 29

Her waggoner, **a small** gray-coated gnat,
Not half so big as a round little worm
Prick'd from the lazy finger of a maid.

NOTES.

A small, put *" is a small ;"* not, *pas.*

III.—1. "In the child," says Macaulay, in speaking of Johnson, "the physical, intellectual, and moral peculiarities which afterwards distinguished the man were plainly discernible: great muscular **strength**, accompanied by much awkwardness and many infirmities; great quickness of parts, with a morbid propensity to **sloth** and **procrastination**; a kind and generous heart, with a gloomy and irritable temper...... 2. Many people had been surprised to see a man of his genius and learning stooping to **every** drudgery, and denying himself almost every comfort, for the purpose **of** supplying a silly, affected old woman with superfluities, which she accepted with **but little** gratitude.

NOTES.

1. Strength (*see* Art., Rule XIII.); sloth, procrastination (*see* Synopsis, Rule I.)
2. Every, put all sorts of; of (*see* Invar. words, Rule XVII.); but little, *fort peu de.*

IV.—"But **now**," says W. Cobbett, "**came rushing into my mind** all at once my pretty little garden, my little blue smock-frock, my little nailed shoes, my pretty pigeons that I used to feed out of my hands, the last kind words of my gentle, tender-hearted and affectionate mother."

NOTES.

Now (*see* Invar. words, Rule XXI.); came rushing into my mind, *me revinrent à l'esprit.*

RULE IV.

In speeches, adjectives preceding the titles given to the people addressed to, generally retain the place they have in English.

Translate.

Most potent, grave, and reverend signiors,
My very noble and **approved good** masters,
That I have ta'en away the old man's daughter,
It is most true. (Shakespeare.)

NOTES.

Most, should be repeated before each adjective; approved good, *excellents.*

RULE V.

The same comparative repeated is translated by the positive expressed once, preceded by **de plus en plus**.

Ex.—It gets **warmer** and **warmer** every day;
Il fait chaque jour **de plus en plus** chaud.

Translate.

1. If **any person** ascends from the base to the top of a **high** mountain, he will find the air growing colder and colder. 2. In very high mountains the cold increases so much towards the summit, that the upper portion is covered **with** snow, which **never** melts. 3. Sometimes, when the sun shines on one of these mountains, a portion of the snow **is loosened** from its sides, and slides down into the valley below; **as** the mass of snow descends, it becomes larger and larger. 4. These falling masses of snow **are called** avalanches.

NOTES.

1. Any person, *quelqu'un;* high (*see* Synopsis, Rule XII.)
2. With (*see* Invar. words, Rule II.) ; never (*see* Invar. words, Rule I.)
3. Is loosened (*see* Verb, Rule V.); as (*see* Invar. words, Rule VI.)
4. Are called (*see* Verb, Rule V.)

PRONOUN.

PERSONAL PRONOUNS.

(*See* Synopsis, Rule XIV. to Rule XVIII., and Rule XXVI.)

RULE I.

He, she, they, him, etc., followed by a relative pronoun, *who, that,* etc., are **lui, elle, eux, elles,** when they represent some particular person, and **celui, celles, ceux, celles,** when they are used in a vague, indefinite sense, or may be turned into *the person, the persons.*

Ex.—**He, who** is your friend, should help you ;
   Lui, qui est votre ami, devrait vous aider.

   He, who is virtuous, is happy ;
   Celui, qui est vertueux, est heureux.

   You have rewarded **him, who** did not deserve it, *i.e.* the one who...
   Vous avez récompensé **celui,** qui ne le méritait pas.

Practically, when " he, she," etc., are *immediately* followed by " who," etc., use " lui, elle," etc., if there is a comma before the relative pronoun, and " celui, celle," etc., if there is none.

Rem.—A personal pronoun must not be followed *immediately* by a reflexive pronoun in French ; either the personal pronoun is suppressed, or, more generally, the verb is put between the two pronouns.

Ex.—**He himself** has done it ;
   Il l'a fait **lui-même** *or* **Lui-même** l'a fait.

Translate.

I.—He that is down needs fear no fall;
He that is low no pride;
He that is humble ever shall
Have God **to be** his guide.

NOTES.

To be his guide, put " for guide."

II.—"Fortune," says Bacon, "makes **him** a fool, **whom** she makes her darling."

NOTES.

Him, whom, (*see* Pron., Rule X., and Verb, Rule LXXXI.)

III.—Places of judicature ought on no account to be sold, for they that buy the office will sell the act; and they that, **at any rate, will** be judges, **will** not, **at an easy rate**, do justice; **nor can they be** easily punished for bribery **whose right to** sit on the **judgment seat was** won by bribery.

NOTES.

At any rate, *à tout prix;* will (*see* Verb, Rule LXIII.); at an easy rate, *à bas prix;* nor can they be punished (*see* Verb, Rule IV.), and translate " nor can " by "*on ne pourra pas non plus* "; whose right (*see* Pron., Rule XVIII.); to, *de* ; the judgment seat, say " the seat of justice;" was, *a été*.

RULE II.

He is, they are, etc., are rendered by **c'est, ce sont**, etc., before a noun preceded by **un, une,** or **des.**

Ex.—**He is** a general, c'est **un** général.
They are generals, ce **sont des** généraux.

Translate.

I.—1. The spirits of Milton are unlike **those** of almost **all other** writers. 2. His fiends, in particular, are **wonderful** creations. 3. They are not metaphysical abstractions. 4. They are not wicked men. 5. They are not ugly beasts. 6. They have **no** horns, no tails, none of the fee-fau-fum of **Tasso** and Klopstock. 7. They have just enough in common with human nature **to** be intelligible to human beings.

NOTES.

1. Those (*see* Pron., Rule XXVI.); all other, put "all *the* other."
2. Wonderful, put "some wonderful."
6. No (*see* Synopsis, Rule VI.); Tasso, *le Tasse*.
7. To (*see* Invar. words, Rule XXXI.)

II.—1. General Poniatowski was a colonel of Stanislaus' Swedish guards. 2. He was a man of extraordinary **merit**, and **had** been induced, by his strong attachment to the person of Charles XII., to follow him into the Ukraine, without any post in the army. 3. He was a man, who, in all the occurrences of life and amidst the greatest dangers, **always** took his measures with despatch, prudence, and success.

NOTES.

1. General (*see* Art., Rule I.)
2. Merit (*see* Art., Rule XIII.); had, put "*who* had."
3. Always (*see* Invar. words, Rule I.)

RULE III.

It is, it was, etc., when followed by a noun determined (*i.e.* preceded by *a, the, my, this*, etc.) or a pronoun (*I, thee, mine*, etc.), is rendered by **c'est, ce sont, c'était, c'étaient**, etc.

Ex.—**It is** my book, c'est mon livre.
It is they, ce sont eux.

RULE IV.

Before an adjective, **it is, it was**, etc., should be rendered by **c'est, c'était**, etc., if they can be turned into *that is, that was*.

Ex.—**It was** very amusing, *i.e. that was*...
C'était très amusant.

It is easy to do, *i.e. that is*...
C'est facile à faire.

If they cannot be so turned, translate **it** by **il, elle**, if it refers to a noun, and by **il** unchangeable, if it does not.

Ex.—Can't you do that translation ? **It is** very easy, though;
Ne pouvez-vous pas faire cette version ? **Elle est** très facile, cependant.

It is easy to do that, **Il** est facile *de* faire cela.

Rem.—Observe from above examples... *C'est* facile *à* faire,
and *Il est* facile *de* faire cela,
that " c'est " requires " à," and " il est " requires " de " when they come before an adjective followed by an infinitive.

RULE V.

Before any other verb but *is*, translate **it** again: 1, by **il, elle**, if it refers to a noun ; 2, by **il** unchangeable, if it does not; 3, by **cela**, if it can be turned into *that*.

Translate.

I.—1. Turn your face *to* the East. **What is it** that shines **so** behind the trees ? 2. Is it a fire ? No, it is the moon. 3. It is very large, and how red it is ! like blood. 4. The moon is round now, but it will not be so round to-morrow night ; it will lose a little bit, and the next night it will lose a little bit **more**, and so on **for** a fortnight, **till** there be no moon at all. 5. **Then,** after that, there will be a new moon; it will be very thin, but it will **grow** rounder and bigger every day, till at last, in another fortnight, it will be a full moon **again** like **this.**

NOTES.

1. What is it, *qu'est-ce que c'est*; so (meaning *thus*), *ainsi*.
4. More, put "another little bit;" for (meaning *during*) *pendant*; till (*see* Invar. words, Rule XXVII.)
5. Then, *puis*; to grow (followed by an adj.), *devenir*; again, *de nouveau* (to be put immediately after the verb); this (*see* Pron., Rule XXVIII.)

II.—1. "Do you imagine," says Burke, in his speech on **conciliation** with **America**, "that it is the Land Tax Act that raises your revenue? that it is the annual vote in the committee of supply which gives you your army? or that it is the Mutiny Bill which inspires it **with** bravery and discipline? 2. No! surely no! It is the love of the people, it is **their** attachment to **their** government, which give you your army and your navy, and infuses into both that liberal obedience, without which your army would be a base rabble, and your navy nothing but rotten timber."

NOTES.

1. Conciliation, put "*the* conciliation;" America (*see* Synopsis, Rule II.); with (*see* Invar. words, Rule II.)
2. Their (*see* Verb, Rule I.)

III.—"It is not very easy," says Johnson, "to fix the principles **upon which** mankind **have agreed** to eat **some** animals and reject **others.**"

NOTES.

Upon, *d'après*; which (*see* Pron., Rule XI.); have agreed (*see* Verb, Rule I.); some, *certains*; others (*see* Pron., Rule XXXIII.)

RULE VI.

Do not express **it** before an adjective or a noun followed by an infinitive.

Ex.—I think **it** useless to write to him.
Do not say: Je *le* crois inutile de lui écrire,
but: Je crois inutile *or* qu'il est inutile de lui écrire.

I think **it** my duty to tell it him;
Je crois qu'il est de mon devoir, *or simply*, Je crois de mon devoir de le lui dire.

Translate.

I.—**Whilst** the inhabitants **continue few**, and lands cheap and fresh, the colonists will find it easier and more profitable to raise corn or rear cattle, and with corn and cattle to purchase woollen **cloth**, for instance, or linen, **than** to spin and weave these articles for themselves.

NOTES.

Whilst (*see* Invar. words, Rule XXXIX. and Verb, Rule XX.); continue few, put "continue *to be* few"; cloth, put it in plural; than (*see* Invar. words, Rule XXIV.)

RULE VII.

"Ye, thou," must be left out before nouns in the vocative when no comma intervenes, and also when joined to an imperative.

Ex.—Ye gods, hear me! Dieux, écoutez-moi!

Translate.

I.—"You dogs," exclaimed Frederick II. of Prussia, at Kolin, **when** the battle was lost, and the few soldiers who remained refused to charge again, "you dogs! do you wish to live eternally?"

NOTES.

When (*see* Verb, Rule XXXVI.)

II.—1. "Go, then," exclaims Robert Hall, in one of his speeches, "go, then, ye defenders of your country, advance with alacrity into the field, where God Himself musters the hosts **to war**! 2. And Thou, sole Ruler among the children of men, gird on Thy sword, thou Most Mighty; go forth with our hosts **in the day of battle**! 3. Pour into their hearts the spirit of departed heroes! 4. And, **while led** by Thine hand, and fighting under Thy banners, open Thou their eyes **to behold** in every valley, and in every plain what the prophet beheld by the same illumination—chariots of fire, and horses of fire!"

NOTES.

1. To war, *pour combattre.*
2. In the day of battle, *au jour du combat.*
3. While led, put "while *they are* led," (and *see* Invar. words, Rule XXXIX., and Verb, Rule XX.); to behold, put "in order that they may behold," (and *see* Verb, Rule XXXIII.)

RULE VIII.

They, men, people, you, etc., and like expressions which do not refer to any particular persons, but are used in a vague sense for the indefinite pronoun "one," must be translated in French by **on** with the *verb* in the *singular*. If there are several verbs, repeat "on" before each of them.

Ex.—**They** say and believe it, *i.e. one* says and believes it; **On** le dit et **on** le croit.

Translate.

THE WONDERS OF CIVILIZATION.

1. The condition of the present inhabitants of this country is very different from **that** of their forefathers. 2. In England, a man of a small fortune may cast his regards around him, and say with truth and exultation : 3. " I am lodged in a house that affords me conveniences and comforts which even a king **could** not **command** some centuries ago... 4. In China, men are gathering the tea-leaf for me ; in America, they are planting cotton for me ; in the West India Islands, they are preparing my sugar and my coffee ; in Italy, they are feeding silk-worms for me ; in Saxony, people are shearing the sheep to make my clothing..."

NOTES.

1. That (*see* Pron., Rule XXVI.)
3. Could (*see* Verb, Rule LXX.) ; command, *obtenir.*

RELATIVE PRONOUNS.

Subject.	Who, that, which .... qui (never qu').
Object.	Whom, that, which .... que *or* qu'.

RULE IX.

Students often find difficulty in distinguishing **which** and **that** subjects, from the same pronouns used as objects. Practically see whether *who* or *whom* would have been used, had these pronouns been employed instead of " which " or " that," and put the corresponding French relative.

RELATIVE PRONOUNS. 39

Rem.—Whenever you come across "**that**," see whether it is a relative pronoun, or a demonstrative adjective (*ce, cette, ces*), or a conjunction (*que*).

Translate.

1. A nation, once the first among the nations, pre-eminent in knowledge, pre-eminent in military glory, the cradle of **philosophy**, of **eloquence**, and of the fine arts, had been **for ages bowed down** under a cruel yoke. 2. All the vices which oppression generates, the abject vices which it generates **in those** who submit to it, the ferocious vices which it generates in those who struggle against it, **had deformed** the character of that miserable race. 3. The valour which had won the great battle of human civilization, which had saved **Europe**, which had subjugated **Asia**, lingered **only** among pirates and robbers.—(Macaulay.)

NOTES.

1. Philosophy, eloquence, (*see* Synopsis, Rule I.); for (meaning *during*), *pendant;* ages, (*see* Synopsis, Rule III.); bowed down (imperf.).
2. In, *chez;* those (*see* Pron., Rule XXVI.); had deformed (*see* Verb, Rule XV.).
3. Europe, Asia, (*see* Synopsis, Rule II.); only, *ne*...(verb)... *que*.

RULE X.

The relative should generally be placed *immediately after* its antecedent. This may easily be done at times by removing one or several words which intervene, and putting them at some other place either before the antecedent, or after the pronoun.

Ex.—I held the **lark** in my hand, **which** was half dead.

Do not say :

Je tenais **l'alouette** dans ma main, **qui** était à demi-morte.

As "qui" refers generally to the nearest noun, it might be understood that it was the *hand* which was half-dead. This ambiguity must be avoided by putting "in my hand" before "the lark," so as to bring the latter noun close to the relative, and the sentence will run thus:

Je tenais dans ma main **l'alouette, qui** était à demi-morte.

Ex.—A **chase** then began, **which** resulted in the capture of the thief.

Put:
Then began a **chase, which**...
Alors commença une **chasse, qui** se termina par la capture du voleur.

Rem.—"Alors une chasse commença, qui," etc., would not be incorrect, as there would be no ambiguity in this sentence; but the other translation is better.

Sometimes, indeed, the relative may be separated from its antecedent by words which cannot be displaced, but then the sentence should be made quite clear. This may often be done simply by *repeating the antecedent* before the relative, or, when the antecedent is followed by a noun of a different gender, by using "*lequel, laquelle,*" instead of "qui."

Ex.—I have seen the husband of your sister, **who** promised to come and see me;
J'ai vu le mari de votre sœur, **lequel** m'a promis de venir me voir.

There is an **authority** much more powerful than that of men, **whose** voice commands to the very bottom of our hearts;
Il y a une autorité beaucoup plus puissante que celle des hommes, **autorité dont** la voix commande jusqu'au fond de nos cœurs.

Translate.

I.—There is a grandeur **about** the productions of **nature** which **art** cannot attain **to**.

RELATIVE PRONOUNS.

NOTES.

About, *dans*; nature, art (*see* Synopsis, Rule I.), to (*see* Pron. Rule XI.)

II.—1. Our **company** were now arrived within a mile from Highgate, when the stranger turned short upon Jones, and, pulling out a pistol, threatened to shoot him, if he did not **deliver** the bank-note that moment. 2. Jones **instantly** caught hold of the fellow's hand, which trembled so that he could scarcely hold the pistol in it, and turned the muzzle **from him**. 3. A struggle then ensued, in which the former wrested the pistol from the hand of his antagonist, and both **came** from their horses on the ground **together**, the highwayman upon **his** back, and the victorious Jones upon him.—(H. Fielding.)

NOTES.

1. Company, *troupe* (f.) (*see* Verb, Rule I.); deliver, put "deliver *to him*."
2. Instantly (*see* Invar. words, Rule I.); from him, *de lui*, would be ambiguous, put "from his own breast."
3. Came, put *fell*, and place "together" immediately after it; his (*see* Art., Rule III.)

RULE XI.

When preceded by a preposition, **whom** is **qui**, or **lequel, laquelle**, etc., whilst **which** can *only* be translated by **lequel, laquelle**, etc., *never* by "qui." The preposition should always be placed *before* the relative, and the relative expressed in French.

The conjunction **that** must never be understood either.

Obs.—Let the student bear in mind that "lequel" being composed of "le *and* quel," *à-le*-quel should be contracted into "auquel," and *de-le*-quel into "duquel," etc.

Rem.—Before translating a preposition, always ascertain if the same is required in French, or if any should be used at all.

Translate.

I.—If we examine all the different parts of the dress and household furniture of a workman, the coarse linen shirt he wears next to his skin, the shoes that cover his feet, the bed he lies on, and all the different parts which compose it, the kitchen-grate at which he prepares his victuals, the coals which he makes use of **for** that purpose, all the other utensils of his kitchen, all the **furniture** of his table, the knives and forks, the earthen or pewter plates upon which he serves up and divides his victuals, the different hands employed in preparing **his** bread and beer, the glass window which lets in the heat and the light, and keeps out the wind and the rain, with all the knowledge and art requisite **for preparing** that beautiful and happy invention, without which these northern parts of the world **could** scarce **have** afforded a very comfortable habitation; if we examine, I say, all these things and consider what **a** variety of labour is employed **about each** of them, we shall be sensible that without the assistance and co-operation of many thousands, the **very meanest** person in a civilised country **could** not be provided, even according to what we very falsely imagine, the easy and simple manner **in which** he is commonly accommodated. (Adam Smith.)

NOTES.

For, *dans*; furniture, *service* (m.); his (*see* Synopsis, Rule VII.); for preparing (*see* Invar. words, Rule XVII.); could have (*see* Verb, Rule LXXIV.); a (*see* Pron., Rule XXII.); about, *pour*; each (meaning *each one*), *chacun*; the very meanest, *la moindre*; could (*see* Verb, Rule LXX.); in which, *dont*.

II.—1. No art could shake the confidence which Elizabeth reposed in Burleigh. 2. She **sometimes** chid him sharply; but he was the man whom she delighted to honour. 3. For him, she relaxed that severe etiquette to which she was unreasonably attached. 4. **Every** other person to whom she addressed **her speech**, or on whom the glance of her eagle eye fell, instantly sank on his knee. 5. For Burleigh alone, a chair was set in her presence.

NOTES.

2. Sometimes (*see* Invar. words, Rule I.)
4. Every, *toute*; her speech, *sa parole*.

RULE XII.

When **which** can be turned into *the one which*, translate it by **celui qui, celui que**, etc.

Translate.

God offers to every mind **its** choice between truth and repose; take which you please, you cannot have **both**.

NOTES

Its, *le*; both, *les deux*.

RULE XIII.

Which, interrogative, is **quel**, etc., when it comes before a noun, and **lequel**, etc., when it does not; in the latter case it may be turned into "which one."

Translate.

. . . He is down! He is down! Who is down? **cried** Ivanhoe; for our Lady's sake, tell me which has fallen?

NOTES.

Cried (*i.e. exclaimed*), *s'écria*.

RULE XIV.

When **which** relates to a whole sentence, or can be turned into "that which, a thing *or* a circumstance which," translate it by **ce qui, ce que**, and if it comes after a preposition, by **ce dont, ce à quoi, après quoi**, etc.

Ex.—They say he is a thief, **which** is true and **which** I knew long ago;

On dit que c'est un voleur, **ce qui** est vrai et **ce que** je savais depuis longtemps.

He is gone, **which** I am very glad of;
Il est parti, **ce dont** je suis très content.

Rem.—For the sake of elegance, the relative may be replaced either by a demonstrative or by a personal pronoun, according to the sense; we might say for instance:

On dit que c'est un voleur; c'est vrai, et je **le** savais depuis longtemps;

i.e. **it** is true and I knew **it** long ago.

"Upon which," may be "sur ce *or* là-dessus."
"After which," après cela, etc.

Translate.

I.—As we **wandered** along, gaping about, a **very decent sort of man** passing by me stopped of a sudden, and took up something, **which** having examined, he presented it to me, with these words: "Sir, you have dropt half-a-crown;" upon which I pulled out my purse, and reckoning my money in my hand, which was now reduced to five guineas, seven shillings and two pence, assured him **I had** lost nothing. (Smollett.)

NOTES.

We wandered (*see* Verb, Rule IX.); a very decent sort of man, *un homme d'un extérieur très convenable*; which, having etc., put "which he examined and presented to me, in saying;" I had, put "*that* I had," (and *see* Verb, Rule XV.)

II.—1. Cromwell, **after inveighing** against the misconduct of the Long Parliament, said one day to the lawyer Whitelock : " **What** if a man should take upon him to be king ? " 2. To which Whitelock replied that the remedy would be worse than the disease.

NOTES.

1. After inveighing (*see* Verb, Rule XLVII.); what, *que penseriez-vous?*

III.—Country Hospitality.

1. As soon as I entered the parlour, **they** put me into the great chair that **stood** close by a huge fire, and kept me there by force **until** I was almost stifled. 2. Then a boy came to pull off my boots, which I in vain opposed. 3. In the meantime, the good lady whispered her eldest daughter, and slipped a key into her hand ; the girl **returned** instantly with a beer-glass half full of *aqua mirabilis* and sirup of gillyflowers. 4. I took **as much** as I had a mind **for**, but Madam **vowed** I should drink it off, and I was forced to obey, which absolutely **took away my stomach.**—(J. Swift.)

NOTES.

1. They, *on* (sing.); stood, *était placé;* until (*see* Verb, Rule XXXIV.)

3. Returned (*i.e.* came back), *revint*, not *retourna*, which would mean *went back.*

4. As much, put "as much *of it;*" for, put " for it, *en* " before the verb; vowed, *désira* (see Verb, Rule XXXI.); took away my stomach, *m'ôta l'appétit.*

RULE XV.

When two clauses are united by a preposition followed by " which " and a noun (as " by which means, during which time," etc.), cut off the sentence before the preposition, and start a fresh one, translating **which** by ce.

" All of which " is " tout cela."

" Both of which " is " tous deux, toutes deux."

Ex.—He might come to-night, **in which case** we had better not go out;

    Il pourrait venir ce soir, dans ce cas nous ferions mieux de ne pas sortir.

Translate.

I.—Baldwin, in his "**African Hunting**," relates that **on one occasion** he went **sea-cow shooting**, and **landing** on a small island, covered with trees, he sat down and went fast asleep, with his feet dangling in the water, in which state his friends found him within a few yards of several enormous crocodiles, which were making towards his resting-place, and would, no doubt, in a few minutes have seized him.

NOTES.

    African hunting, *chasse en Afrique*; on one occasion, *une fois*; sea-cow shooting, *à la chasse aux morses*; landing, put " and *that having landed.*"

II.—1. Catherine, who became Empress of Russia, was fifteen when her mother died ; she **therefore left** the cottage and went to live with the Lutheran minister, by whom she had been instructed **from** her childhood. 2. The old man, who **regarded** her as one of his own children, **had her instructed in dancing** and music by the master who **attended** the rest of the family; thus she continued to improve till he died, by which accident she was once more reduced to pristine poverty.

RELATIVE PRONOUNS. 47

NOTES.

1. Therefore (*see* Invar. words, Rule I.); to leave (a place), *quitter*; from (*i.e.* since), *dès*.
2. Regarded (*see* Verb, Rule IX.); had her instructed in dancing, *lui fit enseigner la dance*; attended (*i.e.* used to attend, *imperfect*), *donnait des leçons à*.

Rem.—The English language admits of a great many combinations by means of relative pronouns, which are inadmissible in French. It would be impossible to reduce them all to rules; therefore our object can only be to put the student on his guard and give him some rules to guide him in the chief cases, leaving to his own industry and judgment the care of finding himself how to deal with difficulties not directly falling under the rules given.

RULE XVI.

The English are rather fond of protracting sentences, the meaning of which is quite complete, by means of relatives or adverbs, whilst the French, on the contrary, prefer shorter sentences, avoiding all combinations which might tend to make them lengthy or obscure; they prefer to start a fresh one, suppressing the adverb, and generally replacing the relative by a personal or demonstrative pronoun (**il, elle, le, la, les,** etc.; *or* **cela, celui-ci,** etc.)

Ex.—I showed him the ring, **which** seeing, he declared it was his own ;

Je lui montrai la bague; en **la** voyant, il déclara que c'était la sienne.

The above English construction could not hold in French.

Translate.

I.—The shape and temper of the camels **show them framed** by nature **to** submit to man, and fitted for his service, who, **therefore, ought** to be more sensible of his wants, and of the divine bounty thus **supplying** them.

NOTES.

Show them framed, put "show *that they are* framed"; to (*see* Invar. words, Rule XXXI.); therefore (*see* Invar. words, Rule I.); ought (*see* Verb, Rule LXI.); supplying (*see* Verb, Rule XLIV.)

II.—1. The waters of the Leeba's are darker than those of **the Zambesi**, and they wind through delightful meadows. 2. Groups of graceful trees stand here and there; all around are the loveliest flowers, in great profusion, from which the bees gather their sweet store. 3. Among the flowers **are some** which have the pleasant flagrance of the hawthorn, inhaling which, the traveller's thoughts fly homeward, and he is a **boy** once more, wandering amongst green lanes and grassy pastures, where the white flocks feed, without fear of the lion or other destroyer.

NOTES.

1. The Zambesi, *le Zambèse.*
3. Are some, *il y en a;* a boy, *un enfant.*

RULE XVII.

Apply Rule XVI. (*see* that Rule) to any sentence in which several sounds of *qui, que* (either a relative or a conjunction), *quand, comme,* etc., would come in succession, such sounds being considered as harsh and disagreeable.

Ex.—I saw the poor man, **who** looked so ill **that** I sent at once for the doctor **whom** you had recommended to me.

Literal translation: Je vis le pauvre homme, *qui* paraissait si malade, *que* j'envoyai de suite chercher le docteur *que* vous m'aviez recommandé.

This sentence would be intolerable; the first relative must be cut off, and the sentence will be as follows:

Je vis le pauvre homme; **il** paraissait si malade, **que** j'envoyai, etc...

Translate.

I.—1. Charles XII. laid siege before Fredericshall in the month of December, 1718. 2. The soldiers, benumbed with cold, **were** hardly **able** to break the ground, which **was** so much hardened by the frost, that **it was** almost as difficult to pierce it as if they had been opening trenches in a rock.

NOTES.

2. Were able, was (*imperfect*) ; it was (imperfect; *see* Pron., Rule IV.)

II.—In this mansion the spider **had** for some time **dwelt** in **peace** and plenty, when **it was the pleasure** of fortune to conduct thither a wandering bee, **to whose** curiosity a broken pane in the glass had discovered itself, and in **he** went; where, expatiating a while, he at last happened to alight upon one of the corners of the spider's citadel, which, yielding to the unequal weight, sunk down **to** the very foundation.— (J. Swift.)

NOTES.

Had dwelt (*see* Verb, Rule XVIII.); peace, plenty, put "the" before each of these two nouns; it was the pleasure of, put "it *pleased*" (past definite); to whose (*see* Rule XX.); he, "*bee*" is fem. in French; to, *jusqu'à*.

RULE XVIII.

When **whose** is not interrogative, and refers to persons, it is **dont, duquel,** etc., **de qui**; if it refers to animals or things, it is **dont** or **duquel,** etc., but *never* " de qui."

Dont is the most usual form of the three; it must *always* be placed next to its antecedent.

Le, la, les, must appear before the noun which comes after "whose," and that noun, if an object, should be placed *after* the verb.

> *Ex.*—The woman **whose son** is gone
> Put: The woman whose *the* son is gone;
> La femme dont **le** fils est parti.
>
> *Ex.*—The woman **whose son** I know;
> Put: The woman whose I know *the son;*
> La femme dont je connais **le fils.**

Rem.—" Of which," when equivalent to "whose" follows the same rule.

> *Ex.*—The table the leg **of which** you broke;
> La table **dont** vous avez cassé **le pied.**

Translate.

I.—O God, whose thunder shakes the sky,
   Whose eye this atom globe surveys,
To Thee, my only rock, I fly,
   Thy mercy in Thy justice praise. (Chatterton.)

NOTES.

To. ⟶ vers

II.—"The author of this volume," says Macaulay, in an article on Gladstone's book on church and state, "is a young man of an unblemished character, and of distinguished parliamentary talents, the rising hope of those stern and unbending Tories, who follow reluctantly and mutinously a leader whose experience and eloquence are indispensable to them, but whose cautious temper and moderate opinions they abhor."

III.—Meanness is a medal the reverse of which is insolence.

IV.—"I should have lived happily enough in that country," says Gulliver, "if my littleness had not exposed me to several ridiculous and troublesome accidents, **some** of which I shall venture to relate."

NOTES.

Some (*i.e.*, some *ones*), *quelques uns*, to be placed after "relate."

RULE XIX.

When **whose** is followed by an *objective personal pronoun* relating to its antecedent, leave out the personal pronoun, and make the relative the object of the verb; besides, precede the noun which stands next to "whose" with **son, sa, ses, leur**, etc., instead of "le, la, les."

Ex.—The man **whose** son has ruined **him**;

Put: The man *whom his* son has ruined;
L'homme **que son** fils a ruiné.

Ex.—The man **whose** ambition has proved fatal **to him**;

Put: The man *to whom his* ambition has proved fatal;
L'homme **à qui** *or* **auquel son** ambition a été fatale.

Translate.

I.—There are a set of people whose cold and **formal** air **stands** them **in stead of** prudence and ability.

NOTES.

Formal, *compassé*; to stand in stead of, *tenir lieu de...(à quelqu'un)*.

RULE XX.

When **whose** is preceded by a *preposition*, "dont" cannot be employed; use then **de qui** or **duquel**, etc., still bearing in mind that "de qui" can only be used in reference to persons.

The noun which in English follows "whose" must be placed in French between the *preposition* and the *relative*, and **le, la, les**, prefixed to it.

Ex.—The man **in whose house** I have lived so long

Put: ......in the house of whom......

L'homme dans la maison $\begin{Bmatrix} \text{duquel} \\ \text{or} \\ \text{de qui} \end{Bmatrix}$ j'ai vécu si longtemps.

Translate.

1. The Puritans **were** men whose minds had derived a peculiar character from the daily contemplation of superior beings and eternal interests. 2. Not content **with acknowledging**, in general terms, an overruling Providence, they **habitually** ascribed every event to the will of the Great Being, for whose power nothing **was** too vast, for whose inspection nothing was too minute.... 3. The meanest of them was a being to whose fate a mysterious and terrible importance belonged, on whose slightest action the spirit of light and darkness looked with **anxious interest**.

NOTES.

1. Were (*see* Verb, Rule IX.)
2. With acknowledging (*see* Invar. words, Rule II. and Rule XVII.); habitually (*see* Invar. words, Rule I.); was, (imperf.)
3. Anxious interest (*see* Art., Rule XIII.)

RULE XXI.

Whose, interrogative, followed by "to be," meaning "to belong," is **à qui**.

Ex.—Whose books are these? Mine or my brother's;

A qui sont ces livres?
or
A qui ces livres sont-ils?
} A moi ou à mon frère.

Observe the construction, and notice that in the answer the noun or pronoun should be construed with " à."

Translate.

I.—1. "In short," said John Lounger, musing, " I shall set myself on the footing of a lord; and who knows **but I may become one**? 2. And then, **for many a mile round**, whenever any traveller **inquires**: "Whose meadows are these?" "Lord Lounger's," will be the answer. "Whose fields are those?" "Lord Lounger's." "Whose castle is that?" "Lord Lounger's." 3. Always "Lord Lounger's!" Just like **what** I have read in the story of "**Puss in Boots**."

NOTES.

1. But I may become one, *si je n'en deviendrai pas un.*
2. For many a mile round, *à plusieurs milles à la ronde;* inquires (*see* Verb, Rule XX.)
3. What (*see* Rule XXIV.); puss in boots, *le chat botté.*

RULE XXII.

What, referring to a noun, is **quel, quelle**, etc.; if there are several nouns, repeat it before each of them.

Ex.—**What** is your age? **Quel** âge avez-vous?
He does not know **what** her age is. Il ne sait pas **quel** âge elle a.
What a pity! **Quel** dommage.

Translate.

I.—Thales the Milesian being asked what **was** the oldest thing? answered, God; what was the largest thing? space; **what** the most lasting? hope; what the best thing? virtue; what the quickest? thought; what the strongest? necessity; what the easiest? advice; what the hardest? self-knowledge; and what the wisest? time.

NOTES.

Thales the Milesian, *Thalès de Milet*; being asked (*see* Verb, Rule VI. and Rem.); was (imperf.); what, put " what *was.*"

II.—Dean Swift in the latter years of his life was looking over his " Tale of a Tub," when **he was suddenly observed** to close the book, and mutter in an unconscious soliloquy: " Good God! what a genius I had when I wrote that book!"

NOTES.

Dean (*see* Art., Rule I.); he was suddenly observed (*see* Verb, Rule IV. and Invar. words, Rule I.); to observe, *voir.*

III.—1. As they **went on**, they **met** two men in raiment that **shone** like **gold**; **also** their faces shone as the light. 2. These men asked the pilgrims whence they came. 3. They also asked them where they had lodged, what difficulties and dangers, what comforts and pleasures, they had met with in **the** way?—(J. Bunyan.)

NOTES.

1. Went on, met, shone, etc. (*see* Verb, Rule IX. and XII.); gold (*see* Synopsis, Rule I.); also (*see* Invar. words, Rule I.)

3. In, to be omitted.

RULE XXIII.

If **what** is put for **the**... [noun] ...**which**, translate it by **le, la, les**... [noun] ...**qui, que**, etc.

Ex.—Give him **what** money you have, *i.e.* the money *which*...
Donnez-lui l'argent **que** vous avez.

Translate.

1. Mr. Gladstone conceives that the duties of governments are paternal. 2. He tells us that "Government occupies in moral the place of τὸ πᾶν in physical **science.**" 3. If government **be** indeed τὸ πᾶν in moral science, we do not understand why rulers should not assume all the functions which **Plato assigned** to them. 4. Why should they not take away the child from her mother, select the nurse, regulate the school, fix the hours of labour and recreation, prescribe what ballads shall be sung, what tunes shall be played, what books shall be read, what physic shall be swallowed?—(Macaulay.)

NOTES.

2. Science, *la science.*
3. Be (*see* Verb, Rule XXV.); Plato assigned, *Platon a assignées.*

RULE XXIV.

When **what** can be turned into **that which**, translate it by **ce qui, ce que, ce dont, ce à quoi**, etc., as the case may require.

Ex.—I know **what** you are talking about, *i.e.* that about which, etc.
Je sais **ce dont** vous parlez.

He is not **what** he ought to be to his father;
Il n'est pas pour son père **ce qu'il** devrait être.

Rem.—However, if "of what" means "*of* that which,"

it is $\begin{cases} \text{de ce qui (subject.)} \\ \text{de ce que (object.)} \end{cases}$

If "to what" means "*to* that which,"

it is $\begin{cases} \text{à ce qui (subject.)} \\ \text{à ce que (object.)} \end{cases}$

Ex.—You did not pay attention **to what** he said, *i.e. to that which*...;
Vous n'avez pas fait attention **à ce qu'**il a dit.

Observe that "ce *que*" is always used before a noun or a pronoun.

Translate.

I.—**He** alone reads history **aright** who, observing **how powerfully** circumstances influence the feelings and opinions of men, **how often** vices pass into virtues and paradoxes into axioms, learns to distinguish what is accidental and transitory in human nature from what is essential and immutable.

NOTES.

He, *celui-là*; aright, *bien* (to be placed immediately after "reads"); how powerfully, *combien*; how often, *combien de fois*.

II.—1. **It is** the great multiplication of the productions of all the different arts, in consequence of the division of labour, which occasions in a well-governed society that universal opulence which extends itself **to** the lowest ranks of the people. 2. Every workman has a great quantity of his work **to** dispose of beyond what he himself has occasion for; and every other workman being exactly in the same situation, he is enabled to exchange a great quantity of his own goods for a great quantity, or, what **comes to the same thing**, for the price of a great quantity of theirs. 3. He supplies them abundantly with what they want, and they accommodate him as amply with what he wants, and a general plenty diffuses itself through the different ranks of society.

NOTES.

1. It is (*see* Pron., Rule IV.); to, *jusqu'à*.
2. To (*see* Invar. words, Rule XXXII.); comes to the same thing, *revient au même*.

III.—1. The conduct of Charles **had proved** that, if **he were suffered** to retain even a small body-guard of his own creatures near his person, the commons would be in danger of **outrage**, perhaps of **massacre**. 2. Would **it** not have been **frenzy in** the Parliament, **under** these circumstances, to raise and pay an army of 15,000 or 20,000 men for the Irish war, and to give to Charles the absolute control of this army ? 3. **Was** it not probable that this army might become, what it is in the nature of armies to become, what so many armies formed under much more favourable circumstances have become, what the army of the Roman Republic became, what the army of the French Republic became, an instrument of despotism ?

NOTES.

1. Had proved (*see* Verb, Rule XV.); if he were suffered (to suffer, *permettre à*...), see Verb, Rule VI. and Rule XXV. ; of outrage, of massacre, put " of being outraged, of being massacred," and *see* Invar. words, Rule XVII.

2. It, *ce*; frenzy, put "*some* frenzy;" in, *de la part de*; under, *dans*.

3. Was (imperf.)

RULE XXV.

What, interrogative and relating to *no noun*, is rendered:—

1. By **qu'est-ce qui,** when it is a *subject*.

   Ex.—**What** is there? **Qu'est-ce qui** est là?

2. By **quoi**, when it stands alone, or is governed by a preposition.

   Ex.—**What** are you speaking **of**? **De quoi** parlez-vous?

3. By **que** or **qu'est-ce que** in other cases.

   Ex.—**What** did you say? **Qu'avez-vous dit?**
   or **Qu'est-ce que** vous avez dit?
   What has become of him? **Qu'est-il devenu?**
   or **Qu'est-ce qu'**il est devenu?

   Observe that **que** or "qu'est-ce *que*," is always used before a noun or a pronoun.

   Rem.—"What," exclamative and standing alone, is "quoi!"

Translate.

I.—Boswell had been **teasing** Johnson **with many** direct questions, such as, "What did you do, sir?" "What did you say, sir?" "And what did you reply, sir?"... **till** the enraged philologist roared, "I **will** not be put to the question; **these** are not the manners of a **gentleman**, sir. You have but two topics, sir, yourself and me, and I am sick of both."

NOTES.

To tease, *ennuyer*; with many, *en lui faisant une foule de*; till (see Invar. words, Rule XXX.); I will not (see Verb, Rule LXIII.); these are (see Pron., Rule XXVIII.)

Rem.—A gentleman (*i.e.* a man of the world), *un homme bien élevé*.

II.—1. This green flowery earth, the trees, mountains, rivers, seas, what are they? 2. That great deep sea of azure that swims over head, the winds **sweeping** through it, the black cloud **now pouring** out fire, now hail and rain, what is it? 3. Ay, what? We call the fire of the black **thunder-cloud**, electricity; but what is it? who **made** it? whence comes it? whither goes it?

NOTES.

2. Sweeping, pouring (*see* Verb, Rule XLIV.); now...now, *tantôt...tantôt.*

3. Thunder-cloud, *nuage qui porte le tonnerre*; made, put "*has made.*"

A SYNOPTIC TABLE OF RELATIVE PRONOUNS.

	PERSONS.	ANIMALS AND THINGS.
Subject (*or* Nominative).	who ...... } qui, (*never* qu'.) that	which ...... } qui. that ...... which (meaning "the one which") ... celui qui. which (referring to a whole sentence) ce qui. what (meaning "that which") ...... ce qui.
Direct object (*or* Accusative).	whom ...... } que, qu'. that	which ...... } que, qu'. that .... which (meaning "the one which") ... celui que. which (referring to a whole sentence) ce que. what (meaning "that which") .... ce que.
Indirect object.	of whom } dont, whose ... } duquel, de laquelle, *etc.*, de qui.*	of which ...... { dont, { duquel, de laquelle, *etc.* of what (meaning "that of which") ... { ce dont, { de quoi.

* Qui, when preceded by a preposition, can only be used in reference to *persons*.

INTERROGATIVE PRONOUNS.

Who	qui *or* qui est-ce qui?	What (*subj.*)	qu'est-ce qui?
Whom	qui *or* qui est-ce que?	What (*obj.*)	que *or* qu'est-ce que?
Of whom	de qui?	Of what...........................	de quoi?
		What (*alone*)	quoi?
Whose .... }	à qui?	What (before a noun)............	quel, quelle? *etc.*
To whom ...... }		Which (before a noun)...........	quel, quelle? *etc.*
		Which (meaning "which one") ...	lequel, laquelle? *etc.*

DEMONSTRATIVE PRONOUNS.

Obs.—There are two cases to be considered:—

1. When " that, those " are followed by a relative or " of."
2. When " that, those " are *not* followed by a relative or " of."

FIRST CASE.—Followed by a relative *or* **" of."**

RULE XXVI.

1. When referring to a noun previously mentioned, **that, those**, are translated by **celui, celle, ceux, celles**. In this case it can generally be turned into *the one* in the singular.

Ex.—Do you see this house? It is **that which** I have bought,
i.e. "*the one* which "...
Voyez-vous cette maison ? C'est **celle** que j'ai achetée.

2. When not referring to a noun previously mentioned, **that** is translated by **ce**.

Ex.—I know **that of which** you speak ;
Je sais **ce dont** vous parlez.

Rem.—Another way of testing whether **that** before "of" should be translated by "celui, celle," is to try if it can be replaced by the possessive case of the next noun.

Ex.—This hat is **that of** your brother, *i.e.* " is *your brother's.*"
Ce chapeau est **celui** de votre frère.

Translate.

1.—The most triumphant death is that of the martyr ; the most awful, that of the martyred patriot ; the most splendid, that of the hero **in** the hour of victory.— (R. Southey.)

NOTES.

In, *à.*

II.—1. Those who are placed among the lower ranks of **men** have little opportunity of **exerting any other** virtue besides those of patience, resignation, industry, and integrity. 2. Those who are advanced into the higher stations, **have full employment for** their generosity, humanity, affability, and charity.— (D. Hume.)

NOTES.

1. Of men, *de l'humanité*; exerting (*see* Invar. words, Rule XVII.); any other, *d'autre*.
2. Have full employment for, *sont à même d'exercer*.

III.—"In short," said the bee to the spider, "the question comes to **this** : **whether** is the nobler being of the two, that which, by a lazy contemplation of four inches **round**, by an overweening pride, feeding and engendering **on** itself, turns all **to** excrement and venom, producing nothing but flybane and a cobweb; or that which, by a universal range, **with long search,** much study, **true judgment** and distinction of things, brings home honey and wax ?"—(J. Swift.)

NOTES.

This (*see* Rule XXVIII., 2.); "whether," leave it out and make an interrogative sentence; round, *de circonférence;* on, *de;* to (*i.e.* "into"), *en;* with, *par;* long search, true judgment (*see* Art., Rule XIII.), and repeat "true" before "distinction."

IV.—1. Dryden **spent** no time in struggles **to** rouse latent powers; he never attempted to **make** that better which was already good, **nor often** to mend that which he **must have known** faulty. 2. He wrote, as he **tells** us, with very little **consideration** ; when occasion or necessity called upon him, he poured out that which the present moment happened to supply.— (S. Johnson.)

DEMONSTRATIVE PRONOUNS. 63

NOTES.

1. Spent (*see* Verb, Rule XII.); to (*see* Invar. words, Rule XXXI.); make (*see* Verb, Rule LXXIX.); nor often, *et rarement*; he must have known, *il devait savoir être*.
2. He tells us, put " he tells *it* us "; consideration, *réflexion*.

RULE XXVII.

If a noun in the possessive case can be turned into **that of...**, **those of...**, translate it by **celui de...**, **celle de...**, etc.

Ex.—This is **your father's** horse, *i.e.* this horse is *that of* your father;
Ce cheval est **celui de votre père**.

Translate.

1. The silly notion that every man has one ruling passion, and that this clue, once known, unravels all the mysteries of his conduct, finds no countenance in the plays of Shakspeare. 2. There man appears as he is, made up of a crowd of passions, which govern him in turn. 3. What is Hamlet's ruling passion? or Othello's? or Harry the Fifth's? or Wolsey's? or Lear's? or Shylock's? or Benedick's? or Macbeth's? or that of Cassius? or that of Falconbridge?—(Macaulay).

SECOND CASE.—*Not followed by a relative or " of."*

RULE XXVIII.

1. If they refer to a noun previously mentioned, in which case they can be turned into *this one, that one*, etc., **this, that,** etc. are translated by **celui-ci, celui-là,** etc.

Ex.—Here are two pens; take **this**, and I shall take **that**.
    i.e. . . . this **one** . . that **one**.
    Voici deux plumes; prenez **celle-ci** *et je prendrai* **celle-là**.

DEMONSTRATIVE PRONOUNS.

2. But if "this, that" refer to *no* noun previously mentioned, in which case they can be turned into *this thing, that thing*, **this, that** are translated by **ceci, cela.**

Ex.—**This** is pretty, but **that** is prettier still;
   Ceci est joli, mais cela est encore plus joli.

Rem.—"This is, that is, these are," when meaning **it is, are** "c'est, ce sont"; when equivalent to **here is, here are,** "voici, voilà;" when to **such is, such are,** "tel est, tels sont," etc.

Translate.

I.—1. Compare the two plans. This is plain and simple, the other full of perplexed and intricate mazes. This is mild, that harsh. 2. This is found by experience effectual for its purposes; the other is a new project. This is universal; that is calculated for certain colonies only. 3. This is immediate in its conciliatory operation; the other remote, contingent, full of hazard. 4. Mine is what becomes the dignity of a ruling people; I have done my duty in proposing it to you. 5. I have indeed tired you by a long discourse; but this is the misfortune of those **to whose influence** nothing **will be conceded**, and who must win every inch of their ground by argument. 6. You have heard me with goodness. May you decide with wisdom. 7. For my part, I feel my mind greatly disburdened by what I have done to-day. 8. I have been **the less** fearful of trying your patience, **because** on this subject I mean to spare it altogether in future... 9. My hold of the colonies is in the close affection which grows from common names, from kindred blood, from similar privileges, and equal protection. 10. These are ties which, though light as air, are as strong as links of iron.—(E. Burke.)

NOTES.

5. To whose influence (*see* Rule XX.); will be conceded (*see* Verb, Rule IV.), and use the present indicative.
8. The less...because (*see* Art., Rule XII., *Rem.*)

DEMONSTRATIVE PRONOUNS. 65

II.—People may say this and that about the advantage of drinking wine to meals : but **take** this **along with you**: if you have more bile than blood, drink water **only**.

NOTES.

Take along with you, *retenez bien* ; only, *ne...que*.

III.—" Great God !" exclaimed Rebecca, " hast thou given men thine own image, **that** it should be thus cruelly defaced by the hands of their brethren!" " Think not of that," said Ivanhoe ; " this is no time for **such** thoughts."

NOTES.

That (*see* Verb, Rule XXXIII.) ; such (*see* Art., Rule XV.)

RULE XXIX.

This, referring to something said before, must be translated by **cela**, *ceci* being only used in reference to what follows.

Ex.—Remember **this** : poverty is no vice ;
Souviens-toi de **ceci**: pauvreté n'est pas vice.
Poverty is no vice, remember **this** ;
Pauvreté n'est pas vice, souviens-toi de **cela**.

Translate.

1. " Are not the present ministers," exclaims J. Fox, in one of his speeches, " ashamed of their temporizing conduct against France ? 2. Look back but a year ago to a letter from one of your Secretaries of State to Holland : ' it is with surprise and indignation ' **your** conduct **is seen, in** something done by a petty governor of an island, while they affect to call the measures of France clandestine. 3. This is the way **that** ministers support the character of the nation, and the national honour and glory... 4. **From** this you may judge of your situation, from this you may know **what a** state you are reduced **to**."

DEMONSTRATIVE PRONOUNS.

NOTES.

2. Your conduct, put "*that* your conduct;" is seen (*see* Verb, Rule IV.); in, *à propos de.*
3. That, *i.e.* " in which," *dont.*
4. From, *d'après*; what a (*see* Rule XXII., Ex.); to (*see* Synopsis, Rule XXV.)

RULE XXX.

Neither the demonstrative, nor the relative pronoun can be suppressed in French after "all," as it is in English.

Ex.—"I know **all** you said," or, "*all that* you said."
Do not translate: "Je sais *tout* vous avez dit," or, "*tout ce* vous avez dit;"
but: "Je sais **tout ce que** vous avez dit," *i.e.* "*all that which* you said."

Translate.

1. Dryden's **performances were** always hasty; he **composed** without consideration, and published without correction. 2. What his mind could supply at call, or gather in one excursion, was all he sought, all he gave. 3. The dilatory caution of Pope enabled him to condense his sentiments, to multiply his images, and to accumulate all that study **might** produce, or chance might supply.—(S. Johnson.)

NOTES.

1. Performances, *productions* (*f.*); were, composed, etc. (*see* Verb, Rule IX.)
3. Might (*see* Verb, Rule LXVII.)

RULE XXXI.

A demonstrative pronoun cannot stand in French next to a past participle, an adjective or a noun used adjectively, but must then be followed by a relative and the auxiliary " to be."

Ex.—Here is your book and **that intended** for your brother;
Do not say: Voici votre livre et *celui destiné* à votre frère,
but: . . . et **celui qui est** destiné à votre frère.

RULE XXXII.

An English relative is often preceded by a demonstrative adjective where the article is sufficient in French.

Ex.—Cherish **those** hearts that hate thee;
Chéris **les** cœurs qui te haïssent.

Translate.

1. The counsel, **in recommending attention to** the public in preference to the private letters, had remarked, in particular, that one letter **should** not be taken as evidence, because it was manifestly private, as it contained in one part the anxieties of Mr. Middleton for the illness of his son. 2. **This was** a singular argument indeed; and **the** circumstance, in my mind, merited **strict observation**. 3. **It went to show** that some at least of those concerned in these transactions, felt the force of those ties, which their efforts were directed to tear asunder: that those who could ridicule the respective attachment of a mother and a son, were yet sensible of the straining of those chords by which they were connected.—(R. Brinsley Sheridan, *Speech against Warren Hastings.*)

NOTES.

1. In recommending attention to, *en appelant l'attention sur;* should (*see* Verb, Rule LXII.)
2. This was (*see* Rule VIII., *Rem.*); the circumstance, put "*that* circumstance;" strict observation (*see* Art., Rule XIII.)
3. It went to show, put "it showed" (imperf.)

A TABLE OF DEMONSTRATIVE PRONOUNS.

			MASCULINE.	FEMININE.
Followed by a relative pronoun or "of."	That Those } referring to a noun		Celui. Ceux.	Celle. Celles.
	That ... referring to *no* noun		Ce.	
Not followed by a relative pronoun or "of."	This That These Those	referring to a noun and meaning "This one," "That one."	Celui-ci. Celui-là. Ceux-ci. Ceux-là.	Celle-ci. Celle-là. Celles-ci. Celles-là.
	This That	referring to *no* noun and meaning "This thing," "That thing."	Ceci. Cela.	

RECAPITULATION ON RELATIVE AND DEMONSTRATIVE PRONOUNS.

Translate.

THE NEVER-FAILING SOURCES OF CHEERFULNESS.

I. A man who uses his best endeavours to live according to the dictates of virtue and right reason, has two perpetual sources of cheerfulness, in the consideration of his own nature, and of that Being on whom he depends. 2. If he looks into himself, he **cannot but** rejoice in that existence which **is** so lately bestowed upon him, and which after millions of ages will be still new and still in its beginning. 3. How many self-congratulations naturally rise in the mind, when it reflects on **this its** entrance **to** eternity, when it takes a view of those improveable faculties which in a few years have made **so considerable a progress**, and which will be still receiving an increase of perfection and consequently an increase of happiness! 4. The consciousness of **such a** being spreads a perpetual diffusion of joy through the soul of a virtuous man and makes him look upon himself every moment as more happy than **he knows how to conceive.** 5. The second source of cheerfulness **to** a good mind is the consideration of that Being **on** whom we depend, and in whom we see every thing that we can imagine as great, glorious, or amiable. 6. We find ourselves everywhere upheld by a Being, whose power qualifies him to **make** us happy by an infinity of means, whose goodness and truth engage Him to **make** those happy who desire it of Him, and whose unchangeableness will secure us in this happiness to all eternity. 7. Such considerations, which every one **should** perpetually cherish in his thoughts, will banish from us that secret heaviness of heart which unthinking men are subject to when they be under no real affliction, all that anguish which we may feel from any evil that actually oppresses us; they will silence those idle bursts of mirth and folly, that are apter to betray virtue than support it, and establish in us such an even and cheerful temper, **as** makes us pleasing to ourselves, to those with whom we converse, and to Him whom **we were made to** please.—(J. Addison.).

NOTES.

2. He cannot but, *il ne peut que;* is, put " has been.".
3. This its, *son;* to, *dans*; so considerable a progress, put it plural.
4. Such a being (*see* Art., Rule XV.); than he knows how to conceive, *qu'il ne peut le concevoir.*
5. To, *pour;* on (*see* Invar. words, Rule II.)
6. Make (*see* Verb, Rule LXXIX.)
7. Should (*see* Verb, Rule LXII.); as, *qu'il;* we were made, *nous avons été créés;* to, *pour.*

INDEFINITE PRONOUNS.

RULE XXXIII.

One, when a numeral, is **un, une** ; if it is not followed by a noun, prefix **en** to the verb ; you should even do so in the case of any word expressive of quantity, as "*deux, trois,* etc..., *plusieurs, beaucoup, un autre,* etc.," when no substantive follows.

    Ex.—Have you a good pen ? Yes, I have **one** ;
    Avez-vous une plume ? Oui, j'**en** ai *une.*

    I have **two** ; I have **several** ;
    J'**en** ai **deux** ; j'**en** ai **plusieurs**.

Rem.—" En " must also be used in a comparison when the noun, which is the object of the first verb, might be repeated after the second.

    Ex.—You have done more work in an hour than I have in a day,
      i.e. than I have done *work ;*
      Vous avez fait plus d'ouvrage en une heure que je n'**en** ai fait en un jour.

Translate.

1. I spent a great deal of time and pains to make an umbrella ; I was indeed in great want of one, and had a great mind to make one. 2. I was a great while **before I could** make something **likely** to hold : nay, **after I thought I had hit the way,** I spoiled two or three before I made one to my mind ; but at last I made one that **answered** indifferently well.—(De Foe's *Robinson Crusoe.*)

NOTES.

    2.—Before I could (*see* Verb, Rule XXXVIII.) ; likely, *qui pût* ; after I thought..., etc., *quand je crus en avoir trouvé le moyen* ; to answer, *faire l'affaire.*

RULE XXXIV.

One, when an *indefinite pronoun* meaning "any body, people," etc., is translated by **on**; if it means **a man, he**, it is rendered by **un homme, celui**.

Rem.—" On " can never be used as an object.

If it can be turned into **a single**, translate it by **un seul, une seule**; if into **the same**, use **le même, la même**.

Translate.

I.—**For** eighteen months, without intermission, this destruction raged from the gates of Madras to the gates of Tinjore, and so completely did Hyder Ali and his more ferocious son absolve themselves of their impious vow, that when the **British** armies traversed the Carnatic, for **hundreds** of miles in **all** directions, they did not see one man, not one woman, not one child, not one four-footed beast of any description whatever.

NOTES.

For, *i.e. during, pendant*; British, *de la Grande-Bretagne*; hundreds, *des centaines*; all, put "*all the*."

II.—1. Sir Nicholas Bacon **was no** ordinary man. 2. He belonged to a set of men whom **it is** easier to describe collectively than separately, whose minds were formed by one system of discipline, who belonged to one rank of society, to one university, to one party, to one sect, to one administration, and who resembled each other so much in talents, in opinions, in habits, in fortunes, that one character, **we had almost said** one life, may, to a considerable extent, serve for them all.

NOTES.

1.—Was no, *n'était pas un.*
2.—It is (*see* Pron., Rule IV.) ; we had almost said, *on pourrait presque dire.*

RULE XXXV.

One, before a proper name, is **un certain, une certaine.** When it comes *after an adjective*, do not translate it at all.

Ex.—You have a good pen, but I have a *bad* **one**;
Vous avez une bonne plume, mais j'en ai une *mauvaise*.

Translate.

I.—1. **Dr. Warburton**, in the preface **to** his Shakespeare, speaking of the poem of Polyolbion, says it **was** written by one Drayton; **a mode of expression** very common with **great men,** when they mean to consign the memory of others over to **oblivion** or **contempt.** 2. Bishop Burnet, speaking of the negociations previous to the peace of Utrecht, says in like manner that one Prior was employed to finish the treaty.

NOTES.

1.—Dr. W. (*see* Art., Rule I.); to, *de*; was, put "has been;" a mode of expression, *manière de parler*; great men, oblivion, contempt (*see* Synopsis, Rule I.)

II.—An **idle** reason lessens the weight of the good ones you **gave** before.

NOTES.

Idle, *frivole*; gave, put "have given."

III.—The old **oracle** said : "All things have two **handles ;** beware of the wrong one."

NOTES.

The old oracle, *la sagesse antique*; handle, *anse* (f.)

RULE XXXVI.

Such as is generally translated by **tel que, telle que,** etc., but render it by **ceux qui, ceux que,** when it can be turned into *those...who, which, whom.*

If a noun intervenes between "such" and "as," render **such** by **le, la, les,** and **as** by **qui** or **que.**

Translate.

I.—Let your employment be such as **becomes a** rational being, and your language always such as becomes a gentleman.

NOTES.

Becomes, *il convient.*

II.—Avoid the company of such as are apt to talk much to little purpose, for such talkers are tedious, and hurtful in vain.

III.—We like only such actions as **have** already **long had** the praise of men, and do not perceive that any thing man can do may be divinely done.

NOTES.

Have long had (*see* Verb, Rule XVII.)

RULE XXXVII.

Something, quelque chose, and its reverse, **nothing,** rien ; **somebody,** quelqu'un, and its reverse, **nobody,** personne ; **what...!** quoi...! and **all that,** tout ce que, require **de** before the next adjective or participle, if immediately followed by it.

Ex.—I have seen **nothing** so pretty;
Je n'ai **rien** vu **de** si joli.

Translate.

1.—"I see nothing great, nothing magnanimous, nothing open, nothing direct in his measures or in his mind," exclaims Sheridan in his speech against Warren Hastings; "on the contrary he has too often pursued the worst **objects** by the worst means... 2. In his mind all **was** shuffling, ambiguous, dark, insidious, and little: nothing simple, nothing unmixed; **all** affected plainness, and actual dissimulation; a heterogenous mass of contradictory qualities, with nothing great **but** his crimes."

NOTES.

1.—Object, *i.e. end, but* (m.)
2.—Was, *i.e.* "used to be," *était*; all, put "all was;" but, *si ce n'est*.

VERB.

RULE I.

The verb, pronoun and adjective connected with collective nouns, as " the crowd, *la foule;* the people (nation), *le peuple;* the assembly, *l'assemblée*," etc., must be put into the *singular* in French.

Ex.—The assembly **have** lost some of **their** most remarkable members;
L'assemblée **a** perdu plusieurs de **ses** membres les plus remarquables.

Translate:

I.—1. In 1792, the Girondist Lasource, replying to one of the Royalist deputies who reproached the Assembly with their indifference, exclaimed : " Let us not insult **the people by** lending them sentiments which they do not possess. 2. The people do not menace **either** the person of Louis XVI. **or** the Prince Royal. 3. **They will not** commit excess or violence. Let us adopt measures of mildness and conciliation ! "— (Lamartine's *Girondists.*)

NOTES.

1. The people, *le peuple* ; by (*see* Invar. Words, Rule XII.)
2. Do not menace either...or, put " menace *neither...nor.*"
3. They will not commit...or, put " they will commit *neither... nor.*

II.—One half of the world are ignorant how the other half lives.—(Goldsmith.)

RULE II.

When two verbs or two adjectives have the same object in English, but govern each a different object, or require a different preposition in French, let the object expressed be that of the first verb or adjective, and use a personal pronoun as an object to the second.

Ex.—They attacked and took possession of *the town.*

" To attack " is in French " attaquer," which requires a *direct* object ; " to take possession of " is " s'emparer *de*," which requires an *indirect* object. So, do not say :

>Ils attaquèrent et s'emparèrent *de la ville*,

but :

>They attacked **the town** and took possession **of it;**
>Ils attaquèrent **la ville** et s'en emparèrent.

>He teased and laughed at **him**;
>Il le taquina et se moqua **de lui.**

>We go **to** and return **from** London in **three** hours;
>Nous allons à **Londres** et **en** revenons en trois heures.

Translate.

I.—1. **In** 1623, Buckingham proposed to **Prince Charles** to give the court of Spain the pleasing surprise of a visit. 2. The Prince and Buckingham set out and travelled in disguise, under the names of John and Thomas Smith. 3. At Paris " John Smith " saw and fell in love with the Princess Henrietta, sister of Louis XIII. 4. This accident and Buckingham's disorderly conduct at Madrid were the cause of the rupture with Spain.

NOTES.

In (*see* Synopsis, Rule XXII.); Prince Charles (*see* Art., Rule I.)

II.—"**While** we control even our feelings by our duty," exclaims G. Canning in one of his speeches, "**let** it not be said that we cultivate peace, either because we fear, or because we are unprepared for war."

NOTES.

While (*see* Invar. words, Rule XXXIX.); let (*see* Invar. words, Rule LXXVII.) *verb,*

RULE III.

If the same verb or adjective has several objects united by a conjunction, they must *all* be *of the same kind*, *i.e.* they must all be either nouns, infinitives, or propositions.

> *Ex.*—I believe **your reasons** excellent, and *that* you will persuade him.
>
> Do not say: Je crois *vos raisons* excellentes et *que* vous le persuaderez.
>
> but: Je crois **que** vos raisons sont excellentes et **que** vous le persuaderez.
>
> *Ex.*—He likes reading and riding.
>
> Do not say: Il aime **la** *lecture* et *à monter* à cheval,
> but: Il aime **la lecture** et **l'équitation,**
> or: Il aime **à lire** et **à monter** à cheval.

Translate.

I.—1. William III. **spoke** little, and very slowly, and most commonly with a disgusting dryness, which was his character at all times, except **in** a day of battle; for **then** he was all fire, though without passion. 2. *élan* He did not like contradiction, nor to have his actions censured; but he loved to employ and favour those who **had the arts** of complaisance; yet he did not love flatterers. 3. He was an attentive hearer of sermons, and was constant in his private prayers and in reading the Scriptures; and when he spoke of religious matters, **which** he did not often, it was with **becoming gravity.**

NOTES.

1. Spoke (*see* Rule IX.); in, leave it out; then, *i.e.* "at that time," *alors*.

2. Who had the arts, *qui possédaient l'art*.

3. Which (*see* Pron., Rule XIV.) becoming gravity (*see* Art., Rule XIII.)

II.—Titus, **after entering** the ruins of Jerusalem, **commanded** his soldiers, wearied **with** slaughter, to cease from carnage, except where any still chanced to resist; that the leaders, concealed in the subterraneous passages, should be sought after; that the youths, distinguished by their beauty and stature, should be reserved for his triumph; the more advanced in years be sent into Egypt to the mines.

NOTES.

After entering (*see* Rule XLVII.); commanded, weary *with*, etc. (*see* Invar. words, Rule II.)

PASSIVE VOICE.

RULE IV.

When a passive verb can be turned in English into the active voice with "one, somebody, they, people," for its subject, use in French the latter form preceded by **on**. If there are several verbs, *repeat* "on" before each of them.

VERB—PASSIVE VOICE.

Ex.—This letter **has been brought** for you, *i.e. one has* brought this letter for you;
On a apporté cette lettre pour vous.

It is said and believed that the king is dead, *i.e. they say* and believe...
On dit et **on** croit que le roi est mort.

Rem.—A passive, followed by an object, is often turned into the active voice in French, by making its object the subject, and its subject the object of the active verb.

Ex.—This house was bought by my father;
Cette maison a été achetée par mon père;
or:
Mon père a acheté cette maison.

Translate.

I.—1. Tea is the leaf of a shrub which grows in China. 2. The leaves of the tea-tree **are not unlike** those of a rose-tree. 3. They are gathered twice a year, in spring and in autumn. 4. The youngest are put by themselves. 5. After **this**, they are thrown into boiling water for a minute, and **when the water is poured from them**, they are left to drain. 6. When they are thoroughly dry, they are put upon large iron plates, placed over very hot stoves. 7. When the leaves have been long enough over the fire, they are spread on large shelves and some workmen begin to roll each leaf separately, while others fan the leaves in order that they may cool more quickly. 8. When each leaf has been separately rolled, the tea is shut up in boxes lined with lead. 9. In these boxes are placed some aromatic herbs, and the tea is covered with fine yellow paper, the workmen taking great care that the boxes should be shut very close in order to exclude the least air, **for** if the air were **allowed** to penetrate, it would spoil the tea. 10. In these boxes the tea is exported **to all** parts of Europe.

NOTES.

2. Are not unlike, *ressemblent assez à.*
5. This (*see* Pron., Rule XXIX.); when the water...etc., put "after having poured the water."
9. To allow, *laisser.*
10. To all, *dans toutes les.*

II.—1. There is no portion of history in which it so much behoves an Englishman to be thoroughly versed as in **that** of Cromwell's age. 2. There it may be seen **to what desperate lengths** men of **good hearts and laudable intentions** may be driven by faction. 3. There may be seen the rise, and the progress, and the consequences of rebellion. 4. There are to be found the highest examples of true patriotism, sound principles and heroic virtue.—(Southey.)

NOTES.

1. That (*see* Pron., Rule XXVI.)
2. To what desperate lengths, *à quelles extrémités terribles*; men of good hearts and laudable intentions, we may say " des hommes de coeur," but we cannot say " *hommes d'intentions*," so, put " ...*et animés d'intentions louables.*"

RULE V.

A passive verb may also be rendered in French by the *reflective form*; this is often the case when the subject is an inanimate object, and particularly when the verb implies an action of " eating, drinking, selling," or a state of " growing, becoming."

Ex.—This fruit **is eaten** green;
Ce fruit **se mange** vert.

These pears **are spoiling**;
Ces poires **se gâtent.**

Human life **is composed** of joys and sorrows;
La vie humaine **se compose** de joies et de chagrins.

VERB—PASSIVE VOICE.

Translate.

THE KNOWLEDGE OF COMMON THINGS.

I.—1. Every boy ought to know that he has five senses; that the year has four seasons; that the world is composed of land and water, and divided into five parts; that there are four cardinal points; that metals such as gold, silver and lead, are **dug out** of the earth, and that diamonds are found on the land, and pearls in the sea. 2. Boys ought at an early age to be acquainted with **such** things **as** are **in** common use; but I have often found **it** necessary to explain to them that sugar is made **from** the juice of the sugar-cane which grows in China; and that chocolate is manufactured **from** the seed of a plant of South America, which is called "cocoa."—(Boys' Week-Day Book.)

NOTES.
1. To dig out, *tirer.*
2. Such...as, *les...qui*; in, *d'un*; it (*see* Pron., Rule VI.); from, avec.

II.—1. A soldier ventured, in the presence of the whole army, to present to Charles XII., with an air of complaint, a piece of bread which **was** black and mouldy. 2. The king received the bit of bread without the least emotion, ate it up, and then said coldly to the soldier: "It is not good, but it may be eaten."

NOTE.
1. Was (imperf.)

RULE VI.

There are some verbs which, though transitive in English, are intransitive in French, such are: "to obey, obéir *à*; to please, plaire *à*," etc.; in this case the passive form can *never* be used.

Ex.—**I was pleased** with the book;
Do not say: *J'ai été plu* avec le livre,
but: The book **pleased** me,
Le livre **m'a plu.**

Rem.—To ascertain this, when you come across a passive verb, put it into the active infinitive and see whether what was its nominative can in French become the direct object; if so, use the passive or active, as you think best; if not, then employ the latter.

Ex.—Somebody **was sent** there.
"To send somebody" is "envoyer quelqu'un,"
So you may say either: Quelqu'un y **fut envoyé**,
or: **On** y envoya quelqu'un.

Ex.—The king **being asked** if he would pardon him said he would not.

"To ask somebody" is "demander à quelqu'un." so "to ask" cannot be construed passively in French with a nominative of person, and we must say:

Comme **on** demandait **au** roi s'il voulait lui pardonner, **il** répondit qu'il ne le voulait pas.

Obs.—There are even some cases in which it may be seen at once whether the passive voice can or cannot be employed.

For instance, if the passive verb is preceded in English by a nominative of person and *immediately* followed by a noun or a pronoun in the accusative, you may be sure that the passive voice must *not* be used.

Ex.—**He** was given **a book**.

From what precedes, you may see at once that you cannot translate literally, but must say:

On lui donna un livre.

Translate.

I.—1. As soon as Montrose **had ended** his discourse, he was ordered to withdraw; and after a short space, was again brought in, and told by the chancellor, "that **he was**, on the morrow, being the one-and-twentieth of May 1650, **to be carried** to Edinburgh cross, and thereto be hanged on a gallows thirty foot high, for the space of three hours, **and then** to be taken down, and his head to be cut off upon a scaffold, and hanged on Edinburgh tollbooth; **and** his legs and arms to be hanged up in other public towns of the kingdom, and his body to be buried at the place where he was to be executed, **except** the kirk should take off his excommunication." 2. He **desired** "that he might say something to them," but was not suffered, and so was carried back to the prison.

NOTES.

1. Had ended (*see* Rule XV.); that he was to be carried (*see* Rule LV.); and then, *puis que*; and (leave it out and repeat " *que.*")
2. He desired that he might say, put "he desired (*voulut*) to say."

II.—1. Our lodger made few stipulations, but the few he made **were** sufficiently comprehensive: He was to be granted the usual privileges of a lodger, **such as** coming and going **whenever he pleased**. 2. He was besides to be allowed the use of any book in the library; to be **forbidden** none of the sitting-rooms; to be asked no questions, nor ever refused whatever he might in his discretion choose to ask.

NOTES.

1. Were, *étaient*; such as, *tels que de* (with the *infinitive*); whenever he pleased, *comme il l'entendait*.
2. To forbid, *interdire*.

RULE VII.

When a passive infinitive may be turned in English into the active form, use the latter voice preceded by " à."

Ex.—This house is **to be let**, *i.e.* " is *to let*,"
Cette maison est **à louer.**

If it may be turned into the active form preceded by "can, could," use again this voice with the present or imperfect of indicative of "pouvoir."

Ex—He is a man not **to be trusted** by anybody, *i.e.* "whom nobody *can trust*;"
C'est un homme à qui personne ne *peut se fier*.

Translate.

CHARACTER OF JOHN HAMPDEN.

I....He was of an industry and vigilance **not** to be tired out, **or** wearied by the most laborious, and **of parts** not to be imposed upon by the most subtle or sharp; and of a personal courage equal to **his best parts**; so that **he was an enemy not to be wished wherever he might have been a friend**; and as much to be apprehended where he was **so** as any man could **deserve to be**.—(Lord Clarendon.)

NOTES.

Not...or, put "neither...nor"; of parts, *d'une intelligence telle*; his best parts, *ses plus grands talents*; he was (*see* Pron., Rule II.); an enemy not to be wished...etc., put "a man whom one *ought* (*devait*) not to wish to have *as an* (*pour*) enemy when one could have him as a friend;" so, *le* (before the verb); deserve to be, put "to be *so*."

II.—"The nuns **in** Vienna," writes Lady Montagu, "receive all visits of women, and play at **ombre** in their chambers **with permission** of their abbess, **which** is easy to be obtained."

NOTES.

In (*see* Synop., Rule XXIII.); ombre, *l'ombre*; with permission, put "with *the* permission"; which, as "*qui*" or "*laquelle*" might relate to "*abbesse*" as well as "*permission*," put "a thing which," (and *see* Synopsis, Rule VIII.)

RULE VIII.

A passive infinitive, coming after "to cause, *faire*," "to order, *faire, ordonner*," "to allow, to suffer, *laisser*," should be put into the active form and placed *immediately after* "to cause, faire," or "to order, ordonner, donner l'ordre de," etc.

 Ex.—He *caused* him **to be punished ;**
  Il le *fit* **punir.**

 Do not *suffer* yourself **to be cast down** by misfortune;
 Ne vous *laissez* pas **abattre** par le malheur.

Translate.

GENEROSITY OF CHARLES XII.

1. After the battle of Narva, Charles XII. caused all the prisoners to be conducted over the river ; **had he** kept them, their number would at least have been five times greater than **that** of the conquerors. 2. After **this**, he entered Narva accompanied by the Duke of Croi, and other general officers of the Muscovites. 3. He ordered their swords to be restored to them all ; and, knowing that they wanted money, he caused five hundred ducats to be given to every Muscovite officer, who could not sufficiently admire the civility of this treatment.—(Voltaire's *History of Charles XII., King of Sweden.*)

NOTES.

1. Had he (*see* Ellipsis, Rule I.) ; that (*see* Pron., Rule XXVI.)
2. This (*see* Pron., Rule XXIX.)

TENSES.

Obs.—The **English preterite** may be rendered in French by three tenses:

1. The **indicative imperfect**;
2. The **preterite definite** (passé défini);
3. The **preterite indefinite** (passé indéfini).

The difficulty consists in knowing when each of these tenses should be used.

RULE IX.

The **imperfect** is used to express an action as being done at the time that another, which is *past*, took place, or something *habitually* or *frequently* performed. Before translating an English preterite, try whether it may be changed into the present participle, preceded by " I was, thou wast," etc. (as: **I was doing**), or into the infinitive preceded by " I used to," etc. (as : **I used to do**). If the change can be effected, put the verb into the imperfect.

Ex..—I **went out** for a walk every morning, *i.e.* I *used to go* out;
J'allais me promener tous les matins.

It **rained** when I went out, *i.e.* it *was raining*;
Il **pleuvait** quand je suis sorti.

Translate.

I.—1. "At school," says Hunt, " our **routine of** life was this. 2. We rose to the call of a bell, at six in summer and seven in winter; and, **after** combing ourselves, and washing **our** hands and **faces**, went, at the call of another bell, to breakfast. 3. All this took up **about** an hour. 4. **From** breakfast we proceeded **to school**, where we remained till eleven, winter and summer, and then had **an hour's play**. 5. Dinner took place at twelve. 6. Afterwards **was** a little play till one, **when** we went again to school, and remained till five in summer and four in winter. 7. At six was supper. We used to play **after it** in summer till eight; in winter we proceeded from supper to bed."

NOTES.

1. Our routine of life, *notre vie.*
2. After (*see* Verb, Rule XLVII.); our (*see* Art., Rule III.); faces, put: "face."
3. About (meaning *nearly*), *environ.*
4. From, *après le;* to school, *en classe;* an hour's play, *une heure de récréation.*
6. Was, *nous avions;* when (*see* Invar. Words, Rule XXVII.)
7. After it, *i.e.* "afterwards," *ensuite.*

II.—The Good Shepherd.

1. A shepherd had a great many sheep and lambs. 2. He took a great deal of care of them, and gave them fresh grass **to** eat, and clear water to drink. 3. **When** they climbed up a steep hill, and the lambs were tired, he used to carry them in his arms; when they were grazing in the field, he used to sit upon a stile, and play them a tune. 4. But every night when it grew dark the shepherd called all his flock together, drove them into the fold, and penned them up, and in the morning he unpenned the fold and let them out again.—(Mrs. Barbauld).

NOTES.

2. To (*see* Invar. Words, Rule XXII.)
3. When (*see* Invar. Words, Rule XXXVI.)

RULE X.

The **imperfect** is likewise used when we speak of the character or of some inherent and distinctive qualities of persons or things no longer existing.

Ex.—Nero **was** cruel, *i.e.* used to be cruel;
Néron **était** cruel.

Translate.

WILLIAM III.

1. William the Third had **a** thin and weak body, **was** brown-haired, and of a clear and delicate constitution. 2. He had **a** Roman eagle nose, bright and sparkling eyes, and a large front. 3. He was always asthmatical, and had a **constant deep** cough. 4. His behaviour was solemn and serious, seldom cheerful, and **but** with a few. 5. He spoke little and very slowly. 6. He had a memory that amazed **all about him**.—(G. Burnet.)

NOTES.

1. A (*see* Art., Rule II.; was, leave it out, and put: " had (*to be understood*) brown hair and a clear..., etc."
2. A, *un.*
3. Constant deep, put: " had a cough deep and constant."
4. But, *i.e. only, seulement.*
6. All about him, put : " all *those who were* about him."

RULE XI.

Use also the imperfect when the action or state spoken of was one of certain duration, and was going on, or, in other words, *imperfect* at the time mentioned or alluded to. It may be that no particular period is stated in the sentence; but in that case you generally may be able to add " then, at that time," or such similar expression, without altering the sense.

Translate.

FRANCE in the SEVENTEENTH CENTURY.

1. France united, during the reign of Louis XIV., almost every species of ascendency. 2. Her military glory was at the height. 3. She had vanquished mighty coalitions. She had dictated treaties. She had sub-

jugated great cities and provinces. 4. Her authority was supreme in all matters of good breeding, **from a** duel **to** a minuet. 5. In literature she gave law to the world. 6. The fame of her great writers filled Europe. 7. No other country could produce a tragic poet equal to Racine, a comic poet equal to Molière, an orator so skilful as Bossuet.—(Lord Macaulay's *History of England.*)

NOTES.

In the, *au* (mind you never put : " *dans le...siècle* ").
4. From... to, *depuis...jusqu'à.*

RULE XII.

If none of the rules previously stated can be applied, either the preterite definite or the preterite indefinite should be employed.

The **preterite definite** is used to denote a thing past at a *named* period of time, *entirely* elapsed. It is called also the narrative or historical tense, and is mostly employed in **narrative** or **historical** style.

Ex.—Richard III. **died** in 1485;
Richard III. **mourut** en 1485.

But: "He went this morning," cannot be translated by "Il *partit* ce matin," as "this morning" is part of the day in which the fact is stated, and so the period of time is not *entirely* elapsed.

Translate.

I.—Historical Style.

1. Alfred the Great, after several unsuccessful actions, withdrew to the Isle of Athelney, where, having heard that the Earl of Devonshire had **obtained** a great victory over the Danes, and had taken their magical standard, he disguised himself as a harper, entered the enemy's camp, and was admitted **to** the

principal generals, who praised his talent for music. 2. Having acquired an exact knowledge of the situation of his enemies, and finding that they **were** divided amongst themselves, he seized the favourable moment, joined the Earl, headed his troops, surprised the Danes at Eddington, in Wiltshire, and obtained a complete victory.

NOTES.

1. "To *obtain* a victory" is not "*obtenir*," but "*remporter une victoire*"; to, *auprès de*.
2. Were, apply Rule XI.

II.—NARRATIVE STYLE.

1. Our troop came through the hedge that **bordered** the road, and rushed forward like wolves, crying, "To the bayonet!" 2. In a second the Cossacks were **in their saddles**, and the veterans in the midst of them. 3. I came up out of breath, and like one mad. 4. I **was** not more **than** fifty paces off, when a Cossack, who was flying, turned on me furious, raising his lance **to** strike, and shouting "Hurrah!" 5. I had **only** just time to stoop, and I felt the whizzing of his lance in the air; yea, I felt a shiver through all my veins, and my very hair stood on end.—(Erckmann-Chatrian. *The Blockade of Phalsburg.*)

NOTES.

1. Bordered, apply Rule IX.
2. In their saddles, *en selle*.
4. I was, apply Rule XI.; than, to (*see* Invar. Words, Rule XXVI. and Rule XXXI.)
5. Only, *ne ... que*.

RULE XIII.

The **preterite indefinite** is used to denote a thing done at a time past which is *not named*; or at a time named, but *not entirely* elapsed.

Ex.—He went this morning;
Il *est* parti ce matin. (*See* Rule XII.)

Do as I *told* you;
Faites comme je vous *l'ai* dit.

The **preterite indefinite** is generally used in *familiar correspondence, conversation, speeches,* especially if the facts alluded to are recent or at least not very distant from the time when they are recorded. It must be observed that, contrary to the English, the French employ that tense even when the time is *completely passed* as in the following example:

I **went** to London *yesterday;*
Je **suis allé** à Londres *hier.*

Translate.

I.—CORRESPONDENCE.

COWPER TO JOSEPH HILL.

Huntingdon, June 24th, 1765.

1. Dear Joe,—I left St. Alban's on the 17th, and arrived **that** day at Cambridge, spent some time there with my brother, and came hither on the 22nd. 2. I am not quite alone, having **brought a servant** with me from St. Alban's, **who** is the very mirror of fidelity and affection for his master. 3. And whereas the Turkish spy says he **kept** no servant, because he **would** not have an enemy in his house, I hired mine because I **would** have a friend. 4. **Men** do not usually bestow encomiums on their lackeys, nor do they deserve **them**; but I had experience of mine, and never saw his fellow...

NOTES.

1. That, put: " the same."
2. Brought, bear in mind that " to bring *somebody* " is not " *apporter quelqu'un,*" as this would mean " to *carry* the person," but " *amener quelqu'un* "; a servant...who (*see* Pron., Rule X.)
3. He kept, apply Rule IX.; would (*see* Rule LXIII.)
4. Men, *on;* them, put: *it.*

II.—CONVERSATION.

1. The mother came into the room; but when she saw the broken basin and the milk spilled, she stopped short, and cried, "Dear, dear, **what a piece of work is here**! Who did this, Robert?" "I don't know, mother," said Robert, in a very low voice. 2. "You don't know, Robert? Tell me the truth, I shall not be angry with you. I ask you, Robert, **did you** break the basin?" 3. "No, mother, I **did** not," said Robert; and he **coloured as red** as fire. 4. "Then where's Frank? **Did he** do it?" "No, mother," said Robert. "How do you know," said his mother, "that Frank did not do it?" 4. "Because—because—because, mother," said Robert, hesitating as liars do **for** an excuse, "because I was in the room all the time, and I did not see him do it." 5. "Then how was the basin thrown down? If you have been in the room all the time, you can **tell**." 6. Then Robert going on from one lie to another, answered, "I suppose **the dog** must have done it." "Did you see him do it?" said his mother. "Yes," said the wicked boy.—(Maria Edgeworth.)

NOTES.

1. What a piece... etc., *voilà de bel ouvrage!*
2. Did you..., put "is it you who broke..."
3. I did not, put "it is not I"; he coloured as red as fire, put "he *became* red as fire" and *see* Synopsis, Rule I.; did he do it, put "is it he who...;" etc.
4. For, put "for *finding*," and *see* Invar. Words, Rule XLVII.
5. Tell, put "tell *it*."
6. I suppose the dog must have done it, put "I suppose it is the dog who did it."

III.—SPEECH.

ATTACK **upon** MR. FLOOD.

1. You began your parliamentary career with an acrimony and personality which **could have been** justified only by a supposition of virtue. 2. After a rank and clamorous opposition, you became on a sudden silent;

you were silent for seven years: you were silent on the greatest questions! ... 3. In 1773, while a negotiation was pending to sell your talents and your turbulence, you absconded from your duty **in Parliament**, you forsook the questions of economy, and abandoned all the themes of your former declamation... 4. Your sale taking place, you supported the rankest measures that ever came before Parliament, the embargo of 1776, for instance... 5. You, sir, who delight to utter execrations against the American commissioners of 1778 on account of their hostility **to** America, you, sir, voted 4,000 Irish troops to cut the throats of the Americans fighting for their freedom, fighting for your freedom, fighting for the great principle, liberty.—(Henry Grattan.)

NOTES.

Upon, *contre.*
1. Could have been (*see* Rule LXXIV.)
3. In Parliament, put "in *the* Parliament."
5. To, *envers.*

RULE XIV.

It was, followed by a verb in the preterite, is generally rendered in French by the present " c'est, ce sont."

Ex.—**It was** you who *did* it;
C'est vous qui avez fait cela.

Translate.

"If the scriptures are rightly understood," writes Lord Byron, "it was in Armenia that Paradise was placed; it was in Armenia that the flood first abated, **and** the dove alighted."

NOTES.

And, "that" should be repeated after "and."

Obs.—It has just been seen that "I had" corresponds to two tenses, the imperfect (j'avais) and the preterite definite (j'eus). This easily accounts for the **English pluperfect** being rendered in French by two tenses:

1. The **pluperfect** (j'avais...)
2. The **past anterior** (j'eus...).

RULE XV.

The **past anterior** is never used except after such conjunctions or adverbs as "when, *quand*," "as soon as, *dès que, aussitôt que*," "after, *après que*," "soon, *bientôt*," "scarcely, *à peine*." So when there is no such conjunction or adverb, you will know at once that the pluperfect must be used.

Let it also be observed that "if, *si*," always requires the *pluperfect*.

Ex.—He told me that he **had seen** you;
Il m'a dit qu'il vous **avait vu**.

If I **had** wished, I might have obtained that situation;
Si **j'avais** voulu, j'aurais obtenu cette place.

RULE XVI.

After such adverbs or conjunctions as those above quoted, use the **pluperfect** if the action has been done *more than once*, and the **past anterior** when it has occurred *once only*.

Ex.—Every morning when I **had** breakfasted, I went out;
Tous les matins quand **j'avais** déjeuné, je sortais. (The action has been repeated.)

Yesterday when I **had** dined I went out;
Hier quand **j'eus** dîné, je sortis. (The action occurred only once.)

Translate.

MARIA.

1. When Maria had **come** a little to herself, I asked her if she remembered a **pale, thin** man, who had sat down betwixt her and her goat about two years before? 2. She said she remembered it upon two accounts; that, **ill as** she was at that time, she saw the person pitied her; and next, that her goat had stolen **his** handkerchief, and she had beat him for the theft; she had washed **it**, she said, in the brook, and kept it ever since in her pocket to restore it **to him** in case she should ever see him again. —(L. Sterne.)

NOTES.

1. Come to herself, *revenue à elle ;* pale, thin (*see* Adj., Rule II.)
2. Ill as, *toute malade que ;* "his handkerchief," if you were to translate by *son mouchoir*, it might mean *her* as well as *his* handkerchief; so, in order to avoid this ambiguity, put "the handkerchief of *that gentleman ;*" it, put "the handkerchief" to make the sense quite clear; to him, put again "to *that gentleman*," for the same reason.

RULE XVII.

In English the *preterite indefinite* is used to mark an action still going on at the time they speak; but in French you should use the **present tense** with **depuis**, so:

Ex.—How long **has** he **been** ill? put "*Since* when *is* he ill?"
Depuis combien de temps **est**-il malade?

He **has been** ill for two years (*or* these two years), put:

"He *is* ill *since* two years."
Il **est** malade **depuis** deux ans.

The literal translation: "Il *a été* malade *pendant* deux ans" would mean, He *was* ill for two years.

Rem.—You may also begin with the time preceded by "il y a" or "voilà," and followed by "que," thus:

"*Il y a*" or "*voilà* deux ans *qu'il est* malade."

Observe that the fact or event expressed by the verb must still be lasting; otherwise the preterite indefinite should be used in French as well as in English.

Ex.—I have not seen him these two years.

The fact of "seeing" him is completely past, is no longer existing, as I saw him two years ago, and neither have I seen him since, nor do I see him at the moment I am speaking; so we must say:

Je ne l'**ai** pas **vu** depuis deux ans,
or Il y a deux ans que je *ne* l'**ai vu**.

Translate.

1. **On all** public solemnities, the Knights of the Garter take precedence of the Knights of the Bath. 2. **Nor** is **this** surprising, **since** the Order of the Garter, instituted by King Edward III., has now been in existence for these five centuries back, whereas that of the Bath, **supposed** to have been instituted by Henry IV., and revived under King George I., has lasted only for some hundred and odd years.

NOTES.

1. On all, put "*in* all *the.*"
2. Nor ..., put "and this is not..."; this (*see* Pron., Rule XXIX.); since (*see* Invar. Words, Rule XXII.); supposed, put " which is supposed " and *see* Rule IV.

RULE XVIII.

The *pluperfect* used in English to mark an action continued up to a certain time mentioned in the sentence should be translated in French by the **imperfect** with **depuis**.

VERB—TENSES. 97

Ex.—How long **had he been playing?** put "*Since* when *was he playing?*"

"**Depuis** quand" or "depuis combien de temps **jouait**-il?"

He **had been playing for** an hour;
Il **jouait depuis** une heure.

Rem.—You may also begin with the time preceded by "Il y avait," and followed by "que," thus:

Il y avait une heure qu'il *jouait*.

Translate.

AN ORIENTAL TALE.

1. I **passed** one day by an ancient and wonderfully populous city, and asked one of its inhabitants how long it had been founded. 2. "**It** is a mighty city," was the reply; "but we know not how long it has existed." 3. Five centuries afterwards I passed by the same place, but the city **was gone**, and upon its site was a peasant gathering herbs; I demanded of him how long it had been destroyed. 4. "The ground," answered the peasant, "has never been different from what you now behold it." 5. "Was there not of old," said I, "a splendid city here?" "Never," answered he, "so far as we have seen, and never did our fathers speak to us of **any such**." 6. **On** my return **there**, five hundred years afterwards, I found a sea, and on its shores a party of fishermen, of whom I inquired how long the land had been covered by the waters. 7. "This spot," said they, "has always been what it is now." 8. I again **returned**, after the same lapse of time, and found there a more populous city than the first. 9. I would fain have informed myself concerning its origin, but the inhabitants answered me, "Its rise is lost in remote antiquity: we are ignorant how long it has existed, and our fathers were on this subject as ignorant as ourselves."

Roulier's Second Book. H

NOTES.
1. Passed (*see* Rule IX.)
2. It (*see* Pron., Rule III.)
3. Was gone, put "had disappeared."
5. Any such, *rien de semblable.*
6. On, *à,* and leave " there " out.
7. " To return," when meaning " to *come back,*" is *revenir,* and not *retourner,* which means "to *go* back again."

RULE XIX.

The future and the conditional may be used in English *to mark a habit;* but in French use the **present indicative** for the future, and the **imperfect** instead of the conditional.

Ex.—He **will** often **remain** silent for hours;
    Il **garde** souvent le silence pendant des heures entières.

    He **would** often **remain**..., etc.
    Il **gardait** souvent..., etc.

Translate.

I.—The Ass.

1. The ass is too often set down as an obstinate, stupid creature ; but **this** is not **right**. 2. The ass is by nature neither stupid nor obstinate; he **only** becomes **so through** blows and **ill treatment**. 3. He has many good qualities which **are** too often **forgotten**. 4. For instance, he will go a long distance without being tired, if you do not hurry him too much. 5. He will be satisfied with food which a horse **would** not eat **if he were ever so hungry**. 6. He will learn very soon to know his master, if he is kindly treated, will come at his call, and toil bravely in his service. 7. **Added** to this, the ass is very sure-footed, and will ascend and descend hills on which a horse could scarcely stand. 8. I think

you will allow, the ass is not really so stupid as **is supposed.** 9. The blame **lies with** those people who beat and ill use a poor dumb creature.

NOTES.

1. This (*see* Pron., Rule XXVII., *Rem.*); right, *juste*.
2. Only (*see* Invar. Words, Rule I.) ; so, *le* (before the verb) ; through, *par suite des* ; ill treatment, make it plural.
3. Are forgotten (*see* Rule IV.)
5. Would (*see* Rule LXIII.); if he were..., etc., *tant affamé fût-il*.
7. Added, put "add."
8. As is supposed, *qu'on le suppose*.
9. Lies with, *retombe sur*.

II.—THE BEAR.

1. A long time since, when I was not so old as you **are**, a man would come to the town **that** I was **in** with a bear **to show**. 2. He led it by a rope, and **it** would get up on its hind legs and walk up and down when the man **told** him to do so. 3. This bear had a long coat of dark hair, and would rest its two fore paws on a strong staff, and sit up to beg for buns or bits of cakes. 4. It was quite tame, and did not wish to hurt you.

NOTES.

1. You are (*see* Verb, Rule XL.); that I was in, put "*where* I *was*;" to show, put "which he showed..."
2. It, *il* would be ambiguous, as it might relate to "man" as well as to "bear"; so see what you must do to avoid that ambiguity; when the man told him, *i.e. whenever* the man told him, so the action was often repeated (*see* Verb, Rule IX.)

RULE XX.

The English often use the indicative instead of the future, especially after "when, as soon as, as long as, whilst, as," etc.; but in French you should use the **future whenever it is meant.**

Ex.—As soon as he **comes**, give him this letter, *i.e.* " as soon as he *will* come..." So put:
Dès qu'il **viendra**, donnez-lui cette lettre.

Do as you **please**, *i.e.* as you *will please*.
Faites comme vous **voudrez**.

I shall give you the book, when I **have** read it, *i.e.* when I *shall have* read it.
Je vous donnerai le livre, quand je l'**aurai** lu.

Translate.

CASTLES **in the Air.**

1. ..." This basket," said Alnaschar to himself, " cost me at the wholesale merchant's a hundred pounds; I shall quickly make two hundred **by** selling it in retail. 2. These two hundred pounds will in a very little rise to four hundred, which will amount in time to four thousand. 3. Four thousand pounds cannot fail of making eight thousand. 4. As soon as by these means I am master of ten thousand pounds, I will lay aside my trade **as a** glassman, and turn **a** jeweller. 5. When I have got together as much wealth as I can **desire**, I will make a purchase of the finest house I can find, with lands, slaves, and horses. 6. I shall then begin to **enjoy myself**, and **make a noise** in the world. 7. I will not, however, stop there, but still continue my traffic **until** I have got together a hundred thousand pounds. 8. When I have thus made myself master of a hundred thousand pounds, I shall naturally set myself on the footing of a prince, and will demand the grand vizier's daughter in marriage. 9. When I have **married** the princess and **brought** her to my house, I shall take particular **care** to breed her in due respect for me. 10. **To** this end I shall confine her **to** her own apartments, make her a short visit, and talk **but** little to her. 11. Her women

will represent to me that she is inconsolable, but I shall remain inexorable. 12. Her mother will then come and bring her daughter to me, **as** I am seated on my sofa. 13. The daughter, with tears in her eyes, will fling herself at my feet, and beg of me to receive her in my favour. 14. Then will I, whilst she is in this attitude, to imprint in her a thorough veneration for my person, spurn her from me with my foot in such a manner that she shall fall down several paces from the sofa."—(Addison.)

NOTES.

In the air, *en Espagne.*
1. By (*see* Invar. Words, Rule XII.)
4. As, *de;* a (*see* Synopsis, Rule IX.)
5. Desire, put " desire *of it.*"
6. "To enjoy one's self" is neither *s'enjouir*, which is not French, nor *se réjouir*, which means " to rejoice," but *s'amuser;* to make a noise, *faire* **du** *bruit.*
7. Until (*see* Verb, Rule XXXIII.)
9. " To marry " is not *marier*, which means " to give in marriage," but *épouser;* brought (*see* Rule XIII., I., Note 2); care, put " *a* care."
10. To, *dans* ; but, *ne...que.*
12. As, *i.e. whilst,* tandis que.

RULE XXI.

In English the preterite may be used for the conditional present, and the pluperfect for the conditional past, particularly after " when, as soon as," etc. ; but in French you should express the **conditional whenever it is meant.**

> *Ex.*—I was told I could see him when he **came** back, *i.e.* " when he *should come* back ; "
> On m'a dit que je pourrais le voir quand il **reviendrait.**

> He said he would come when he **had finished**, *i.e.* " when he *should have* finished ; "
> Il dit qu'il viendrait lorsqu'il **aurait** fini.

Translate.

"**Wast thou** in my own land," says Sterne to Maria, "where I have a cottage, I would **take** thee to it, and shelter thee; thou shouldst eat of my own bread, and drink **of** my own cup; when the sun went down, I would say my prayers; and when I had done, thou shouldst play thy evening song upon thy pipe; **nor** would the incense of my sacrifice be worse accepted for entering heaven along with that of a broken heart."

NOTES.

Wast thou (*see* Ellip., Rule I.); "to take *somebody* somewhere" is not "*prendre*" but "*mener*" *quelqu'un quelque part*; of, *à*; "nor" at the beginning of a sentence and when *not* preceded by "neither" is to be rendered like "and...not."

RULE XXII.

The preterite may also be used in English for the pluperfect; when such is the case, put in French the pluperfect or the past anterior according to Rule XV.

Ex.—He had been very unhappy since he **left** me, *i.e.* "since he *had left* me;"
Il avait été très malheureux depuis qu'il **m'avait** quitté.

He was very unhappy after he **left** me, *i.e.* "after he *had left* me;"
Il fut très malheurex après qu'il m'**eut quitté.**

Translate.

1. On the 31st of May, 1854, Livingstone came in sight of the Portuguese settlement, called St. Paul de Loanda. 2. It was pleasant to the white man to think

that he should once more enjoy communion with educated christian men, and the comforts of civilization. 3. Since he parted from his family at Cape Town, and turned his face once more to the north, **he had been a sojourner** in the forest and the wilderness, **either** in solitude, **or** with some strange faces around him.

NOTES.

3. He had been a sojourner (*see* Subst., Rule I.); either...or, *soit...soit.*

RULE XXIII.

After "si, *if*," use in French the **present** tense instead of the *future*, and the **imperfect** instead of the *conditional*.

Ex.—**If** he **should come, I shall** go, *i.e.* "if he *comes*;"
   S'il vient, je m'en irai.

   If you **should see** him, would you tell it him?
   Si vous le **voyiez,** voudriez-vous le lui dire?

But the future and conditional are retained after "si, *whether.*"

Ex.—I do not know **whether** he **will come;**
   Je ne sais s'il **viendra.**

Translate.

I.—1. The very negative blessings which we commonly enjoy, deserve the thanksgivings of a whole life. 2. If God should send a cancer upon **thy** face, or a wolf into thy side, if he should spread a crust of leprosy upon thy skin, what wouldst thou give **to** be but as thou now art?

NOTES.

2. Thy (*see* Art., Rule III.); to (*see* **Invar.** Words, Rule XXXI.)

II.—The obligation which we all **deem we lie under** of **consulting ourselves whether** we shall do one thing rather than another, is a certain proof of the liberty of our choice, **for** we do not **consult** as to things which we deem **matters of necessity**, as, for instance, whether we shall have to die one day.

NOTES.

We deem we lie under, put " we deem to have ; " consulting with ourselves whether, put " consulting ourselves to (*i.e. in order to*) know whether ; " for, *i.e.* " *because*," *car* ; to consult, *délibérer* ; matter of necessity, put " necessary."

RULE XXIV.

When " if," placed at the beginning of a sentence, is followed by several verbs having different subjects, put **si** before the first with the *indicative*, and **que** before each of the others with the *subjunctive*.

Ex.—If he **should** come and I **should** be out...
S'il **venait** et **que** je **fusse** sorti...

Rem.—If the verbs have the same subject, you may either apply this rule or translate literally, so :

Ex.—If my friend *calls* and *asks* for me...
Si mon ami *vient* et me *demande*...

or : *Si* mon ami vient et *qu'il* me demande...

Translate.

NECESSITY OF LAW.

If nature should intermit her course, and leave altogether, **though** it were only for a while, the observation of her own laws ; if the frame of that heavenly arch erected over our heads should loosen and dissolve itself; if the prince of the lights of heaven should begin to stand and to rest himself; if the moon should wander from her **beaten** way, the times and seasons of the year blend themselves by disordered and confused **mixture**, the winds breathe out their last gasp, the clouds yield no rain, the earth be defeated of heavenly influence, the fruits of the earth pine away; what would become of man himself, whom these things do now **all** serve ?—(R. Hooker.)

NOTES.

Beaten, *ordinaire*; mixture, put " *a* mixture ;" all, construe " all these things."

RULE XXV.

After a verb of **motion** (to go, to come, to run, etc.,) put the next verb into the infinitive, "**and**" being left out.

Ex.—Go **and** fetch my brother, put go *to fetch* my brother; Allez **chercher** mon frère.

Translate.

Leonidas replied proudly to Xerxes, who asked him to give up his arms: " **come** and take them."

NOTE.

Come (2nd person singular.)

MOODS.

INDICATIVE AND SUBJUNCTIVE.

RULE XXVI.

It is rather a common error with students to believe that the conjunction " that, que," governs the subjunctive in French ; they should bear in mind that, except in two cases, stated hereafter (*see* Rule XXXIII. and Rule XXXV.), it *cannot have* any influence over the mood to be subsequently employed ; that mood depends entirely upon the verb or expression which precedes and governs the conjunction.

Ex.—He told me **that** you **were** arrived;
    Il m'a dit **que** vous **étiez** arrivés; *not* " que vous *fussiez*," as " dire " governs the indicative.

Rem.—" That " should *never* be omitted in French.

Translate.

1. At the **time** of the establishment of the diligences in England, many persons were, as usual, disposed to clamour against the innovation simply because **it was** an innovation. 2. **It was argued** that this mode of conveyance would be fatal to the breed of horses and to the noble art of horsemanship ; that the Thames, which **had long been** an important nursery for seamen, would cease to be the chief thoroughfare from London **up** to Windsor and **down** to Gravesend ; that saddlers and spurriers would be ruined by hundreds ; that numerous inns would be deserted, and would no longer pay any rent; that the new carriages were too hot in summer and too cold in winter ; that the passengers were grievously annoyed by invalids and **crying children** ; that the coach

sometimes reached the inns so late that it was impossible **to get supper**; and sometimes started so early that it was impossible to get breakfast.—(Macaulay.)

NOTES.

1. Time, *époque*; it was (see Pron., Rule III.)
2. It was argued (*see* Verb, Rule IV.); had long been (*see* Verb, Rule XVIII.); up...down (to be left out); crying children, *les cris des enfants;* to get supper, *d'avoir à souper.*

RULE XXVII.

Bearing in mind that the conjunction "that" does not necessarily govern the subjunctive, it remains to see how it can be ascertained when that mood must be employed.

The subjunctive expresses **doubt** and **indecision**; so, if the action or event spoken of is *uncertain*, use the **subjunctive**; if the action is *certain*, or simply if *affirmation* or *belief* is expressed as to its existence or accomplishment, use the **indicative**.

Ex.—I wish that he **may come.**

It is uncertain whether my wish will be fulfilled, it is not sure at all that he will come; so, "he may come" must be put into the subjunctive.

Je désire qu'il **vienne.**

Ex.—It is necessary you **should do** it.

Though it be necessary, is it certain that the thing will be done? No; so use the subjunctive.

Il est nécessaire que vous le **fassiez.**

Ex.—I hope, I think, I am sure you **will succeed**;
J'espère, je crois, je suis sûr que vous **réussirez.**

RULE XXVIII

When once you know that you must employ the subjunctive mood, you still have to determine on the *tense*. It is a question which is regulated by the preceding verb, on which the subjunctive is always dependent.

1. If the verb in the principal clause is in the *present* or in the *future*, use the **present of the subjunctive**.

>   *Ex.*—I **doubt, I shall doubt** whether he **will come**;
>   Je **doute**, je **douterai**, qu'il **vienne**.

2. If the verb in the principal clause is in the *imperfect indicative*, the *past definite*, in short in any *past tense*, or in the *conditional*, use the **imperfect of the subjunctive**.

>   *Ex.*—I *doubted*, I *have doubted*, I *should doubt* whether he **would come**;
>   Je *doutais*, j'*ai douté*, je *douterais*, qu'il **vînt**.

>   *Obs.*—We will now lay down a few rules to guide the student, but he should bear in mind that they refer only to particular cases of the general principle previously established, and that in each of them the use of the indicative or the subjunctive will be determined by *belief*, *likeliness*, or *certainty* on the one hand, and *doubt* or *uncertainty* on the other.

RULE XXIX.

The subjunctive is used:

1. After most impersonal verbs, as **il faut, il convient, il est juste, il est bon**, etc. Those are excepted which imply *certainty* or *likeliness*, as " il est certain, il est vrai, il est évident, il parait, il me, te, lui,...semble, il est probable," etc.

>   *Ex.*—*It is certain* that he **is** arrived;
>   *Il est certain* qu'il **est** arrivé.

>   *It is good* that he **should be** punished;
>   *Il est bon* qu'il **soit** puni.

2. After the **superlative** or an adjective equivalent to a superlative, as **le seul, l'unique, le premier**, etc.; after a **relative pronoun,** "qui, que, dont, où," etc., when the sense is doubtful; also after **whatever,** quelque ... que (adj.), quoi que (pron.), **whoever,** qui que ce soit qui, **however,** si...que."

Ex.—This is *the best* picture that I **have** ever seen;
Voici *le meilleur* tableau que **j'aie** jamais vu.

The affirmation in this case is not positive; it is simply meant to express our admiration for the thing which is before our eyes; but it is obvious we cannot sufficiently remember all the pictures we have seen previously to the time when we speak, to be able to pronounce the one we look at to be really the best. *Doubt* is therefore implied, and the subjunctive should be used. But we say with the indicative:

Of these men it is *the tallest* **I know**;
De ces hommes c'est *le plus grand* que je **connais**;

for the thing is quite certain.

I wish to find a house *which* **may please** me;
Je désire trouver une maison *qui* me **plaise**;

as I do not know whether I shall find it.

But the indicative must be used in the next sentence:

I have found a house *which* **pleases** me;
J'ai trouvé une maison qui me **plaît**;

because there is no doubt implied.

Translate.

I.—1. **After** having paid my passage with half my moveables, I found myself, **as if** fallen from the skies, a stranger in one of the principal streets of Amsterdam

2. In this situation, I was unwilling to let any time pass unemployed in teaching. 3. I addressed myself, therefore, to two or three of those I met, but it was impossible to make ourselves understood. 4. **It was not till** this moment **I recollected** that, in order to teach the Dutchmen **English**, it was necessary that they should teach me Dutch. 5. How I came to overlook so obvious an objection is to me amazing, but **certain it is** I overlooked it.—(O. Goldsmith.)

NOTES.

1. After (*see* Invar. Words, Rule XVII.); as if, *comme*; a (to be left out).
4. It was not till, *ce n'est qu'à*; I recollected, put: "*that* I recollected"; English, put: "*the* English."
5. Certain it is, put: "it is certain."

II.—Mind your diction. In whatever language you may **either** write or speak, **contract a habit of** correctness and elegance.

NOTES.

Either (to be left out); contract a habit of, *habituez-vous à*.

III.—The example of a good life is the best lesson one can give to the human kind.

IV.—Nothing can be more narrow-minded than the contempt with which, **in the** last century, it was fashionable to speak of the pilgrimages, the sanctuaries, the crusades, and the monastic institutions of the middle ages. 2. **In times when** men were scarcely ever induced to travel by liberal curiosity, or by the pursuit of gain, it was better that the rude inhabitant of the North should visit Italy and the East **as a** pilgrim, **than that** he should never see anything but those squalid cabins and uncleared woods amongst which he was born. 3. In times when life and honour were exposed to risk daily from tyrants and marauders, it was better that the precinct of a shrine should be regarded with an irrational awe, **than that there should be** no refuge inaccessible to cruelty and licentiousness. 4. In times when statesmen were incapable of forming extensive political combinations, it was better that the Christian nations should be roused and united for the recovery of the Holy Sepulchre, than that they should, one by one, be overwhelmed by the Mahomedan power. 5. Whatever reproach may at a later period have been justly thrown on the indolence and luxury of the religious orders, it was surely good that, in an age of ignorance and violence, there should be quiet cloisters and gardens, in which the arts of peace could be safely cultivated, in which gentle and contemplative natures could find an asylum, in which one brother could employ himself **in** transcribing the **Æneid** of **Virgil**, and another in meditating the Analytics of **Aristotle**, in which **he who** had **a genius for** art might illuminate a martyrology or carve a crucifix, and in which he who had a turn for natural philosophy might make experiments on the properties of plants and minerals.—(Macaulay.)

NOTES.

1. In the, *au*.

2. In times when, *à une époque où* ; **as a** (*see* Art., Rule XIV.) ; than that he, *que de* (with the infinitive).

3. Than that there should be, *que de ne pas avoir*.

5. In, *à* (*see* Invar. Words, Rule XVII.) ; the Æneid of Virgil, *l'Enéide de Virgile*; Aristotle, *Aristote;* he who (*see* Pron., Rule I.) ; a genius for (*see* Art., Rule XIII., Rem.).

RULE XXX.

The subjunctive is used :

3. After **interrogative** and **negative** verbs followed by "que" or a relative, and denoting **something uncertain.**

Ex.—Do you think he **will come**;
Croyez-vous qu'il **vienne** ?

I do **not** think he **will go** so soon;
Je **ne** crois **pas** qu'il **parte** si tôt.

But say with the indicative :

Do you know **that** he **is arrived** ?
Savez-vous qu'il **est arrivé** ?

as there is no doubt as to his having arrived.

I do not know **whether** he **will come**;
Je ne sais pas **s**'il **viendra**.

as "sais" is not followed by "que."

Obs.—It must be observed that even verbs which generally do not govern the subjunctive (as "croire, espérer," etc.), do so, when negative or interrogative, if doubt or uncertainty is implied.

Translate.

FROM LORD ERSKINE'S SPEECH ON THE TRIAL OF STOCKDALE.

1. Gentlemen, I tremble with indignation to be driven to put **such a** question in England. 2. **Shall it be endured** that a subject of this country may be impeached by the Commons for the transactions of twenty years, that the accusation shall spread as wide as the region of letters, that the accused shall stand day after day, and year after year, as a spectacle before the public, which shall be kept in a perpetual state of inflammation against him ; yet that he shall not, without the severest penalties, **be permitted** to submit anything to the judgment of mankind in his defence ?...

NOTES.

1. Such a (*see* Art., Rule XV.)
2. Shall it be endured (to endure, *souffrir*, *see* Verb, Rule IV.); to be permitted, *pouvoir*.

RULE XXXI.

The subjunctive is used:

4. After verbs expressing **doubt**, or **wish, will, command.**

> *Ex.*—I **doubted** whether he **would come;**
> Je **doutais** qu'il **vînt.**
>
> I **wish** you **to do** it;
> Je **désire** que vous le **fassiez.**

Observe that "whether" after "douter" is rendered by *que*.

Translate.

I.—**On** hearing that Charles XII. was killed, the Prince of Hesse gave **instant orders** that no one should stir out of the camp, and that all the passes to Sweden should be strictly guarded, **that** he **might have time** to take the necessary measures **for** placing the crown on his wife's head.

NOTES.

On (*see* **Invar. Words,** Rule XXXVI.); gave instant orders, put "gave immediately the order;" that (*see* Rule XXIII.); might (*see* Rule LXVII.); have time, put "have *the* time;" for (*see* Invar. Words, Rule XVII.)

II.—1. A German lady, one of the keepers of the Queen's robes, retired, and her Majesty offered the vacant post to Miss Burney. 2. **What was demanded** of her was that she should consent to be almost as completely separated from her family and friends as if she had gone to Calcutta; that with talents which had instructed and delighted the highest minds, she should now be employed only **in** mixing snuff and sticking pins; that she should pass her whole life under the restraints of a paltry etiquette, should sometimes fast till she was ready to swoon **with** hunger, should sometimes stand till her knees gave way with fatigue; that she should not dare to speak or move without considering how her mistress might like her words or gestures.—(Macaulay.)

NOTES.

2. What (*see* Pron., Rule XXIV.); was demanded (*see* Rule XI.); in (*see* Invar. Words, Rule II.); with, *de*.

III.—Death of Henry VIII.

1. Shortly before his death the king desired that Cranmer **might be sent for**; but **before** the prelate arrived he was speechless, **though** he still seemed to retain his senses. 2. Cranmer desired him to give some sign **of his dying** in the faith of **Christ**; he squeezed the prelate's hand, and immediately expired.

NOTES.

1. Might be sent for (*see* Rule IV.); before (*see* Rule XXIII. and *Rem.*); though (*see* Rule XXXIII.)
2. Of his dying (*see* Rule XLII.); Christ, *le Christ*.

RULE XXXII.

The subjunctive is used:

5. After verbs expressing **joy, pleasure, sorrow, fear, pity, surprise**, in fact *any emotion*, as "être content, être charmé, être bien aise, regretter, craindre, trembler, s'étonner," etc.—"**Espérer**, to hope," must be excepted. (*See* Rule XXVII.)

    Ex.—I **was afraid** you **were** unwell;
        Je **craignais** que vous *ne* **fussiez** malade.

    I **am glad you told** it him;
        Je **suis bien aise** que vous le lui **ayez** dit.

Rem.—**Craindre, appréhender, avoir peur, trembler,** require **ne** before the subjunctive; this particle is the same as the Latin "*ne*, lest," which is put after "*timere*, to fear."

"Lest" after those verbs is rendered by **que.**

Translate.

I.—1. "**It has been** judiciously **remarked,**" says Hume, "that we attach ourselves more by the services we perform than by those we receive, and that a man is in danger of losing his friends **by** obliging them **too far.** 2. I should therefore choose **to lie in the middle way**, and to have my commerce with my friend varied both by obligations given and received. 3. I have too much pride **to** be willing that all the obligations should be on my side, and should be afraid that, if they all lay on his, he would also have too much pride **to be entirely easy under them**, or have a perfect complacency in my company."

NOTES.

1. It has been remarked (*see* Rule IV.); by (*see* Invar. Words, Rule XII.); too far, put "too much."

2. To lie in the middle way, *rester dans le juste milieu.*

3. To, *pour*; to be entirely...etc., *pour n'en être nullement incommodé.*

II.—1. When Charles I. heard of the transaction which had been concluded between the Scotch and the English, he declared that he was bought and sold. 2. "Yet," **he added**, "if I am sold by the Scots, I may justify them **to all the world**, for I never **trusted** them farther **than to men.** 3. I am only sorry they have done it, and that my price should be so much above **my Saviour's.** 4. **Better** others should betray me **than myself**, and **that** the price of my liberty should be my conscience."

NOTES.

2. He added (*see* Synopsis, Rule XVIII.); to all the world, *aux yeux du monde entier*; I trusted (to trust, *avoir confiance en*, *see* Rule XIII.); than to men, *qu'il ne convient d'en avoir dans les hommes.*
3. My Saviour's (*see* Pron., Rule XXVII.)
4. Better, *mieux vaut*; than myself, *que de me trahir moi-même*; that, *que si.*

III. The Norman Conquest.

1. The English were not sensible that they had surrendered themselves without resistance, to a tyrant and a conqueror. 2. **Though** the early confiscation of Harold's followers might seem iniquitous, yet **were these rigours excused** on account of the urgent necessities of the prince, and those who were not involved in the present ruin hoped that they should henceforth enjoy, without molestation, their possessions and dignities.—(D. Hume.)

NOTES.

2. Though (*see* Rule XXXIII.); were these...etc., put "these rigours were excused," and *see* Rule IV.

RULE XXXIII.

The subjunctive is used:

6. After **that,** meaning "**in order that**, afin que, pour que," and the following conjunctions:

```
although, though ...quoique, bien que,
before ..................avant que,
in order that .........afin que, pour que,
lest, for fear...........de peur que, de crainte que,
provided ...............pourvu que,
unless ..................à moins que,
till, until ...........jusqu'à ce que,
whether ...............soit que,
without ...............sans que.
```

Ex.—I give you this book **that** you **may read** it, *i.e.*, *in order that...*
Je vous donne ce livre **pour que** vous le **lisiez**.

Rem.—The three conjunctions **à moins que, de peur que, de crainte que**, require *ne* before the subjunctive. **Avant que** should also be followed by *ne*, but only when doubt is implied.

Ex.—I shall not be able to do it, **unless** you **help** me ;
Je ne pourrai pas faire cela, **à moins que** vous **ne m'aidiez**.

Translate.

I.—When a troop of wild swans fly away, one is sure to take the lead; the bird is an old **one** who knows his way **well**; and **as** they **all fly** from one lake to the next, he **will cry out** from time to time that none of them may be lost.

NOTES.

An old one, put "an old swan;" "well," place it immediately after "knows;" as, *pendant que*; all fly, put "fly all;" he will cry out (*see* Rule XIX.)

II.—" I dare say," says D'Israeli, " that among **all orders of Englishmen**, there is not a man who, in his toils and perplexity, **has** not sometimes thought of the Duke of Wellington, and found in his example support and solace. 2. Though **he lived so much** in the **hearts** and **minds** of his countrymen, though he occupied eminent posts and fulfilled august duties, **it was not till** he died that we felt **what a** place he **filled** in the feelings and thoughts of the people of England."

NOTES.

1. All orders of Englishmen, *les Anglais de tous rangs*; has (*see* Rule XXIX.)
2. He lived so much, put "he was incessantly;" hearts... minds, use the singular; it was not till, put "it was only when;" what a (*see* Pron., Rule XXII.); he filled, *il tenait*.

III.—My Lord wept that now my tears might be wiped away; He bled that I might now rejoice; He was forsaken that I might not now be forsook; **He then** died that I might now live.—(J. Hall.)

NOTE.

He then, *puis ñ.*

IV.—Rooks are cunning; if they see a man with a gun, or even a stick, they fly off to their nests **in great uproar**, and **and will not leave** them till the cause of their fright has gone.

NOTES.

In great uproar, *en grand émoi*; will not leave (*see* Rule XIX.)

V.—1. "Agur's prayer," says Hume, "is sufficiently noted: **Two things have I required of** Thee; deny me them not before I die. 2. Remove far from me vanity and lies; give me neither poverty nor riches; feed me with food convenient for me, lest I be full and deny Thee, and say, who is The Lord? or, lest I be poor, and steal, and take the name of my God in vain."

NOTES.

1. Two things...etc., *construe* "I have required two things;" of (*see* Invar. Words, Rule II.)

RULE XXXIV.

The subjunctive is also used after **that**, beginning an *exclamative sentence* and followed by "*should.*" "That" in this case is rendered by **faut-il que, se peut-il que.**

Ex.—**That** I **should** have such a son!
Faut-il que j'aie un tel fils!

Translate.

"O God," exclaims the unhappy Cassio, " that men should put an enemy in their mouths **to** steal away their brains ! that we should, with joy, pleasance and applause, transform ourselves into beasts !"

NOTE.

To (*see* Invar. Words, Rule XXXI.)

RULE XXXV.

The **subjunctive** coming after "if" must be rendered by the *indicative* in French ; if there are two verbs, use " que " before the second with the subjunctive mood,

Ex.—**If** he **come** and his brother *be* out...
 S'il **vient** et **que** son frère **soit** sorti.

Translate.

1. "Every man who has seen the world," says Macaulay, "knows that nothing is so useless as a general maxim. 2. If it be moral and very true, it may **serve for** a copy to a **charity-boy**. 3. If, like those of La Rochefoucault, it be sparkling and whimsical, it may make an excellent motto for an essay. 3. But few indeed of the **many** wise apophthegms which have been uttered from the time of the Seven Sages of Greece to that of **Poor Richard**, have prevented a single foolish action."

NOTES.

2. To serve for, *servir* **de** ; a charity-boy, *un élève de l'école gratuite*.
2. Many (when preceded by *the*), *nombreux*.
3. Poor Richard (*see* Art., Rule I.)

RULE XXXVI.

Si, if, instead of being repeated, may be rendered the second time by *que* with the following verb in the subjunctive, as has been said in preceding Rule.

If any other conjunction is followed by several verbs, put likewise " que " before each of them except the first, only in this case take care to put the verbs following " que " in the *same mood as the first.*

> *Ex.*—As your friend is here and you cannot go out, send for him ;
>
> Comme votre ami *est* ici et **que** vous ne *pouvez* pas sortir, envoyez le chercher.
>
> Though he was here and lived close to me, I never saw him ;
>
> Quoiqu'il *fût* ici et **qu'il** *demeurât* près de moi, je ne l'ai jamais vu.

Rem.—As the two verbs have the same subject, it might also be said:

> **Quoiqu**'il fût ici et demeurât près de moi...

Translate.

I.—1. Stanley **arrived** at Unyanyembe **on the 23rd of** June, 1871. 2. **After resting** for a few days, he prepared to push on for Ujiji, but found that the King of Ujowa had lately declared that no caravan should pass through his territory. 3. The Arabs had taken alarm at the king's announcement, and had declared war **with** him. 4. " We say war," said they, " until we have got his beard under our feet, and we can again travel through any part of the country **with only** our walking canes in our hands."

NOTES.

1. Arrived (*see* Rule XII.); on the 23rd of (*see* Synopsis, Rule XIII.)
2. After resting (*see* Rule XLVII.)
3. With (*see* Invar. Words, Rule II.)
4. With only, *sans autre chose que*.

II.—1. Livingstone having **introduced** Stanley to the Arabs who **stood** around him, conducted him to his house, and **conversation** began. 2. Stanley heard from the doctor's lips an outline of the strange story of his wanderings in that wild African land. 3. After he **had listened for** some time to the narration, and the Arabs had withdrawn, Livingstone's letter-bag was produced. 4. The doctor took it, and when he had opened it and glanced at its contents, he read one or two of his children's letters; then he laid the rest aside and asked **for** news of the world.—(H. G. Adams, *Dr. Livingstone.*)

NOTES.

1. "To introduce some one" is not "*introduire*" but "**présenter**" *quelqu'un;* stood (*see* Rule IX.); conversation, put "*the* conversation."
3. Had listened (*see* Rule XVI.); for (i.e. *during*), *pendant*.
4. For (*see* Invar. Words, Rule II.)

III.—"When I see," says Addison, "kings lying **by** those who **deposed** them, and I consider rival wits placed side by side, or the holy men that divided the world with their disputes, I reflect with sorrow and astonishment on **the little** competitions, factions, and debates of mankind."

NOTES.

By (i.e. *by the side of*), *à côté de;* deposed, put "have deposed"; the little, repeat both the article and the adjective before each noun.

IV.—A child knows if an arm or a leg be distorted in a picture, if the attitude be natural, or grand, or mean, though he has never received any instruction in drawing, or heard any conversation on **the** subject, **nor can** himself draw with correctness a single feature.

NOTES.

The, *ce*; nor can, put " and cannot."

RULE XXXVII.

In speaking of the conditions of a treaty, of the articles of a decree enacted by a sovereign or an assembly, and the like, the future or conditional is used, the will of the agents being in this case considered as a command which must be executed.

> *Ex.*—The ringleaders demanded that the minister *should* be dismissed, but the king answered that he **should** not do it;
> Les chefs de l'émeute demandèrent qu'on *renvoyât* le ministre, mais le roi répondit qu'il ne le **ferait** pas.

The *subjunctive* is used in the first instance, as the ringleaders are uncertain whether their request will be granted, and the *indicative* in the second case, because the king has the power to dismiss the minister and will not do so.

Translate.

I.—1. The parliament in the reign of Edward III. framed an act **to** confirm the great charter **anew**, and to oblige all the chief officers of the law and of the state to swear to the regular observance of it. 2. **They** enacted that no peer should be punished **but** by the award of his peers **in parliament**; that the chief officers of **state** should be appointed by the advice of parliament; and that they should answer before parliament to **any** accusation brought against them.

NOTES.

1. To (*see* Invar. Words, Rule XXXI.); anew, to be placed next to "confirm."
2. They (*see* Rule I.); but, *si ce n'est;* in parliament, put "*of the* parliament;" state, put "*the* state;" any, *toute.*

II.—In 1544 Henry VIII. ordered that the litany should be celebrated in **the** vulgar tongue.

NOTE.

The (to be left out).

III. –1. The most considerable officers of the army, and even Fleetwood, brother-in-law **to** the protector, were entering into cabals against him. 2. Richard, who **possessed** neither resolution nor penetration, **was prevailed** to give an unguarded consent for **calling** a general council of officers, who proposed that the whole military power should be entrusted to some person in whom they might all confide. 3. The parliament, **no** less alarmed than the protector **at** the military cabals, voted that there should be no meeting or general council of officers, except with the protector's consent, or by his orders. 4. This vote **brought affairs** immediately **to** a rupture. 5. The officers hastened to Richard and demanded **of** him that the parliament should be dissolved.—(D. Hume.)

NOTES.

1. To, *de.*
2. Possessed (*see* Rule X.); was prevailed to, *fut amené à;* to call (an assembly), *convoquer* and *see* Invar. Words, Rule XVII.
3. No, *non;* at (*see* Invar. Words, Rule II.)
4. Brought affairs to a rupture, put "brought a rupture."
5. Of him, *lui.*

IV.—The principal articles of the treaty of Utrecht, **as between** France and England, **were**, that Louis should abandon the Pretender, acknowledge the queen's title and the protestant succession; should raze the fortifications of **Dunkirk**; and should cede **Newfoundland**, Hudson's Bay, and **St. Christopher's.**

NOTES.

As between, *concernant*; were (imperf.); Dunkirk, *Dunkerque*; Newfoundland, *Terre-Neuve*; St. Christopher's (*see* Pron., Rule XXVII.)

RULE XXXVIII.

The indicative or subjunctive are sometimes replaced by *the infinitive*, for the sake of elegance; this is particularly the case when the subject is the same for the two verbs, or when the first may be followed by " de " with the infinitive, provided this should lead to no ambiguous meaning.

Ex.—**I** wish **I** had done it;
Je voudrais l'**avoir fait.**

But

I wish **he** had done it;
Je voudrais qu'il l'**eût fait,**

as the verbs have different subjects.

He fell ill before **he could** return;
Il tomba malade avant *de* **pouvoir** revenir.

He ordered **that they should** be dismissed;
Il ordonna **de** les **renvoyer** (or *qu'on les renvoyât*).

Obs.—It must be observed that in the latter instance the second verb may also be replaced in English by an infinitive; it might be said, for instance, " He ordered them **to be dismissed.**" This might be for the student a way to test when he may use the infinitive. whenever the two verbs have *not* the same nominative.

Translate.

I.—1. Hampden **moved** that the question should be put, " Whether **the House** would consent to the proposition made by the King, **as** contained in the message ?" 2. Hyde interfered, and proposed that the question should be divided ; that the **sense of** the House **should be taken** merely on the point whether there should be a supply or no supply ; and that the manner **and the amount** should be left for subsequent consideration.

NOTES.

1. Moved, *proposa* ; the House, *la Chambre* ; as, *telle qu'elle était.*
2. To take the sense of, *consulter* ; on the point, *pour savoir.*
3. And the amount, put " and the amount *of it.*"

II.— . . . . My story being done,
She gave me for my pains a world of sighs :
She swore, in faith, 'twas strange, 'twas passing strange;
She **wish'd** she had not heard it ; yet she wish'd
That Heaven had made **her** such a man : she thank'd me ;
And bade me, if I had a friend that loved her,
I should but teach him **how** to tell my story,
And that would woo her. (*Othello.*)

NOTES.

She wished, *elle aurait voulu* ; her, put " of her;" how (*see* Invar. Words, Rule XVI.)

III.—When the Florentine magistrates proposed to Dante that he should return on condition **of** apologising and paying a fine, he answered with **vivid indignation** : "If I cannot return without calling myself guilty, I will never return."

NOTES.

Of (*see* Synopsis, Rule VII., and Invar. Words, Rule XVII.)
vivid indignation (*see* Art., Rule XIII.)

IV.—1. Hardy stood over Nelson in silence **for a** moment or two, then kissed his forehead and left him for ever. 2. Nelson **now** desired to be turned upon his right side, and said: "I wish I had not left the deck, **for** I shall soon be gone."

NOTES.

1. For (i.e. *during*), *pendant.*
2. Now (when referring to the past), *alors*; for (i.e. *because*), *car.*

RECAPITULATION ON THE INDICATIVE AND THE SUBJUNCTIVE.

Translate.

DEATH OF NELSON.

I.—1. Nelson, wounded to death, did not for a moment lose his presence of mind. 2. He observed, as they were carrying him down the ladder, that the tiller ropes, which had been shot away, were not yet replaced, and ordered that new ones should be rove immediately; then, that he might not be seen by the crew, he took out his handkerchief, and covered his face and his stars. 3. It was soon perceived upon examination, that the wound was mortal. 4. **He himself** being certain that no human care could avail him, insisted that the surgeon should leave him, and attend to those to whom he **might** be useful... 5. He became impatient to see Hardy; and as that officer, though he had been often sent for, could not leave the deck, Nelson feared that some fatal cause prevented him. 6. An hour and ten minutes elapsed **from the time when** Nelson received his wound, before Hardy could come to him. 7. They shook hands in silence. "Well, Hardy," said Nelson, "**how goes the day with us**?" "Very well," replied Hardy, "ten ships have struck, but five of the van have tacked, and show an intention to bear down upon the Victory. 8. I have called two or three of our fresh ships round, and I have no doubt but that I shall give them a drubbing." 9. "I hope," said Nelson, "none of our ships have struck." Hardy answered, "There was no fear of that"... 10. **Upon the surgeon inquiring** whether his pain was great, Nelson replied, "So great, that I wish I was dead"... 11. He said to Hardy, "Don't throw me overboard;" and he desired that he might be buried by his parents, unless it should please the king **to order** otherwise... 12. And, after a short pause, he added, "Remember that **I leave** Lady Hamilton and my daughter Horacia **as a legacy** to my country"... 13. His articulation now became difficult; but he was disdistinctly heard to say, "Thank God, I have done my duty!"... 14. He expired at thirty minutes after four —three hours and a quarter after he had received his wound.—(R. Southey.)

NOTES.

4. He himself (*see* Pron., Rule I., Rem.); he might (*see* Rule LXVII.)
6. From the time, *depuis le moment*; when (*see* Invar. Words, Rule XXXIV.)
7. How goes the day with us, *Comment la journée s'annonce-t-elle pour nous?*
10. Upon the surgeon inquiring (*see* Verb, Rule XLII.)
11. To order, *d'en ordonner.*
12. I leave as a legacy, put "I bequeath."

II. "**Grieved am I**," exclaims W. Pitt, in his speech on the abolition of the slave trade, "to think that there should be a single person in this country, much more that there should be a single member in the **British** Parliament, who can look on the present state of the African continent as a ground **for continuing** the slave trade."

NOTES.

Grieved am I, construe "I am grieved"; British, *de la Grande-Bretagne;* for continuing (*see* Invar. Words, Rule XVII.)

III.—1. The press of England is still free. It is guarded by the free constitution of our forefathers. 2. It is guarded by the hearts and arms of Englishmen; and I trust I may venture to say that, if it be to fall, it will fall only under the ruins of the British Empire... 3. Believing, then, that we are on the eve of a great struggle, that you have now in your hands the only remains of free discussion in Europe; convinced that the unfettered exercise of reason depends more on your present verdict than on any other that was delivered by a jury, I trust I may rely with confidence on the issue; 4. I trust that you will consider yourselves as the advanced guard of liberty, as having this day to fight the first battle of free discussion against the most formidable enemy that it ever **encountered**!—(Sir J. Mackintosh.)

NOTE.

Encountered, put "*has* encountered."

IV. 1. Though his judges had condemned him to die, Essex did not renounce all hope. 2. Once Elizabeth had given him a ring, saying: "Provided you return this ring to me, I promise to pardon you, though you might have merited my anger; not that I suspect your fidelity, **as** you have given me too many proofs of it that I may doubt it; you might, however, be accused of imprudence **without your being guilty.**" 3. **So** Essex entrusted this precious pledge to the Countess of Nottingham, that she might place it into the hands of Elizabeth before it were too late. 4. But whether because the countess was a secret enemy **to** Essex, or she was influenced by her husband, she kept the ring until she was on her death-bed, two years after the execution of the favourite. 5. Then, having begged the queen to come, she confessed her treason. "I cannot die in peace," she said, "unless your majesty pardon me!" 6. "Ask pardon **of** God," answered the queen, beside herself, "but not of me, lest I should curse you. 7. I leave you for fear you should make me do something unworthy of a queen." 8. Elizabeth died a very short time after that interview.

NOTES.

2. As (*i.e. because*), *car;* without your being guilty (*see* Rule XLII.)
3. So, *donc* (to be placed after "entrusted.")
4. To, put "of."
6. Of (*see* Invar. Words, Rule II.)

INFINITIVE AND PARTICIPLES.

RULE XXXIX.

An English infinitive preceded by an object is generally rendered by the indicative or the subjunctive preceded by "que." If you can turn it into **that I, he**, etc....**should**..., use the *subjunctive;* if into **that I, he**, etc., with the **indicative mood**, use the *indicative*.

Ex.—I wish **you to do** it, i.e. *that you should* do it;
Je désire **que** vous le **fassiez**.

I know **him to be** unhappy, i.e. *that he is* unhappy;
Je sais **qu'il est** malheureux.

Rem.—The infinitive may be used when the preceding verb may be followed by " de."

He allowed **me to go;**
Il me permit **de** *partir.*

It might also be said:

Il permit *que je partisse*;

but the former translation is preferable.

Translate.

I.—1. Robert and William, sons of **the Conqueror**, besieged their brother in the fortress of St. Michael's Mount, in Normandy, and had nearly reduced him by the scarcity of water; when the elder, hearing of his distress, granted him permission to supply himself. 2. **Being reproved by William** for this ill-timed generosity, he replied: "What! shall I suffer my brother to die of thirst? Where shall we find **another when he is dead?**"

NOTES.

1. The Conqueror, *Guillaume le Conquérant.*
2. Being reproved by W. (*see* Rule IV.); another (*see* Pron. Rule XXXIII.); when he is dead (*see* Rule XX.)

Roulier's Second Book.   K

II.—The crow **will** only **live** with its mate, and **will** not **let** any bird of its own kind come near its nest, **nor does it like** a rook to build in a tree near it.

NOTES.

Will live..., will let... (*see* Rule XIX.); nor does it like, *il n'aime pas non plus.*

III.—The swan makes his nest by the side of a pool, in the reed beds, when they grow high, for he does not like his nest to be seen.

RULE XL.

An infinitive preceded by **for him, for me, for us**, etc., or by **for** and a **noun**, must be rendered by the **subjunctive** with *que*, if it can be turned into **that** *or* **till I, he**..., etc., and with *pour que, afin que*, if it can be turned into **in order that I, he**..., etc.

Ex.—It is necessary **for you to go**, i.e. *that* you should go;
Il faut **que vous partiez.**

He sends it **for me to keep** it, i.e. *in order that* I may keep it;
Il l'envoie **pour que je le garde.**

Wait **for me to come** back, i.e. *till* I come back;
Attendez **que je revienne.**

Rem.—The infinitive may also be used for the sake of elegance.

Ex.—It was necessary **for us to go.**

Instead of saying:

Il fallut *que nous nous en allassions,*

which would sound badly and seem pedantic, it is much better to say with the infinitive:

Il fallut **nous en aller.**

Translate.

I.—While you have everything to fear from the success of the enemy, you have **every means** of preventing that success, so that it is next to impossible for victory not to crown your exertions.—(R. Hall.)

NOTE.

Every means, put "all the means."

II.—The white bear eats fish, and **will lie** for a long time **at** a hole **in** the ice waiting for a seal to **come up for air, when** he will kill the seal and eat it.

NOTES.

Will lie (*see* Rule XIX.); at, *près de*; in, *pratiqué dans*; come up for air, put "come to the surface *to* breathe;" when, *et alors*.

III.—The world **was** made for man to use it, and not for him to misuse it.

NOTE.

Was, put "has been."

IV.—Livingstone learning that it would be difficult for him to obtain food beyond Kebrabassa, before the new crop came in, determined on delaying his departure for the interior **until May**.

NOTE.

Until May, put "until *the month of* May."

V.—" I **insisted**," says Portia to Brutus, " **yet you**
   answer'd not ;
But, with an angry wafture of your hand,
Gave sign for me to leave you."

NOTE.

I insisted (*see* Rule XIII.)

RULE XLI.

The *present participle* used in English as subject or object of a verb, is translated in French by **the infinitive**.

Ex.—**Reading** aloud is a good exercise for young people;
Lire à haute voix est un bon exercice pour les jeunes gens.

He does not like **walking**;
Il n'aime pas à **marcher**.

Sometimes it may also be rendered by a noun; for instance, we might say as well:

La lecture à haute voix est, etc.
Il n'aime pas *la marche*.

Rem.—If there are several participles, they must all be translated in the same way, *i.e.* be all either nouns or adjectives.

Ex.—Riding and shooting are his only occupations;
Do not say: **L'équitation** et *chasser* sont ses seules occupations;
but say: **L'équitation** et la **chasse** sont ses seules occupations;
or: **Monter à cheval** et **chasser**, voilà ses seules occupations.

Translate.

I.—1. A trade is an occupation by which a man gets his living. 2. The word "trade" **is** also **applied** to the exchange of the products of various countries. 3. Bringing in goods from foreign parts **is called** "importing," and sending out goods from our own country is called "exporting."

NOTES.

2 and 3. Is applied, is called (*see* Rule V.).

II.—Diseases of the body may have appropriate exercises; bowling is good for the stone and reins, shooting for the lungs and breast, gentle walking for the stomach, riding for the head and the like.—(F. Bacon.)

RULE XLII.

An English **present participle** preceded by an **article, a possessive adjective**, or a **noun in the possessive or any objective case**, cannot be translated literally, but should be replaced by an equivalent. It is impossible to give any fixed rule, but it will be found generally that the participle will have to be turned into some tense of the indicative or of the subjunctive, or into the infinitive. It may also be rendered by a noun, especially when it is preceded by **the**.

Ex.—What is the reason of **your being** so late? *i.e.* Why are you so late?
Pourquoi êtes-vous si en retard?

I am astonished at **your brother's being** so fond of that dog;
Put: . . . . . . *that* your brother is so fond, etc.
Je m'étonne **que votre frère aime** tant ce chien.

Do you remember **my telling** it? *i.e.* that I told it;
Vous souvenez-vous **que je l'ai dit?**

Perhaps **my being** here prevents **his coming**;
Put: . . . my *presence* here prevents *him from coming*;
Peut-être **ma présence** ici l'empêche-t-elle de **venir**.

The shooting of the volunteers was excellent;
Le tir des volontaires fut excellent.

Rem.—**There is no**, with a present participle, is rendered in French by **il n'y a pas moyen de**, and by the present participle turned into the infinitive.

Ex.—**There is no** *discussing* with you;
Il n'y a pas moyen de *discuter* avec vous.

VERB—INFINITIVE AND PARTICIPLES.

Translate.

I.—1. When the trial began, Lord Kilmarnock and Lord Cromartie pleaded guilty, Balmerino not guilty, saying he could prove his not being at the taking of the castle of Carlisle. 2. Lord Kilmarnock is a Presbyterian, **with four earldoms in him**, but very poor since Lord Wilmington's stopping a pension that my father had given him. 3. Lord Cromartie **was** receiver of the rent's of the king's second son in Scotland... 4. **On** Wednesday they were again brought to Westminster Hall **to receive sentence**, and on their being asked what they had to say, Lord Kilmarnock made a very fine speech, confessing the extent of his crime, but offering his principles as some alleviation. 5. He insisted much on his tenderness **to** the English prisoners, which some deny, and say that **he was the man** who proposed their being put to death.—(H. Walpole: *Letter to Sir Horace Mann.*)

NOTES.

2. With four earldoms in him, put "possessing four earldoms."
3. Was (*see* Rule IX.)
4. On (*see* Synopsis, Rule XIII.); to (*see* Invar. Words, Rule XXXI.); receive sentence, *entendre prononcer le jugement.*
5. To, *pour;* he was the man, put " it was he," and *see* Rules XIV., XIII., and XXXI.

II.—1. People judge of travellers exactly with **the same** candour and impartiality they judge of their neighbours **upon all** occasions. 2. For my part, I am so well acquainted with the morals of all my dear friends and acquaintances, that I am resolved to tell them nothing at all, to avoid the imputation of my telling too much. 3. But I depend upon your knowing me enough to believe whatever I seriously assert **for truth**.— (Mr. W. Montagu : *Letter to the Countess of Mar.*)

NOTES.

1. The same (should be repeated before " impartiality "); upon all occasions, put " *in* all *the* occasions."
3. For truth, *pour vrai.*

III.—"Most of the time," says Charles Lamb, in speaking of the Quakers, "the meeting is broken up without a word having been spoken. But the mind has been fed."

IV.—1. In April, 1797, a mutiny broke out in the fleet at Spithead. 2. Upon the signal being given to weigh, the crew of the Queen Charlotte, the flagship, instead of obeying, ran up the shrouds and gave three cheers, **which were answered** from the other ships.

NOTE.

2. Which were answered (*see* Rule VI.).

V.—Charles XII., wounded and incapable of acting, saw himself cooped up between the Boristhenes and the river that runs to Pultowa, in a desert country, without any places of security, or ammunition, in the face of an army, which at once cut off his retreat, and prevented his being supplied with provisions.

VI.—The child's being able to speak is no proof of his being able to think.

VII.—1. The first remedy is **to** remove, by all means possible, that material cause of seditions whereof **we spake**; which is, want and poverty in the State. 2. To which purpose serveth the opening and well balancing of trade, the cherishing of manufactures, the banishing of idleness, the repressing of waste and excess by sumptuary laws, the improvement and husbanding of the soil, the regulating of prices of things vendible, the moderating of taxes and tributes, and the like.—(Bacon).

NOTES.

1. To, *de*; we spake, put "we *have spoken*."

RULE XLIII.

The **present participle preceded by another verb** is generally rendered by the *infinitive* in French.

> *Ex.*—He left off *reading;*
> Il cessa de *lire.*

Translate.

1. "I was surprised," writes Lady Montagu, "to find in the convent of St. Lawrence the only beautiful young woman I have seen at Vienna. 2. I could not forbear shewing my surprise at seeing a nun like her. 3. She made me a thousand obliging compliments, and **desired me to come** often. 4. "It would be an infinite pleasure to me," said she, **sighing**, "but I avoid, with the greatest care, seeing any of my former acquaintances; and, whenever they come to our convent, I lock myself in my cell."

NOTES.

3. Desired me to come (*see* Rule XXXIX.)
4. Sighing (*see* Invar. Words, Rule XVIII.)

RULE XLIV.

If you can turn the present participle in English into a **relative pronoun followed by the present or imperfect of indicative**, use one of these two tenses preceded by "qui."

> *Ex.*—There is your father **coming**, *i.e.* "*who is coming,*"
> Voilà votre père **qui vient.**

Translate.

1. **What a** pretty sight a poultry-yard is ! 2. There is the hen clucking, the cock strutting about, the peacock spreading his tail, the drake showing his fine plumage **as he sails** in the pond, the turkeys gobbling, and the guinea-hens crying, " Come back, come back." —(Mrs. Barbauld.)

NOTES.

1. What a (*see* Pron., Rule XXII.)
2. As he sails, *tout en nageant.*

RULE XLV.

If the present participle can be replaced in English by the infinitive as well as by a relative pronoun with the present or imperfect indicative, as is often the case after "to see, *voir*," "to hear, *entendre*," "to feel, *sentir*," and the like, either the **infinitive** or the **indicative mood**, preceded by **qui**, may be used, the latter being more precise.

Ex.—I hear him **singing**,
put : I hear him *sing—or—who is singing*,
Je l'entends **chanter—or—qui chante.**

Translate.

1. The sense of sight is, indeed, the highest bodily privilege, the purest physical pleasure, which man has derived from his Creator ; to see the wandering fire, after he has furnished his journey through the nations, coming back to us in the eastern heavens ; to see the earth waking from deep slumbers, the day flowing down the sides of the hill till it reaches the secret valleys, the little insect returning to life, the bird trying her wings, man going forth to his labour ; each created being moving, thinking, acting, contriving, according

to the scheme and compass of its nature, by force, by cunning, by reason, by necessity. 2. Is it possible to joy in this animated scene, and feel no pity for the sons of darkness, the blind?

RULE XLVI.

Should the present participle be **blended with past participles**, as in the next piece, it is better to preserve the present participle in French, and not paraphrase it, as in Rule XLIV.

Translate.

CHARACTER OF PAUL.

1. Here, then, we have a man of liberal attainments, and, in other points, **of sound judgment**, who had addicted his life to the service of the gospel. 2. We see him, in the prosecution of his purpose, travelling from country to country, enduring every species of hardship, encountering every extremity of danger, assaulted by the populace, punished by the magistrates, scourged, beat, stoned, left for dead; expecting, wherever he came, a renewal of the same treatment and the same dangers; yet, **when driven** from one city, preaching in the next; spending his whole time in that employment, sacrificing to it his pleasures, his ease, his safety; persisting in this course **to** old age, unaltered by the experience o perverseness, ingratitude, prejudice, desertion; unsubdued by anxiety, want, labour, persecutions; unwearied by long confinement, undismayed by the prospect of death. Such **was** Paul.—(W. Paley.)

NOTES.

1. Of sound judgment (*see* Art., Rule XIII.)
2. When driven (*see* Ellipsis, Rule II.); to, *jusqu'à la*; was (*see* Rule IX.)

RULE XLVII.

Put into the *infinitive perfect* the present participle, preceded by **after**, *après*.

> *Ex.*—After **singing**;
> Après **avoir chanté**.

RULE XLVIII.

Use likewise the *infinitive perfect* after **for**, *pour*, when the verb expresses a *past* action, and can be turned in English into the *participle perfect*.

> *Ex.*—He was punished **for talking**, *i.e.* for *having talked*;
> Il fut puni pour **avoir parlé**.

Translate.

I.—1. Boileau **thought it** probable that, in the best modern Latin, a writer of the Augustan age would have detected ludicrous improprieties. 2. And who can think otherwise?...Has any modern scholar understood **Latin** better than Frederick the Great understood French? 3. Yet is it not notorious that Frederick the Great after reading, speaking, writing French, and nothing but French, during more **than** half a century, after unlearning his mother tongue in order to learn French, after living familiarly during many years with French associates, could not, to the last, compose in French without imminent **risk** of committing some mistake which would have moved a smile in the literary circles of Paris?—(Macaulay.)

NOTES.

1. Thought (*see* Rule IX.); it (to be left out).
2. Latin...French, names of languages generally take the definite article, and are spelt with a small initial.
3. Than (*see* Invar. Words, Rule XXVI.); risk, put "the risk.'

II.—No man ever **perished** who **followed** first the will of God and then the will of his superiors; but thousands have been lost merely for following their own will, **and** relying upon their own judgments, **and** choosing their own work, and doing their own fancies. —(Jeremy Taylor.)

NOTES.

Perished...followed, put "*has* perished, *has* followed"; and (to be omitted, except before the last verb).

RULE XLIX.

The **infinitive perfect** coming in English after a *past tense* should be rendered in French by the *infinitive present*.

Ex.—He **was** the most worthy **to have reigned;**
Do not say : Il était le plus digne **d'avoir régné**,
but say : Il était le plus digne de **régner.**

Translate.

1. "I forgot to tell you," says the disabled soldier, " that in an engagement I was wounded in two places; I lost four fingers of the left hand, and my leg was shot off. 2. If I had had the good fortune to have lost my leg and use of my hand on board a king's ship, and not aboard a privateer, I should have been entitled to clothing and maintenance during the rest of my life."

RULE L.

A past participle, coming after " to *get*, to *make*, to *have* " (meaning " to make, to get "), is rendered in

French by the **infinitive active**, and put immediately after the above-mentioned verbs. " To get, to have," must then be translated by **faire**.

> *Ex.*—I shall *make* it **known;**
> Je le *ferai* **savoir.**
>
> I shall *get* it **done** ;
> Je le *ferai* **faire.**

RULE LI.

After " to see, *voir* ; to perceive, *apercevoir* ; to hear, *entendre* ; to feel, *sentir*," and such others as denote perception, both the **present** and **past participles** are translated by the infinitive, when they express an *action*, and by the past participle, when they express a *state*.

> *Ex.*—I saw him **killed** (state) ;
> Je l'ai vu **tué.**
>
> I saw him **killed** by his brother (action) ;
> Je l'ai vu **tuer** par son frère.
>
> I saw him lying on the grass (state) ;
> Je l'ai vu **étendu** sur l'herbe.
>
> I heard the bird **singing** (action) ;
> J'ai entendu l'oiseau **chanter.**
>
> I heard it **said**;
> Je l'ai entendu **dire.**

Translate.

1. Fontenelle, **a** witty French writer of the eighteenth century, hearing sung at Madame de Tencin's a nonsensical couplet, thought he understood it, and wished to have it sung again **to** understand it better. 2. Madame de Tencin interrupted the singer, and said to Fontenelle : "**You** great fool, do you not see that this couplet is

mere nonsense?" 3. "It resembles so much all the verses I hear read or sung here," replied the wit, maliciously, "that it is not surprising **I should have been** mistaken."

NOTES.

1. A (*see* Synopsis, Rule VIII.); to, *pour.*
2. You (*see* Pron., Rule XXXI.)
3. I should have been (*see* Rule XXIX.)

AUXILIARIES AND OTHER VERBS.

RULE LII.

The verb **to be**, before an infinitive should not generally be translated literally, but ought to be interpreted and translated according to the sense.

If it denotes an *intention*, translate it by **devoir**.

If it implies *necessity*, and can be replaced by " must, should, ought," etc., it may be rendered either by **devoir**, or by **falloir**, with the infinitive or subjunctive.

Ex.—He **was** to come with us, *i.e.* " he *intended* to come;"
Il **devait** venir avec nous.

This work **is** to be finished to-day, *i.e.* "*must* be finished."
So say: Ce travail **doit** être fini aujourd'hui,
or, Il **faut** finir ce travail aujourd'hui,
or, Il **faut que** ce travail soit fini aujourd'hui.

Translate.

I.—Some books are to be tasted, others to be swallowed, and some few to be chewed and digested; that is, some books are to be read only in parts, others to be read, but not **curiously**, and some few to be read wholly and with diligence and attention.—(F. Bacon).

NOTE.

Curiously, *attentivement.*

II.—**For** more **than** ten years the people had seen **their** rights infringed by the perfidious king who had recognised them. 2. At length **circumstances** compelled Charles to summon another Parliament : another chance was given to our forefathers. 3. Were they again to be cozened by *le Roi le veut*? 5. Were they again to advance their money on pledges which had been forfeited over and over again?...6. They were compelled to choose whether they would trust a tyrant or conquer him. We think that they chose wisely and nobly.—(Macaulay.)

NOTES.

1. For (*i.e. during*), *pendant;* than (*see* Invar. Words, Rule XXVI.); their (*see* Rule I.)
2. Circumstances, put "*the* circumstances."

RULE LIII.

If "to be" **may be** replaced by "**can, could**," translate it by **pouvoir**, and put the passive infinitive into the *active* voice, thus:

Ex.—There **was** no bread to be got; *or*, No bread **was** to be got, *i.e.* No bread *could* be got ; or, *one could* get no bread ;
 On ne **pouvait** pas **se procurer** de pain.

Translate.

1. From Grodno to the Boristhenes, eastward, there is nothing but morasses, deserts, and immense forests.

2. In the cultivated spots there are no provisions to be had, the peasants burying under ground all their grain, and whatever else can be preserved in these subterranean receptacles. 3. In order to discover these hidden magazines, the earth **must be pierced** with long poles, **pointed with iron.** 4. The Muscovites and the Swedes alternately made use of these provisions; but they were not always to be found, and even then were not sufficient.

NOTES.

3. Must be pierced, put "one must (*il faut*) pierce;" pointed with iron, *garnis d'une pointe de fer.*

RULE LIV.

When **to be**, before a passive infinitive, can be replaced by the indicative, or imperfect passive of the verb which is in the infinitive, render it by **on** with the *active indicative.*

Ex.—This **is** not **to be seen** anywhere else, *i.e* "this *is* not seen;"
On ne **voit** cela nulle part ailleurs.

Sometimes the reflexive form may also be used; for instance, we might say here:

Cela ne **se voit** nulle part ailleurs.

Translate.

1. **From what** has been said we may infer that, as there are two kinds of sentiments, the natural and the sublime, which **are** always **to be pursued** in a heroic poem, there are also two kinds of thoughts which are carefully to be avoided. 2. The first are **such** as are affected and unnatural; the second such as are mean and vulgar. 3. As for the first kind of thoughts, we

meet with little or nothing that is like them **in** Virgil: he has none **of those** trifling points and puerilities that are so often to be met with in Ovid, none of the epigrammatic turns of **Lucan**; none of those swelling sentiments which are so frequently to be observed in **Statius** and Claudian, none of those mixed embellishments of Tasso. Everything is just and natural.

NOTES.

1. From, *d'après*; what (*see* Pron., Rule XXIV.); are to be pursued (*see* Rule IV.).
2. Such as (*see* Pron., Rule XXXVI.); in, is generally translated by *dans* before an author's name; of those (*see* Synopsis, Rule VII.); Lucan, *Lucain*; Statius, *Stace*.

RULE LV.

The verb **to be** may also be rendered by the future, or conditional of the verb before which it stands, which is especially the case in a **command**.

Ex.—You **are** not to **stir** out of the house, *i.e.* "you *shall* not stir;"
Vous ne **bougerez** pas de la maison.

He was told that he **was to be** banished from the kingdom;
On lui dit qu'il **serait banni** du royaume.

Translate.

SHE STOOPS TO CONQUER.

Act ii.

Hardcastle (to three or four awkward servants).—Well, I hope you are perfect in the **table exercise I have been teaching** you these three days. You all know your posts and places and can show that you have been used to **good company**.

Roulier's Second Book.   L

Omnes.—Ay, ay.

Hard.—When company comes you are not to pop out and stare, and then run in again like frighted rabbits in a warren.

Omnes.—No, no.

Hard.—You, Diggary, whom I have **taken** from the barn, are to make a show at the side-table; and you, Roger, **whom I have advanced from the plough**, are to place yourself behind my chair. But you are not to stand **so** with your hands in your pockets. Take your hands from your pockets, Roger, and from your head, **you** blockhead, you...

NOTES.

Table-exercise, *service de la table;* I have been teaching (*see* Rule XIII.); good company, *à la bonne société;* taken, *tiré;* whom I have advanced from the plough, *que j'ai arraché à la charrue et fait monter en grade;* so (*i.e.* **thus**), *ainsi;* you (*see* Pron., Rule VII.)

RULE LVI.

He will have that, he will have it that, etc., is rendered by *prétendre, soutenir, vouloir absolument.*

Translate.

1. As soon as the two knights were sufficiently recovered, the Druid began to inquire into the occasion of their quarrel. 2. "Why, this man," **cried** the black knight, "will have it that yonder shield is **silver**." 3. "And he will have it," replied the white knight, "that it **is** gold."

NOTES.

2. Cried (*i.e. exclaimed*), *s'écria*; silver, put "*of* silver."
3. Is (*see* Rule XXXI.)

RULE LVII.

The verb **to do**, when placed before another to emphasize its meaning, in which case it could be expressed by *indeed* or *it is true*, should in French be rendered by **en effet, il est vrai,** or some similar expression.

Ex.—You say that he travels too much: he **does** travel, but for the sake of his health, *i.e.* "he travels *indeed*," or "*it is true*;"

Vous dites qu'il voyage trop: il voyage **en effet** *or* **il est vrai**, mais c'est pour sa santé.

Translate.

1. The ostrich **has been said to be** a bad mother, but **this is not the case.** 2. She does leave her eggs, as travellers **have always told**, on the sand to be warmed by the sun in the day; but she never fails to return and sit on them when the shades of night have fallen on the desert.

NOTES.

1. Has been said to be (*see* Rule VI.); this is not the case, *il n'en est pas ainsi.*
2. Have always told, put "have always told *it*."

RULE LVIII.

Do, don't, joined to an *imperative*, are generally rendered by **de grâce, je t'en prie, je vous en prie.**

> *Ex.*—**Do** come with me;
> Venez avec moi, **je vous en prie.**

"**Do**" may also be joined to a verb to express a strong affirmation or contradict a negative statement, in which case it is generally rendered by adding "*si,* yes," or *je vous dis que* before the verb.

> *Ex.*—You **do** want money, though you will not own it;
> **Si,** vous avez besoin d'argent, quoique vous ne vouliez pas l'avouer.
>
> I do not want any money.—Why not own it? You **do** want some;
> Je n'ai pas besoin d'argent.—Porquoi ne pas l'avouer? **Je vous dis que** vous en avez besoin.

Translate.

I.—**How** delightful **it is** for a foreigner who has studied ancient **Greek,** to be seated at a modern Greek table, and listen to **such** immortal names and classical phrases as these: "Themistocles, my love, do **avoid fighting.**" — "Alcibiades, sit still now, do!" — "Socrates, do put down that cup!" — "Oh, fie! Aspasia, don't! oh! don't be naughty!"

NOTES.

How (*see* Invar. Words, Rule XIV.); it is (to be placed before "delightful," *see* Pron., Rule IV.); Greek (*see* Rule XLVII., Note 2); such (to be placed before "as"); avoid fighting (*see* Rule XLIII.)

II.—**I see it all**; you do need aid, you do need protection, though you do not own it.—(W. Scott.)

AUXILIARIES AND OTHER VERBS. 149

NOTE.

I see it all, *je vois ce que c'est.*

III.—" You jest," cried my wife, " we can **walk it** perfectly well; we want no coach to carry us now." "You mistake, **child**," returned I, " we do want a coach."—(Goldsmith.)

NOTES.

Walk it, *faire la route à pied*; child, put "*my* child."

RULE LIX.

The auxiliary **to do** is sometimes *redundant*, and might be left out in English, in which case it should not be rendered in French.

Translate.

In Lapland, **for** one half of the year, the sun does not rise, and all that time it is dark and very cold. When at last the sun does rise, he does not set for the rest of the year, and all that time it is day.

NOTE.

For, *i.e. during.*

RULE LX.

The auxiliaries **do, be, have,** used in the second term of a comparison, may be left out in French whenever the same thing might be done in English.

Ex.—I am older than **he is**, *i.e.* " older than *he* ;"
Je suis plus âgé que **lui.**

Translate.

I.—Elizabeth, the Queen of England, **once** said: "**It is** very singular that every person who is taller than I am **looks** too tall, and that every person who is **shorter** than I am looks too short."

NOTES.

Once (*see* Invar. Words, Rule I.); it is (*see* Pron., Rule IV.); to look (*i.e.* to *seem*), *avoir l'air* or *paraître*; short (when speaking of the stature of a person), *petit*.

II.—The king is but a man, as I am; the violet **smells to him** as it doth to me; **the element shows to him** as it doth to me;...... **his ceremonies** laid by, in his nakedness he appears but a man; and though his affections are higher mounted than ours are, yet, when they stoop, they stoop with the like wing; therefore, when he sees **reason of fears**, as we do, his fears, out of doubt, be of the same **relish** as ours are; yet, in reason, no man **should possess him with any** appearance of fear, **lest** he, **by** showing **it**, should dishearten his army.—(Shakspeare: *King Henry V.*)

NOTES.

Smells to him, *a le même parfum pour lui*; the element shows to him, put "the elements act upon him;" his ceremonies, *sa pompe*; reason of fear, *quelque motif de crainte*; relish, *nature*; should (*see* Rule LXII.); possess him with any..., put "show him the least...;" lest (*see* Rule XXXIII. and Rem.); by (*see* Invar. Words, Rule XII.); it, put "his."

RULE LXI.

When you come across **will, would, shall, should,** you ought to consider whether they are mere signs of the future and conditional, or whether they are to be translated separated from the verb.

RULE LXII.

When **shall** and **should** can be turned into *must, ought*, render them by the indicative, the conditional, or the imperfect indicative of **devoir,** as the case may be, with the next verb in the infinitive.

> *Ex.*—Everybody **should** do his duty, *i.e*, "*must do.*"
> Chacun **doit** faire son devoir.

We might also say:—

> *Il faut que* chacun fasse son devoir.

> You **should** tell it him, *i.e.* "you *ought* to tell,"
> Vous **devriez** le lui dire.

Translate.

I.—1. Works of the intellect are great only by comparison with each other; but nothing is great, not even **mighty Homer** and Milton, beside the infinite Reason. It carries them away as a flood. 2. **Thus** is justice **done** to **each** generation or individual, wisdom, teaching man that he shall **not** hate, **or** fear, **or** mimic his ancestors; that he shall not bewail himself as if the world were old and thought were spent; for by the virtue of the Deity, thought renews itself inexhaustible every day.—(Emerson.)

NOTES.

1. Mighty Homer (*see* Article, Rule I.).
2. Thus, *c'est ainsi que*; is done, *est rendu;* each (to be repeated before "individual"); not...or...or, put "neither...nor...nor."

II. "This **great savage** country," says Emerson in his *Young American*, "should be furrowed by the plough, and combed by the harrow; these rough **Alleganies** should know their master; these foaming torrents should be bestridden by proud arches of stone;

these wild prairies should be loaded **with** wheat; the swamps with rice; the hill-tops should pasture innumerable sheep and cattle; the interminable forests should become **graceful parks**, for use and for delight."

NOTES.

Great savage (*see* Adjective, Rule II.); Alleganies, *Allégany;* with, *de* (*see* Synopsis, Rule VII.); graceful parks, put "*some* graceful parks."

III.—THE DUTIES OF A STATESMAN.

1. Touching matters of revenue, a statesman should be acquainted with the various branches of the public income, its sources and amount, so that if any one has been overlooked **it may be turned** to account, or **if less productive than** it ought to be, it may be enlarged. 2. He ought also to be conversant with the public expenditure; for a nation is not less enriched by retrenchment of expenditure than by addition of income. 3. In matters of peace and war **he should** know the national force, its present amount and condition, as well as the amount it may be **raised to**, and the improvement it may **admit of**. 4. He should be familiar, too, with the wars in which not only his own country but the neighbouring states have been engaged. 5. And, with a view to the security of the territory he should understand well what places are best suited for posts, and what amount, as well as what kind of force, is best calculated to defend them.—(Bacon.)

NOTES.

1. It may be turned (*see* Rule IV.); if less productive than (*see* Invar. Words, Rule XXV., and Ellipsis, Rule II.).

3. "He should" may also be translated by "*il faut qu'il;*" raised to..., admit of (*see* Synopsis, Rule XIX.).

RULE LXIII.

When **will** and **would** may be turned into "*to wish, to be willing,*" translate them by **vouloir**, with the next verb in the infinitive. **Will** is generally put into the *present tense*, whilst **would** is rendered by one of the next four tenses, *viz.*, the imperfect, the preterite definite, the preterite indefinite, and the conditional present, as the case may require.

Ex.—**Will** you do it ? *i.e.*, " *are* you *willing* to do it;"
Voulez-vous le faire ?

I told him to stop, but he **would** go;
Je lui ai dit de rester, mais il **a voulu** partir.

Rem.—The verb **to have** is *not* translated after "will" and "would." If "have" is followed by another verb, that verb is put into the subjunctive.

Ex.—I **will** not **have** it;
Je ne le **veux** pas.

I will not **have** you **do** that;
Je ne **veux** pas *que vous fassiez* cela.

Obs.—When "will" may be changed into "I am going to, he is going to," etc., render it by " je *vais*, il *va*," etc.

Ex.—You wish to see it? Come, I **will** show you, *i.e.* I am *going* to show it you,
Vous désirez le voir? Venez, je **vais** vous le montrer.

Translate.

I.—I will tell you a short anecdote. The Duchess of Marlborough was very ill, and lay in bed without speaking. The physicians said she **must** be blistered or she would die. Suddenly she called out: "I won't be blistered, and I won't die !"

NOTE.

Must (*see* Rule LXIX.).

I. 1. There is no wise or good man that would **change persons** or **conditions entirely** with any man in the world. 2. It may be he would have one man's wealth added to his own, or the power of a second, or the learning of a third; but still he would **receive these** into his own person, because he loves that best. 3. Would any man be **Dives to** have his wealth, or Judas for his office, or Saul for his kingdom, or Absalon for his bounty, or Achitophel for his policy? 4. It is likely he would wish **all these**, and yet he would **be** the same person still.

NOTES.

1. Change, *changer de*; persons..., conditions, to be put into the singular; entirely (to be placed immediately after *changer*).
2. Receive these, *fondre tout cela*; he loves tha best, put " he prefers it to everything."
3. Dives, *le mauvais riche*; to (*see* Invar. Words, Rule XXXI.).
4. All these, put " all *that*;" be, *rester*.

III.—What you do.
Still better, what is done. When you speak, sweet,
I'd have you do it ever: when you sing,
I'd have you buy and sell **so**; so give alms;
Pray so . . . .

NOTE.

So, *en chantant*.

RULE LXIV.

Would, like **should,** may be used in English instead of the *present indicative*, but in that case it must be put into that tense in French.

Translate.

I.—Reader, would'st thou know what true peace and quiet mean; would'st thou find a refuge **from** the noises and clamours of the multitude; would'st thou enjoy at once solitude and society; would'st thou be alone, and yet **accompanied**; solitary, **yet not** desolate? . . . . come with me **into** a Quaker's meeting.

NOTES.

From, *contre*; accompanied, *en compagnie*; yet not, put "without being;" into, *à*.

II.—**He who** would act **like** a wise man, and build his house on the rock and not on the sand, should view human life, not only **in the sunshine** but also in the shade.

NOTES.

He who (*see* Pron., Rule I.); like, *en*; in the sunshine, *du côté du soleil*.

RULE LXV.

I had rather, I would rather, etc., are translated by the conditional present of *préférer* or *aimer mieux*, with the next verb in the infinitive.

Ex.—I **had rather** come to-morrow :
Je **préfèrerais** venir demain.

RULE LXVI.

To **wish**, followed by *was*, *were*, or any verb conjugated with the auxiliaries *would*, *could*, *might*, is generally translated by the conditional present of

vouloir with the subjunctive, if the two verbs have different subjects, and with the infinitive if they have the same subject.

Ex.—I **wish** *he was* here;
Je **voudrais** bien qu'il *fût* ici.

I **wish** *I could* come;
Je **voudrais** bien *pouvoir* venir.

Translate.

1. My father would have gone on **ever so** long, **probably**, in this train, **had not** the servant entered with a note from Mrs. Meekin inviting them to dinner for the following Saturday. 2. "Do you mean **to go**?" says my mother.—"Go?" says my father; "why, I suppose **we must**."—3. "I wish they were further," says my dear mother.—"I wish they were at Jericho," says my dear father.—4. "I had rather do anything **than go on** Saturday," says my mother.—"I had rather be hanged than ever go," says my father; "it is **such an intolerable** bore."

NOTES.

1. Ever so (to be left out); probably (*see* Invar. Words, Rule I.); had not (*see* Ellipsis, Rule I.).
2. To go, put "to go *there* (*y*);" we must, *il le faut*.
4. Than go, put "than go *there* (*y*)" (and *see* Invar. Words, Rule XXIV.); on (*see* Synopsis, Rule XIII.); such an intolerable (*see* Art., Rule XV.).

RULE LXVII.

May and **might**, when preceded by a verb or a conjunction, and if mere auxiliaries, are rendered by putting into the indicative or the subjunctive mood the verb to which they are prefixed.

Ex.—I still hope he **may come**;
J'espère encore qu'il **viendra**.

I wish he **might come**;
Je voudrais qu'il **vînt**.

But when they express permission or possibility to do something, **may** is rendered by the indicative present, and **might** by the imperfect indicative or subjunctive, or the conditional present of **pouvoir**; the verb before which they stand is then put into the infinitive.

Ex.—He told me I **might** come with you;
Il m'a dit que je **pouvais** venir avec vous.

I believe I **might** do it;
Je crois que je **pourrais** le faire.

He did not think I **might** do it;
Il ne croyait pas que je **pusse** le faire.

Obs.—Practically we should advise the student, when he does not know into which tense to put "might," to see by what tense of the verb "to be able" it could be replaced, supposing those two verbs should be equivalent, and to put "might" into that tense.

Rem.—When **may** and **might** are preceded neither by a verb nor a conjunction, they are always translated separately.

Ex.—**May** I go;
Puis-je m'en aller.

You **might** be wrong;
Vous **pourriez** avoir tort.

Translate.

I.—1. In the republics of Greece and Rome the art **of speaking** was the powerful engine **of patriotism** or ambition. 2. When the liberty of **public debate** was suppressed, the orator, in the honourable profession of an advocate, might plead the cause of innocence and justice; he might abuse his talents in the more profitable trade of panegyric ; and the same precepts continued to dictate the fanciful declamations of the sophist, and the chaster beauties of historical composition. 3. The systems, which professed to unfold the nature of God, of man, and of the universe, entertained the curiosity of the philosophical student ; and according to the temper of his mind, he might doubt with the Sceptics, or decide with the Stoics, **sublimely speculate** with **Plato,** or severely argue with **Aristotle.**—(E. Gibbon.)

NOTES.

1. Of speaking (*see* Invar. Words, Rule XVII.) ; of patriotism (*see* Synopsis, Rules I. and VII.).
2. Public debate, *la tribune.*
3. Sublimely speculate, *se livrer à des spéculations sublimes*; Plato, *Platon* (proper names ending in *o* end generally in *on* in French) ; Aristotle, *Aristote.*

II.—1. " Such has been your conduct," exclaims H. Grattan in the conclusion of his attack upon Mr. Flood, " and **at** such conduct **every order of your fellow-subjects** have **a right** to exclaim ! 2. The merchant may say to you, the constitutionalist may say to you, the American may say to you, and I, I now say, and **say** to your beard, Sir, you are not an honest man."

NOTES.

1. At (*see* Invar. Words, Rule II.) ; every order of, etc., put " your fellow-subjects of every order " (*rang, m.*) ; a right, put " *the* right."
2. Say, put " say *to you.*"

RULE LXVIII.

Must, implying supposition, is translated by the present or the imperfect indicative of **devoir** ; by the *present* if the supposition refers to the present or the future, by the *imperfect* if it refers to the past.

Ex.—You **must** be tired;
Vous **devez** être fatigué.

I thought you **must** be wrong;
Je pensais que vous **deviez** avoir tort.

RULE LXIX.

When implying *necessity, obligation,* **must** may be rendered by **devoir**, but is more generally rendered by **falloir**. Besides, if the idea conveyed by the sentence is general, or if there cannot exist any ambiguity as to who must or must not do the thing spoken of, suppress the pronoun subject and put the next verb into the infinitive; otherwise use **il faut que,** etc., with the next verb in the subjunctive.

Ex.—We **must** be honest, *i.e., everybody* must be honest;
Il faut être honnête.

Mary **must** not go out to-day;
Il ne **faut** pas que Marie *sorte* aujourd'hui.

Translate.

I.—1. In the latter part of the seventeenth century the authority of France was supreme in all matters of good breeding, **from** a duel **to** a minuet. 2. She determined how a gentleman's coat must be cut, whether his heels must be high or low, and whether the lace of his hat must be broad or narrow.

NOTE.

From...to, *depuis...jusqu'à.*

II.—1. As the dark winter days come on, the farmer finds work of a different kind to engage his attention. 2. He fattens sheep and oxen, and these creatures require to be managed with much care and judgment. 3. Fuel must be provided for the cold months; the fences which have fallen into decay must be mended; drains must be constructed to carry off superfluous moisture from the land; and manure to render the ground fertile must be procured. 4. A man who wishes to cultivate a farm must be intelligent as well as industrious. 5. He must not **be satisfied with** working only. 6. He must think and observe, or a great portion of his labour will be thrown away and lost.

NOTE.

5. To be satisfied with, *se contenter de.*

III.—1. Charles XII. went reconnoitring, and, as he was returning to his camp, he received **a shot from a** carbine, which pierced his boot and shattered the bone of his heel. 2. The surgeons examined the wound and were of opinion that the leg must be cut off, **which** threw the army into the utmost consternation.

NOTES.

1. A shot from a, *un coup de.*
2. Which (*see* Pron., Rule XIV.).

RULE LXX.

Could may be rendered by the imperfect, the preterite definite or indefinite, or the conditional present of **pouvoir.** In order to ascertain which of these tenses must be used, turn it into *to be able.*

Ex.—You say you cannot do it, but I believe you **could**, *i.e.* you *would be able* to;
Vous dites que vous ne pouvez pas le faire, mais je crois que vous le **pourriez.**

I **could** not come yesterday, *i.e.* I *was not able* to;
Je **n'ai pas pu** venir hier (*see* Rule XIII.).

Rem.—It may also be put into the subjunctive if it is preceded by some expression governing that mood.

Ex.—I was afraid he **could** not come;
Je craignais qu'il ne **pût** pas venir.

Translate.

I.—1. **Fire** is one of the most valuable possessions of **man**. 2. By means of fire our food **is prepared**; by its assistance homes **are made** warm and habitable. 3. There are still more important **objects effected** by the aid of fire. 4. No blacksmith could make a nail, no ironfounder could cast a vessel of iron, no machine could be constructed without the employment of fire. 5. Even if machines could be made, they would be almost useless if fire were not applied to them, for nearly every engine is now worked by the aid of steam. 6. Then, again, **if it were not for** fire, we could not see to read or work during the long nights of winter.

NOTES.

1. Fire...man (*see* Synopsis, Rule I.).
2. Is prepared...are made (*see* Verb. Rule IV. and Rule LXXIX.).
3. To effect an object, *obtenir un résultat*.
6. If it were not for (*i.e., without*), sans.

II.—1. The pastoral writers of other countries **appear as if they had** paid nature an occasional visit, and become acquainted with her general charms; but the **British** poets appear as if they had lived and revelled with her—they have wooed her in her most secret haunts, they have watched her minutest caprices. 2. A spray could not tremble **in** the breeze; a leaf could not rustle to the ground; a diamond drop could not patter in the stream; a fragrance could not exhale from the humble violet, nor a daisy unfold its crimson tints, **but it has been** noticed by these impassioned and delicate observers.—(W. Irving: *Sketch Book*.)

NOTES.

1. Appear as if they had, put "seem to have;" British, *de la Grande-Bretagne*.
2. In, *au souffle de*; but it has been, put "without being."

RULE LXXI.

Must have, preceding a past participle, is rendered by the preterite indefinite of "devoir" (j'ai dû, tu as dû, etc.), and the participle put into the *present infinitive*.

Ex.—You **must have been** glad to see him again; Vous **avez dû être** content de le revoir.

Translate.

1. The woollen coat which covers the day-labourer, **as** coarse and rough **as** it may appear, is the produce of the joint labour of a great multitude of workmen. 2. The shepherd, the sorter of the wool, the woolcomber or carder, the dyer, the scribbler, the spinner, the weaver, the fuller, the dresser, with many others, must all join their different arts in order to complete even this homely production. 3. How many merchants and carriers, besides, must have been employed **in** transporting the materials from some of those workmen to others, who often **live** in a very distant part of the country! 4. How much commerce and navigation, in particular, — how many ship-builders, sailors, sail-makers, rope-makers, must have been employed in

order to bring the different drugs made use of by the dyer, **which** often come from the remotest corners of the world!—(Adam Smith.)

NOTES.

1. As...as, *tout...que.*
3. In (*see* Invar. Words, Rule XVII.); live, *demeurer* (not *vivre*).
4. Which (as *qui* might be supposed to refer to "dyer," put "*and* which.")

RULE LXXII.

Ought to have, preceding a past participle, is rendered by the conditional past of "devoir" (j'aurais dû, etc.), and the participle translated by the *present infinitive.*

Should have, before a past participle, is rendered in the same manner, if it can be turned into "ought to have;" otherwise it is translated by putting the verb, before which it stands, into the conditional past.

Ex.—I **should have** come, had I known you were here;
Je **serais venu**, si j'avais su que vous étiez ici.

In this case "should have" is a mere auxiliary.

You **should have** come, *i.e.* you *ought to have* come;
Vous **auriez dû** venir.

Translate.

1. It would be amusing to make a digest of the irrational laws which bad critics have framed for the government of poets. 2. "Shakspeare," says Rymer, "ought not to have made Othello black; for the hero

of a tragedy ought always to be white." 3. "Milton," says another critic, "ought not to have taken Adam for his hero; for the hero of an epic poem ought always to be victorious." 4. "Milton," says another, "should not have put so many similes into his first book; for the first book of an epic poem ought always to be the most unadorned. There are no similes in the first book of the Iliad." 5. A law of heroic rhyme, which, fifty years ago, was considered as fundamental, was that there should be a pause—a comma at least—at the end of every couplet. 6. It was also provided that there should never be a full stop except at the end of a line. 7. We do not see why we should not make a few rules of the same kind, why we should not enact that the number of scenes in every act shall be **three** or some multiple of three; that the number of lines in every scene shall be an exact square; that the *dramatis personæ* shall never be more or fewer **than** sixteen; and that, in heroic rhymes, every thirty-sixth line shall have twelve syllables.—(Macaulay.)

NOTES.

7. Three, *de trois;* than (*see* Invar. Words, Rule XXV.).

RULE LXXIII.

May have, followed by a past participle, is rendered by the past indefinite of " pouvoir " (j'ai pu, etc.), and the participle put into the *present infinitive.*

Ex.—I **may have** *said it;*
  J'**ai pu** le *dire.*

Translate.

1. "I speak," exclaims Curran in one of his speeches, "in the spirit of the British law, which proclaims even to the stranger, **the** moment he sets his foot upon British earth, that the ground on which he treads is holy, and consecrated by the genius of Universal Emancipation. 2. No matter in what language his doom may have been pronounced; no matter in what disastrous battle his liberty may have been cloven down; no matter with what solemnities he may have been devoted upon the altar of slavery,—the moment he touches the sacred soil of Britain, the altar and the god sink together in the dust......, and he stands redeemed, regenerated, and disenthralled by the irresistible genius of Universal Emancipation."

NOTE.

1. The, put "at the."

RULE LXXIV.

Could have, might have, before a past participle, are rendered by the conditional past of "pouvoir" (j'aurais pu, etc.), and the participle, turned into the *present infinitive*.

> *Ex.*—You **could have** *done* it;
> Vous *auriez* **pu** le *faire*.
>
> You **might have** *seen* him there;
> Vous **auriez pu** le *voir* là.

Translate.

To His Grace the Duke of Bedford.

1. My Lord,...You are, indeed, a considerable man. The highest rank, a splendid fortune, and a name glorious,

till **it was** yours, were sufficient **to have supported** you with meaner abilities **than you think you possess**. 2. The use you have made of these uncommon advantages might have been more honourable **to** yourself, but could not be more instructive **to** mankind. 3. We may trace it in the veneration of your country, the choice of your friends, and in the accomplishment of every sanguine hope, which the public might have conceived from the illustrious name of Russell. 4. Compare the natural dignity and importance of the richest peer of England, the noble independence which he might have maintained in Parliament, and the real interest and respect which he might have acquired through the whole kingdom; compare these glorious distinctions with the ambition of holding a share **in government**, and though you **may** not regret the virtues which create respect, you may see, with anguish, how much real importance and authority you have lost.—(*The Letters of Junius.*)

NOTES.

1. It was (*see* Rule XXXIII.); to have supported (*see* Rule XLIX.); than you think you possess, " than those which you believe to possess."
2. To, *pour.*
4. In government, put " in *the* government;" may (*see* Rule XXXIII.).

RULE LXXV.

The auxiliaries **do, have, shall, will**, etc., are often used *elliptically* in English, particularly in answers; but in French you should supply the words which are wanting to make the sentence complete.

Ex.—Do you know him? I **do** not, *i.e.* I *do not know* him;
 Le connaissez-vous? Non, je ne **le connais** pas.

Rem.—You may also use simply **oui, non**, when the auxiliaries might be replaced in English by " yes, no;" only you should generally add " Monsieur, Madame," etc., after " oui *or* non."

RULE LXXVI.

When the auxiliaries are in the *interrogative* form, they are rendered by **vraiment**, if, in an answer, they express *surprise*, and are equivalent to "indeed! really!" etc.; otherwise translate them by **n'est-ce pas** unchangeable.

Ex.—She is one hundred years of age.—**Is she**? *i.e.* really!
Elle a cent ans.—**Vraiment?**

Yo know your lesson, **do you not**?
Vous savez votre leçon, **n'est-ce pas**?

Obs.—It may be observed that "n'est-ce pas" is used when the auxiliary is part of one sentence uttered by the same person, whilst "vraiment" is employed when it forms, with what precedes, two sentences said by two different persons.

Translate.

1. "**Well**, Nickleby," said Squeers, **eyeing** him maliciously, "you think Smike has run away, I suppose?"
2. "I think it extremely likely," replied Nicholas, **in** a quiet manner.
3. "Oh, you do, do you? May be you know he has?"
4. "I know nothing of the kind."
5. "**He did not tell** you he was going, I suppose, did he?"
6. "He did not," replied Nicholas; "I am very glad **he did not**, for it would then have been my duty **to have warned** you in time."
7. "**Which** no doubt you would have been very sorry to do," said Squeers, in a taunting fashion.
8. "I should, indeed," replied Nicholas.—(Dickens.)

NOTES.

1. Well, *eh bien !* eyeing (*see* Rule XVIII.).
2. In (before " way, manner, fashion "), *de*.
5. He did not tell (*see* Rule XIII.).
6. He did not (*see* Rule XXXII.); to have warned (*see* Rule XLIX.).
7. Which (*see* Pron., Rule XIV.).

RULE LXXVII.

When **let**, followed by an infinitive, can be turned into *allow*, it must be translated by **laisser**.

Ex.—**Let** me do it ; *i.e.*, *allow* me to do it;
Laissez-moi faire cela.

When it cannot be so turned, it is a mere auxiliary and must then be translated by putting the next verb into the imperative.

Ex.—**Let** us go;
Partons.

Let him come ; **let** them come;
Qu'il vienne ; qu'ils viennent.

Translate.

I.—1. Let our readers think over these circumstances. 2. Let them take into the account **the sweating sickness** and the plague. 3. Let them consider the state of the northern counties, constantly the scene of robberies, rapes, massacres, and conflagrations. 4. Let them add to all this the fact that seventy-two thousand persons suffered death by the hands of the executioner during the reign of Henry VIII., and judge between the nineteenth and the sixteenth centuries.—(Macaulay).

NOTE.

2. The sweating sickness, *la suette.*

II.—1. "Oh, for pity's sake, let me go home!" cried Kate. "Let me leave this house and go home."
2. "Yes, yes," said Ralph. "**You shall.** But you must dry your eyes first, and compose yourself. Let me raise your head. There—there......Come, let us walk about."

NOTE.

2. You shall (*see* Rule LXXV.)

RULE LXXVIII.

To get has no direct equivalent in French, and should be translated by the verb for which it has been substituted, as

Ex.—I **got** back; *i.e. I came* back;
Je revins.

The following piece taken from "Wither's *Aristarchus,*" is a curious illustration of the chief uses of that verb, and will afford the student an opportunity of dealing with them all at once.

Translate.

1. I got on horseback within ten minutes **after I had got** your letter. 2. When I got to Canterbury, **I got** the waiter at the inn to get me a chaise for **town.** 3. But I got wet through before I got to Canterbury,

and I have got such a cold as I shall not be able to get rid of **in a hurry**. 4. I got to the Treasury about noon, but first of all **I got shaved** and dressed. 5. I soon got into the secret of getting a memorial before **the board**, but I could not get an answer then. However, I got intelligence from the messenger that I should most likely get **one** the next morning. 6. As soon as **I got back** to my inn, I got my supper and got to bed; it was not long before I got to sleep. 7. When I got up in the morning, I got my breakfast, and then got myself dressed, that I might get out in time **to** get an answer to my memorial. 8. As soon as I got it, I got into the chaise, and got to Canterbury by three; and about tea-time I got home. 9. I have got nothing particular **for you, and so** adieu.

NOTES.

1. After I had got (*see* Rule XXXVIII.)
2. I got, *j'obtins que* (with the *subj.*); town, put *the* town.
3. In a hurry, *de longtemps*.
4. I got shaved (*see* Rule L.)
5. The board, *le conseil;* one (*see* Pron., Rule XXXIII.)
6. I got back (*see* Rule XXII.)
7. To (*see* Invar. Words, Rule XXXI.)
9. For you, *à vous dire;* and so, *ainsi donc.*

RULE LXXIX.

To make, followed by an adjective, is translated by "*rendre.*"

Ex.—This news will **make** him **unhappy**.

Do not say: Cette nouvelle le *fera* malheureux,

But: Cette nouvelle le **rendra** malheureux.

RULE LXXX.

When **to make, to cause, to get** are followed by an objective personal pronoun and the active infinitive of a *transitive* verb, put the pronoun into the dative and place it before " make, cause, or get," all of which are then rendered by **faire**.

If the object is a noun, prefix **à** to it and place it *after* the infinitive.

> *Ex.*—I will make **him do** it;
> Je le **lui** ferai faire.

> I will get the **servant** to **do it**;
> Je le ferai faire **à la servante**.

Should the verb in the infinitive be *intransitive*, no alteration must take place with regard to the *case;* translate the object literally, only place it as indicated above.

> *Ex.*—I will make **him** *go* ;
> Je **le** ferai *partir*.

> I will make **your father** *consent* to your departure ;
> Je ferai *consentir* **votre père** à votre départ.

Rem.—The object " votre père " is placed after " consentir," as " faire " always requires to be followed immediately by the infinitive active of the next verb.

Translate.

I.—Anger.

1. Of **all** passions anger endeavours **most** to make reason useless. 2. It makes a man's body monstrous, deformed, and contemptible ; the voice horrid ; the eyes

cruel; the face pale or fiery; the speech clamorous or loud. 3. It makes friendships and societies intolerable. 4. It multiplies the evils of drunkenness, and makes the levity of wine run into madness. 5. It makes **innocent gesting** the beginning of tragedies... 6. It makes a man lose his reason...7. It makes a prosperous man to be envied, and the unfortunate to be unpitied. 8. And lastly, though it be very troublesome to **others**, yet it is most troublesome to **him that** hath it.—(J. Taylor.)

NOTES.

1. All, put " all *the;*" most, put "*the* most."
5. Innocent gesting (*see* Rule LXXXI.)
8. Others, **les** *autres*; him that (*see* Pron., Rule I.)

II.—" Madame," said Ruthven to **Queen Mary, pointing out** to Ritzio, " he has offended your honour; he has caused your Majesty to banish a great part of the nobility **that** he might be **made a lord**; he has been the destroyer of the Commonwealth, and **must** learn his duty **better**."

NOTES.

Queen Mary (*see* Art., Rule I.); pointing out (*see* Invar. Words, Rule XVIII.); that (*see* Rule XXXIII.); made *a* lord (*see* Art., Rule I..) ; must (translate it by "*falloir* "); better (must be placed immediately after "learn").

RULE LXXXI.

An active verb cannot have two direct objects unless they be united by a conjunction.

From this, **to make**, followed by a pronoun and a noun, or by two nouns, requires the pronoun or first noun to be turned into an *indirect* object preceded by of."

Ex.—That event made **him an honest man**, put " made *of* him ;" Cet évènement **en** fit (*or* fit **de lui**) un honnête homme.

Translate.

I.—" My greenhouse," writes Wm. Cowper, " is never so pleasant as when we are just upon the point of being turned out of it. The gentleness of the autumnal sun, and the calmness of this latter season make it a much more agreeable retreat as we ever find it in the summer."

II.—An hour **in** every day withdrawn from frivolous pursuits would, **if** profitably **employed**, enable a person of ordinary capacity to go far towards mastering a complete science. 2. It would make an ignorant man a well-informed man in ten years.

NOTES.

In (to be left out); if...employed (*see* Ellip., Rule II.)

INVARIABLE WORDS.

RULE I.

In French, the adverb is generally placed after the verb in simple tenses, and between the auxiliary and the participle, if the tense is compound.

Ex.—I **often** see him;
Je le vois **souvent**.

I have **often** spoken to him;
Je lui ai **souvent** parlé.

Rem.—Adverbs of time or place, like **aujourd'hui** (to-day), **hier** (yesterday), **ici** (here), etc., are placed after the participle.

Ex.—I saw him **yesterday**;
Je l'ai vu **hier**.

Mieux (better) must be placed immediately after the verb, if it is in a simple tense; if the tense is compound, "mieux" follows the general rule stated above.

Ex.—I like this horse **better** than that one;
J'aime **mieux** ce cheval-ci que celui-là.

Translate.

MARY, QUEEN OF SCOTS, ON HEARING THE WARRANT FOR HER EXECUTION.

1. Mary heard the warrant **to** the end without emotion, and, crossing herself in the name of the Father, of the Son, and of the Holy Ghost: "That

soul," said she, " is not worthy the joys of **Heaven**, which repines because the body must endure the stroke of the executioner. 2. I willingly submit to the decrees of that which Providence has decreed to be my lot." 3. And laying her hand on a Bible, which happened to be near her, she solemnly protested she was innocent of that conspiracy which Babington had carried on against Elizabeth's life. 4. She then earnestly entreated, that now, in her last **moment**, her almoner **might be suffered** to attend her. 5. Even this favour, which is usually granted to the vilest criminal, was absolutely denied.—(W. Robertson.)

NOTES.

1. Heaven, put " *the* Heaven."
4. Moment, put " moments;" might be suffered (*see* Verb, Rule VI.).

RULE II.

The French do not always use the same prepositions as the English (to fill *with*, remplir *de;* to rejoice *at*, se réjouir *de*, etc.); moreover, they sometimes drop altogether the English preposition (to wait *for*, attendre; to look *at*, regarder; to listen *to*, écouter, etc.), and, on the other hand, insert one where there is none in English (to obey, obéir *à*; to disobey, désobéir *à*; to resist, résister *à*, etc.). It is a thing the student cannot be too careful about, and which he should always ascertain, before translating, by means of a good grammar or dictionary.

Ex.—I am astonished **at** it;
Je suis étonné **de** cela, *or* j'**en** suis étonné.

Fill the bottle **with** water;
Remplissez la bouteille d'eau.

I shall have much pleasure **in** seeing you;
J'aurai grand plaisir à vous voir.

This is the very thing I wished **for**;
Voilà précisément ce **que** je désirais.

I have not answered **his** letter yet;
Je n'ai pas encore répondu à **sa** lettre.

Translate.

LETTER FROM A CITIZEN OF THE WORLD.

1....When I survey the absurdities and falsehood with which the books of the Europeans are filled, I thank **Heaven** for having been born in China. 2. The Europeans reproach us **with** false history and fabulous chronology; **how should they** blush to see their own books filled with the most monstrous fables, and attested with the utmost solemnity. 3. The bounds of a letter do not permit me to mention all the absurdities of this kind which in my reading I have met with. 4. I shall confine myself to the accounts which some of their lettered men give **of the persons** of some of the inhabitants on our globe.

5. A Christian doctor says that **it was** not impossible for a whole nation to have **but** one eye in the middle of the forehead. 6. He is not satisfied with leaving it in doubt, but assures us that the fact **was** certain, and that **he himself was** an eye-witness of it.

7. You will, no doubt, be surprised, reverend Fum, at this author's effrontery; but, alas! he is not alone in this story—he has only borrowed it from several others who **wrote** before him. 8. Solinus tells us of a people of India who have but one leg and one eye, and yet are extremely active, run with great swiftness, and live by hunting. 9. These people we scarcely know **how** to pity or admire; but the men whom **Pliny** calls **Cyna-**

molci, who have got **the heads of dogs**, really deserve our compassion. 10. Solinus confirms **what** Pliny mentions, and Simon Mayole, a French bishop, talks of them as of familiar acquaintances. 11. "**After passing** the deserts of Egypt," says he, "we meet with the Kunokephaloi. They live by hunting; they cannot speak, but whistle; their chins resemble a serpent's head; their hands are armed with long sharp claws; their breast resembles that of a greyhound; and they excel in swiftness and agility. 12. These people," continues our faithful bishop, "never refuse wine; love roast and boiled meat; they are particularly curious in having their meat well dressed, and spurn at it **if** in the least **tainted**."—(Goldsmith.)

NOTES

1. Heaven, put "*the* Heaven."
2. With, put "with *having a;*" how should they, put "how they should," and *see* Rule XIII.
4. Of the persons (put it singular).
5. It (*see* Pron., Rule IV.); was (*imperf.*); but (*i.e., only*), ne... que.
6. Assures us that the fact was, put "assures us that the fact *is;*" he himself was, put "himself *has been*."—In French a personal pronoun cannot be immediately followed by a reflexive pronoun (as "myself, himself," etc.); if the personal pronoun is of the third person, you may either leave it out or express it—only if you express it, put the reflexive pronoun after the verb, and say, for example: "*Il* l'a vu *lui-même*," or "*Lui-même* l'a vu." If the pronouns are of the first or of the second person, both of them are generally expressed and placed as said above; for example: "*Nous* l'avons vu *nous-mêmes.*"
7. Wrote (*see* Verb, Rule XIII.).
9. How, put "if we must;" Pliny, *Pline;* Cynamolci, *Cynamolces;* the heads of dogs, put "a dog's head."
10. What (*see* Pron., Rule XXIV.).
11. After passing (*see* Verb, Rule XLVII.); Kunokephaloi, *Cynocéphales.*
12. If...tainted (*see* Ellipsis, Rule II.).

RULE III.

See Article, Rule XIV.

As is generally **comme**; if the next verb implies *futurity*, put it into the **future**.

Ex.—Do **as** you **please**;
Faites **comme** vous **voudrez**.

RULE IV.

When **as** means *for*, *because*, translate it by **car**.

Ex.—I do not believe you, **as** you never speak the truth, *i.e.*, *because* you...
Je ne vous crois pas, **car** vous ne dites jamais la vérité.

"As well as," meaning *and also, the same as,* is "ainsi que."

RULE V.

In a comparison, translate the *first* "as" by **aussi**, and the *second* by **que**.

Ex.—I am **as** tall *as* you;
Je suis **aussi** grand *que* vous.

Translate.

1. I **deny** not **but** that it is of greatest concernment **in** the Church and commonwealth to have a vigilant eye **how** books demean themselves, as well as men, and thereafter to confine, imprison, and do sharpest justice on them as malefactors; as books are not absolutely

dead things, but do contain **a progeny** of life in them **to be** as active as that soul **was whose progeny they are**; nay, they do preserve, as in a vial, the purest efficacy and extraction of that living intellect that **bred** them. 2. I know they are as lively and productive as the fabulous dragon's teeth, and, being sown, may chance to spring up armed men. 3. And yet, on the other hand, **as good** almost kill a man as kill a good book. 4. Who kills a man kills a reasonable creature, God's image; but he who destroys a good book, kills reason itself—kills the image of God, as it were, in the eye.—(J. Milton.)

NOTES.

1. Deny...but, *nier...que* (with the *subj.*, as "to deny" is equivalent to a negative verb; *see* Verb, Rule XXX.); in, *pour;* how, put "on the manner in which;" a progeny, *un germe;* to be, put "which will be;" was, *l'était;* whose progeny they are (*see* Pron., Rule XVIII.); bred (*see* Verb, Rule XIII.).

3. As good, put "it would be as well" (*autant vaudrait*).

RULE VI.

"As," meaning "in proportion as," is translated by "à mesure que."

Translate.

As we grow older, we grow wiser.

RULE VII.

As, after an adjective, is translated by **tout...que**, with the indicative mood, and the adjective placed between "tout" and "que."

Ex.—Rich **as** he is, he has never shown any pride;
  Tout riche **qu'**il est, il n'a jamais montré d'orgueil.

After an adverb **as** is generally turned into *although*, and translated by **quoique** with the subjunctive.

Ex.—Greatly **as** we love you, we cannot approve your conduct;

  Say: *Although* we love you greatly...

  Quoique nous vous aimions beaucoup, nous ne pouvons pas approuver votre conduite.

Rem.—We might also say:

  Quelque grande que soit notre affection pour vous..., *i.e.* however great our love to you;

  or: *Tout en* vous aimant beaucoup..., *i.e.* whilst loving you greatly...

Translate.

I.—**Telemachus**, admirable enough as it is, could never obtain amongst us to be called a poem.

NOTE.

Telemachus, *Le Télémaque.*

II.—Much as I regret the accident, it has had pleasant consequences after all.

RULE VIII.

As, before a verb in the indicative mood, may sometimes be turned into **in** with the *present participle*, and should then be rendered thus in French.

>*Ex.*—He could not help crying **as he told** this sad story, *i.e.*, *in* telling;
>Il ne put s'empêcher de pleurer **en racontant** cette triste histoire.

Translate.

The Accusing Spirit, which flew up to Heaven's chancery with the oath of **Uncle Toby**, blushed as he gave it in, and the Recording Angel, as he wrote it down, dropped a tear upon the word, and blotted it out for ever.—(Sterne.)

NOTE.

Uncle Toby (*see* Art., Rule I.).

RULE IX.

So...as, the former preceding an adjective and the latter following it, are **assez...pour**, or **si...que de**.

>*Ex.*—I am not **so** silly **as** to believe that;
>Je ne suis pas **si** sot **que de** croire cela;
>
>or: Je ne suis pas **assez** sot **pour** croire cela.

Translate.

Anger is a universal passion, of an infinite object; for no man was ever so amorous as to love a toad;

none so envious as to repine at the condition of the miserable; none so timorous as to fear a dead bee; but anger is troubled at every thing, and every man, and every accident.—(Jeremy Taylor.)

NOTE.

None so, put " none *was* so."

RULE X.

1. **But**, when meaning *only*, is translated by **seulement**, and more generally by **ne... que**, when joined to a verb.

Ex.—He is **but** three years old;
Il a **seulement** trois ans;

or: Il **n'a que** trois ans.

2. **But**, when meaning *except*, is rendered by **excepté**, and when meaning *if not*, by **si ce n'est, sinon**.

They all came **but** him;
Ils vinrent tous **excepté** lui.

What is sleep **but** an image of death?
Qu'est-ce que le sommeil **sinon** l'image de la mort?

RULE XI.

No one but, nothing but, when used as subjects, are rendered by **il n'y a que... qui**, with the subjunctive, and when used as subjects, by **ne... que** only.

Ex.—**None but** your father can do it; *i.e., there is only your father who...*
Il n'y a que votre père **qui** puisse le faire.

You will speak to **no one but** to him;
Vous **ne** parlerez **qu'**à lui.

INVARIABLE WORDS. 183

When a noun stands between "no" and "but," use **il n'y a pas un** (noun) **qui ne...** with the next verb in the subjunctive negative.

Ex.—**No** man **but** is more or less dissatisfied with his own condition; *i.e., there is no man who* is not...
Il n'y a pas un homme **qui** ne *soit* plus ou moins mécontent de son sort.

Translate.

I.—None but the brave deserve the fair.

II.—Nothing but virtue can supply the place of merit.

III.—What are spring and autumn, youth and old age, morning and evening, but real images of life and death?

IV.—No man can be a slave but he that fears pain, or fears to die.

V.—No man but is convinced of the brevity of life, yet no man but live as if life was eternal.

RULE XII.

By, when before a present participle, and implying the *means* or the *end*, is rendered by **en**.

Ex.—He made a fortune **by** working;
Il fit sa fortune **en** travaillant.

Translate.

1. "Our rulers," says Macaulay, "will promote the improvement of the nation by strictly confining themselves to their **own** legitimate duties, by leaving **capital** to find its most lucrative course, industry and intelligence their natural reward, idleness and folly their natural punishment, by maintaining peace, by defending property, by diminishing the price of law, and by observing strict economy in every department of the state. 2. **Let** the Government do **this**: the People will assuredly do the rest."

NOTES.

1. Own (to be left out when before an adjective); capital, industry... etc, (*see* Synopsis, Rule I.).
2. Let (*see* Verb, Rule LXXVII.); this (*see* Pron., Rule XXIX.).

RULE XIII.

How, preceding a verb, is **comment**, and in an *exclamative* sentence **comme**.

Ex.—**How** could you do it?
Comment avez-vous pu faire cela?

How he runs!
Comme il court!

RULE XIV.

Before an adjective or an adverb, **how** is translated by **comme** *or* **combien**, and if the sentence is exclamative, by **comme** *or* **que**. The verb and its subject should be placed between "comme, combien, que" and the adjective or adverb.

Ex.—I cannot tell you **how** good he is ;
Je ne peux pas vous dire **comme** *or* **combien** il est *bon*.

How cold it is !
Comme il *or* **qu'il** fait froid !

How *well* she sings !
Qu'elle chante *bien !*

Translate.

I.—1. Everything which another man would have hidden, **was matter** of gay and clamorous exultation **to** Boswell. 2. What silly things he said, what bitter retorts he provoked, how at one place he was troubled with evil presentiments which came to nothing, how he went to see men **hanged** and came away maudlin, how he was frightened out of his wits at sea, and how the sailors quieted him as they would have quieted a child, how tipsy he was at Lady Cork's one evening, and how much his merriment annoyed the ladies, how impertinent he was to the Duchess of Argyle, and with what stately contempt she put down his impertinence ; **all these things he proclaimed** to all the world, as if they had been subjects **for** pride and ostentatious rejoicing.

NOTES.

1. Was (*see* Verb, Rule IX.) ; matter, put " a cause ;" to, *pour*.
2. Hanged (*see* Verb, Rule LI.) ; all these things... etc. (*see* Emphasis, Rule VII.) ; subjects for, put " subjects *of*."

II.— . . . . How profound
The gulf ! and how the giant element
From rock to rock leaps **with delirious bound** !...—
(Byron.)

NOTES.

With, *de* ; delirious bound (*see* Art., Rule XIII.).

III.—What a **piece of work** is man ! **how noble** in reason, **how infinite** in faculty ! in form and moving **how express** and admirable ! **in action** how **like** an angel ! **in apprehension** how like a god !

NOTES.

Piece of work, *chef-d'œuvre que ;* how noble..., how infinite..., how express..., put " how noble his reason is, how infinite his faculties are,..." etc. ; in action, put " in his actions ;" how like, put " how he resembles ;" in apprehension, *dans ses pensées.*

RULE XV.

For the sake of elegance the *adjective*, but especially the adverb, following "how," may be turned into a noun, preceded by **quel, quelle**, in the first case, and by **avec quel**, etc., in the second. This change occurs frequently with adverbs ending in *ly*, or when there are several in the same sentence. The verb should then remain at the place it occupies in English.

Ex.—**How eloquently** he speaks !
Avec quelle éloquence il parle !

How innocent, **how** careless, **how** secure is infancy !
Que l'enfance est innocente, *qu'elle* est insouciante, *qu'elle* est confiante !

Or : **Quelle** innocence, **quelle** insouciance, **quelle** confiance chez l'enfant !

Translate.

I.—1. " The increase of wealth," says Macaulay, " under **Queen Elizabeth**, the progress of knowledge, and the reformation of religion, produced a great change ;

...a new and remarkable species of politicians appeared. 2. **It is** needless to relate how dexterously, how resolutely, how gloriously she directed the politics of England during the eventful years which followed...."

NOTES.

1. Queen Elizabeth (*see* Art., Rule I.)
2. It is (*see* Pron., Rule IV.)

II.—1. Let us leave those dull climates, so little favoured by the sun, for those happier regions on which he looks more kindly, making perpetual **summer**.... 2. We see a country rich **with** gems, but richer **with** the fragrant spices it affords. 3. How gravely move the largest of land-creatures on the banks of this fair river. 4. How sumptuously apparalled, gay, and splendid are all the various insects which feed on the plants of this warm region! 5. How beautiful the plants themselves...(Lord Shaftesbury.)

NOTES.

1. Summer, put " *a* summer."
2. Rich with (if no article follows), *riche* **en**, and (before an article), *riche* **par**.

RULE XVI.

How, before an infinitive, and preceded by to **know**, to **learn**, to **teach**, to **instruct**, is *not* expressed in French.

Ex.—She does not know **how** to *swim;*
Elle ne sait pas **nager**.

Translate.

I.—Horace instructs how to combat our vices and to regulate our passions, how to give bounds to our desires, how to distinguish between truth and falsehood, how to come back from our prejudicate opinions, and to understand exactly the principles and motions of all our actions.

II.—1. **Queen** Charlotte **knew** how to dispense, gracefully and skilfully, those little civilities which, **being paid** by a sovereign, are prized **at many times** their intrinsic value; she knew how to pay a compliment, how to lend a book, how to ask after a relation. 2. But she seems to have been utterly regardless of the comfort, the health, the life of her attendants when her own convenience was concerned.

NOTES.

1. Queen (*see* Art., Rule I.); knew (*see* Verb, Rule IX.); being paid, put " when they are paid;" at many times, *bien au-delà de.*

RULE XVII.

En, in, is the *only* preposition which requires the present participle.

The others require the *present infinitive*, with the exception of **après**, after, and **pour**, for, but the latter only when referring to the past, which govern the *infinitive perfect* (*see* Verb, Rule XLVII. and XLVIII.).

Ex.—I met him **in** travelling;
Je le rencontrai **en** voyageant.

He passed **without** seeing me;
Il passa **sans** me **voir.**

Rem.—Before a division of time, **en** means "*within the space of,*" and **dans**, *after* such a time.

Ex.—I can go there **in** three days; *i.e. within* three days;
Je puis y aller **en** trois jours.

I shall start **in** three days; *i.e. after* three days;
Je partirai **dans** trois jours.

Translate.

CHARACTER OF CHARLES XII., KING OF SWEDEN.

1. Charles XII., King of Sweden, died at the age of thirty-six years and a half, after experiencing all the grandeur of prosperity and all the hardships of adversity, without being **either** softened by the one or the least disturbed by the other... 2. He carried all the virtues of the hero to **such an** excess **as render** them no less dangerous than the opposite vices.... 3. He never was the aggressor, but in taking vengeance on those who had injured him, his resentment got the better of his prudence. 4. He was the first man who ever aspired to the title of conqueror, without the least desire of enlarging his dominions. 5. His only end in subduing kingdoms was to have the pleasure of giving them away. 6. His passion for glory, for war and revenge, prevented him from being a good politician; **a** quality without which the world had never seen before any one a conqueror.—(Voltaire, *History of Charles XII.*)

NOTES.

1. Either (to be left out).
2. Such a (*see* Art., Rule XV.); as render, put "that he rendered."
6. A (*see* Synopsis, Rule VIII.)

RULE XVIII.

When **in** might be supplied before a present participle, express it in French.

Ex.—He went away **laughing**; *i.e. in* laughing.
Il s'en alla **en** riant.

Translate.

1. The populace had invaded the palace...One of the multitude handed a *bonnet rouge* to Louis XVI. at the end of a pike. 2. The king **made a signal** to one of his grenadiers to hand him the *bonnet rouge*, and, smiling, he put it on his head, and then arose shouts of "*Vive le Roi!*"...3. However, fresh orators, mounting on the shoulders of their comrades, demanded incessantly of the king, sometimes by entreaties, sometimes by threats, to promise the recal of Roland and the sanction of the decrees. Louis XVI. refused to surrender to violence. 4. "Do not fear, Sire," said a grenadier of the National Guard to him. "My friend," replied the king, taking his hand and placing it on his breast, "see if my heart beats quicker than usual."

NOTE.

2. Made a signal, *fit signe*.

RULE XIX.

Neither...nor, before an infinitive, are **ni...ni**, and require *ne* to be placed before the preceding verb in the indicative mood. If there are several infinitives, put "ni" before *each* of them.

Ex.—He can **neither** read, write, **nor** count;
Il *ne* sait **ni** lire, **ni** écrire, **ni** compter.

Translate.

There are many objects of our mind which we can neither see, hear, feel, smell, nor taste, and which no sense **could** ever **have introduced** into the mind.

NOTE.

Could have introduced (*see* Verb, Rule LXXIV.)

RULE XX.

Nor, when not preceded by *neither*, is translated by **et ... ne** (and not), and the *affirmative* turn used in French, instead of the interrogative employed in English.

    Ex.—I have never heard it, **nor** can I believe it; *i.e.* "and I cannot..."
    Je n'ai jamais entendu dire cela, **et** je **ne** peux pas le croire.

Neither, when not followed by *nor*, is rendered by **ne ... non plus**, with the verb in the affirmative turn.

    Ex.—If you do not do it, **neither** will I;
    Si vous ne le faites pas, je **ne** le ferai pas **non plus**.

Translate.

I.—I am positive I have a soul; nor **can** all the books with which the materialists have pestered the world ever convince me of the contrary.

II.—When the innocence of the citizens is not secure, neither is liberty.

NOTE.

    I. Can (use the future).

RULE XXI.

Now, adverb of time, when in a sentence, the verb of which is in the *past tense*, must be translated by **alors**, not by "maintenant," the latter expression being used only with the present.

Ex.—His father came, and **now** he *told* him the whole affair; Son père vint, et **alors** il lui *conta* toute l'affaire.

Rem.—When "now" means neither "at present" nor "at that time" translate it by **or**.

Translate.

I.—1. After the victory of Preston Pans many of the Highlanders had returned home with their booty; and as Charles could now muster only about 1,500 men, **he was advised** to wait and recruit his army. 2. He **therefore** returned to Holyrood-house. 3. He might now be considered master of all Scotland, except some of the country beyond Inverness, the Highland forts, and the castles of **Edinburgh** and Stirling.

NOTES.

1. He was advised, *il se laissa persuader.*
2. Therefore (*see* Rule I.)
3. Edinburgh, *Edinbourg.*

II.—One of the chiefs of Robin Hood's merry men was John Little, whom Robin one day met on a narrow bridge. Now as neither **would** allow the other to pass peaceable, they fought with sticks **until** they were tired.

NOTES.

Would (*see* Verb, Rule LXIII.); until (*see* Verb, Rule XXXIII.)

RULE XXII.

Since, before a date, is **depuis**; after a date, and being equivalent to *ago*, or *before*, it must be translated by **il y a**, or **auparavant**, and placed first.

>*Ex.*—Since yesterday;
>**Depuis** hier.
>
>Two years since;
>**Il y a** deux ans.

Before a verb, translate it by **depuis que**, with the indicative, if you can turn it into *since the time when* . . . ; otherwise use **puisque** with the same mood.

>*Ex.*—I never heard of him **since** he left us, *i.e.* "since the time when."
>Je n'ai jamais entendu parler de lui **depuis qu**'il nous a quittés.
>
>I will go there, **since** you wish it;
>J'irai, **puisque** vous le désirez.

RULE XXIII.

After the impersonal "to be, *y avoir*," followed by a date, **since** is to be rendered by **que ne**, with the indicative.

>It is a month **since** I saw him,
>Il y a un mois **que** je **ne** l'ai vu.

Translate.

I.—Since poetry is of all human learning the most ancient; since it is so universal that no learned nation doth despise it, no barbarous nation is without it; since its effects **be so** good **as** to teach goodness and delight to the **learners** of it; since the Holy Scripture **hath** whole parts **in it poetical**, and that even our Saviour vouchsafed to use the flowers of it; I think the laurel crown appointed for triumphant captains, doth worthily honor the poet's triumph.—(Sir Philip Sydney.)

NOTES.

Be, put " are;" so good as (*see* Rule IX.); the learners of it (*see* Substantive, Rule I.); hath in it, put "contains;" poetical, say "*which are* poetical."

II.—**It is** curious **to** remark **how heartily** men, as they **grow** towards **middle age**, despise themselves as they were a few years since.

NOTES.

It is...to (*see* Pron., Rule IV.); how heartily (*see* Rule XV.); as (*see* Rule VI.); they grow, *ils avancent;* middle age, put " the middle of life."

III.—It is **nearly** three hundred years since Mary, Queen of Scots, was beheaded.

NOTE.

Nearly (before a number), *près* **de.**

RULE XXIV.

Than, preceded by a comparative and followed by an infinitive, or a present participle, is rendered by **que de**, with the *present* infinitive.

Ex.—There is nothing better **than** to practise virtue;
Il n'y a rien de meilleur **que de** pratiquer la vertu.

INVARIABLE WORDS. 195

Translate.

I.—Nothing, **we are told** on good authority, is more erroneous than supposing the Hindoos **are prohibited** the use of animal food.

NOTES.

We are told (*see* Verb, Rule VI.) ; are prohibited, put " that the use of animal food is prohibited to the Hindoos."

II.—There is no more interesting spectacle than to see the effects of wit upon the different characters of men, than to observe it expanding caution, relaxing dignity, unfreezing coldness, and charming even the pangs of grief.

RULE XXV.

If **than**, after a comparative, comes before a verb in the indicative mood, translate it by **que**, and put **ne** before the verb ; should the verb be preceded by a conjunction, use **que** only.

Ex.—He is richer **than** you think;
Il est plus riche **que** vous **ne** pensez.

I am more glad **than if** I had been given a thousand pounds;
Je suis plus content **que** *si* l'on m'avait donné mille livres.

Translate.

I.—**Would** you know wherein lies the secret strength of our elder writers, it lies in this : they always say less than they think, and never write more than they know.

NOTE.

Would (*see* Verb, Rule **LXIV.**)

II.—I am better satisfied with his apology than if he had paid the damage.

Rem.—When, in a comparison, the noun, which is the object of the first verb, might be repeated after the second, precede the latter with **en**.

Ex.—You have done more work in an hour than I have **in a day**,
i.e. than I have done *work;*
Vous avez fait plus de travail en une heure que je **n'en** ai fait en un jour.

III.—Xenophon reaped more glory **from** his celebrated retreat than many generals of the present time have obtained from their brilliant victories.

NOTE.

From, *par.*

RULE XXVI.

Than, preceding a cardinal number, is **de**.

Ex.—This man is more **than** 90 years old ;
Cet homme a plus **de** quatre-vingt-dix ans.

I went there more **than** once ;
J'y suis allé plus **d'**une fois.

Translate.

Amongst the sovereigns of England, Elizabeth is one of those who remained longest on the throne ; she reigned more than forty-four years.

RULE XXVII.

Till, or **until**, when a verb follows, is **jusqu'à ce que**, with the subjunctive.

Before a noun, when no verb follows, and being then equivalent to *as far as, as late as*, it is **jusqu'à**, and before a year **jusqu'en**. " To," when having the same meaning, is translated in the same way.

Ex.—Wait **until** to-morrow...**until** 1890;
    Attendez **jusqu'à** demain,...**jusqu'en** mil huit cent quatre-vingt-dix.

He would have remained **to** this hour, *i.e. until...as late as;*
Il serait resté **jusqu'à** maintenant.

He stayed with us **until** his father came back;
Il resta avec nous **jusqu'à ce que** son père fût revenu.

Obs.—Sometimes the verb following the conjunction may be elegantly replaced by a noun; for instance, we might say here:

"Il resta avec nous *jusqu'au retour* de son père.

RULE XXVIII.

Between " to wait " and another verb, **till** should be rendered by **que** only, with the subjunctive.

Ex.—Wait **till** I have seen him;
    Attendez **que** je l'**aie** vu.

Translate.

I.—The senate spoke to Nero of its gratitude; the prince, then a youth, replied " **To** rely upon it, I shall wait till I have deserved it."

NOTE.

To, (*see* Rule XXXI.)

II.—More was Lord High Chancellor **from** 1530 until 1538, and, although unjustly accused of cruelties, he did support in controversy the fierce policy of persecution.

NOTE.

From, *depuis.*

RULE XXIX.

If **until**, coming before a noun, is preceded by a negative, translate it by **ne...que**, or **ne...pas avant**. If the noun does not immediately follow, " ne ... que " alone can be used.

Ex.—I shall not see him **till** next month;
    Je **ne** le verrai **que** le mois prochain; *i.e.* " I shall see him *only* next month."

    Or: Je **ne** le verrai *pas avant* le mois prochain; *i.e.* " I shall *not* see him *before* next month."

    But say, with " ne...que " only:
    Je **ne** le verrai **que** *dans* le courant du mois prochain.

Rem.—Between two verbs, the first of which is negative, " until" should be translated by " before," to which it is then equivalent.

Translate.

I.—Henry VII. levied a benevolence in 1491; but appears not to have succeeded **in** obtaining the money till he had procured an Act a few years afterwards.

NOTE.

In (*see* Rule II.)

II.—The cotton manufacture did not acquire any importance in France until 1787, **when** the French Government established cotton spinning machines at Rouen; but it was not, however, until under the Empire, that, thanks to the efforts of Richard Lenoir, this branch of industry became prosperous.

NOTE.

When (*see* Rule XXXVII.)

RULE XXX.

Till may sometimes either be suppressed or turned into *at last*, in which case either leave it out in French, or translate it by **enfin**, as you think it best, and begin a fresh sentence.

Translate.

1. After leaving Zanzibar, Livingstone travelled along the left bank of the Rovuma. 2. To the difficulty of the route **was added** the unwillingness of a portion of his party to work. 3. The sepoys gave the doctor **immense trouble**; until at last, unable to bear with their murmurings and complainings any longer, he sent them back to the coast.

NOTES.

2. Was added (*see* Verb, Rule V.)
3. Immense trouble (*see* Art., Rule XIII.)

RULE XXXI.

To, before an infinitive, is rendered by **pour**, when it can be turned into **in order to, for the purpose of, with a view to**.

Ex.—I wrote **to** ask him to come; *i.e. in order to* ask;
Je lui ai écrit **pour** lui demander de venir.

Translate.

HOWARD, THE PHILANTHROPIST.

1. "I cannot name this gentleman," says Burke, "without remarking that his labours and writings have done much to open the eyes and hearts of all mankind. 2. He has visited all Europe, not to survey the sumptuousness of palaces, or the stateliness of temples, nor to collect medals, or collate manuscripts, but to dive into the depths of dungeons, to plunge into the infection of hospitals, to survey the mansions of misery, depression, and contempt; to remember the forgotten, to attend to the neglected, to visit the forsaken, and compare the distresses of all men in all countries."

RULE XXXII.

To, before an infinitive active, is translated by **à**, when that infinitive can be turned into the passive voice.

Ex.—I have a lesson **to** learn; *i.e. to be* learnt;
J'ai une leçon **à** apprendre.

Translate.

1. The Indian squaw's inferiority **to** the hunter is like **that** of the horse to his master. 2. While she has a thousand toils to endure, she has scarcely any rights **as either a** woman or a wife.

NOTES.

1. To, *vis-à-vis de*.
2. As either..., construe " either as woman or as wife."

RULE XXXIII.

The verb " avoir," followed by a noun requires **de** before the next infinitive, if that infinitive can be turned in English into the present participle preceded by " of."

Ex.—I shall **have the pleasure** *to see* you on Monday; *i.e.*,
"the pleasure *of seeing* you;"
J'aurai le plaisir **de** vous **voir** lundi.

Translate.

CHARACTER OF CROMWELL.

1. Is it not most extraordinary that a **person** of **mean birth, no fortune**, no eminent qualities of body, or of mind, should have the courage **to attempt**, and the happiness **to succeed in, so improbable** a design as the destruction of one of the most ancient monarchies? 2. That he should have the power or boldness to put his prince and master to an infamous death; to banish that numerous and strongly-allied family; to do all this under the name and wages of a

parliament; to trample upon them, too, as he pleased, and spurn them out of doors when he grew weary of them,...to oppress all his enemies by arms, and all his friends afterwards by artifice; to be feared and courted by all foreign princes; to have the estates and lives of three kingdoms as much at his disposal as the little inheritance of his father; and, lastly, to die with peace at home and triumph abroad; to be buried among kings, and to leave a name behind him, **not to be extinguished**, but with the whole world.—(Abraham Cowley.)

NOTES.

1. A person, put "*a man;*" mean birth (*see* Art., Rule XIII.); no fortune, no eminent qualities, put "*without* fortune, *without*, etc."; to attempt, and...to succeed in (*see* Verb, Rule II.); so improbable a (*see* Art., Rule XV.)

2. Not to be extinguished, but..., put "which will not be extinguished but," and *see* Verb, Rule V.

RULE XXXIV.

When or **in which**, coming after an expression of time (such as "day, year," etc.), are rendered by **où**. "One day" is an exception (*see* next Rule).

Ex.—I remember the day **when** I first saw you;
   Je me souviens du jour où je vous ai vu pour la première fois.

Translate.

I.—1. Gentlemen, the question you have to try upon all this matter is extremely simple. It is neither more nor less than this: 2. At a time when the charges against Mr. Hastings were in every hand and on every table ; when the lightning of eloquence was incessantly consuming him; when every man was with perfect impunity saying and writing just what he pleased **of** the supposed plunderer and devastator of nations,—would it have been criminal **in** Mr. Hastings himself to remind the public that he was a native of this free land, entitled to the common protection of her justice?— (Thomas, Lord Erskine: *Speech on the trial of Stockdale.*)

NOTES.

2. Of (*i.e.* about), *sur*; in, *de la part de*.

II.—1. Whatever any man ardently desires, he very readily believes he shall some time **attain**. 2. Every man thinks **the day coming** in which he shall be gratified with all his wishes, in which he shall leave all his competitors behind him ; **the day is always coming to the servile** in which they shall be powerful, to the obscure **in which** they shall be eminent, and to the deformed in which they shall be beautiful.

NOTES.

1. He shall attain (*see* Ellipsis, Rule VI.).
2. The day coming, put "that the day arrives;" the day is always coming to the servile, put " the servile always see coming the day," etc., and *see* Verb, Rule XLIII. ; in which, put "*that* in which," and *see* Pron., Rule XXVI.

RULE XXXV.

After " hardly, scarcely, one day," **when** is rendered by **que** with the indicative.

Ex.—*Scarcely* had I seen him **when** he went away
A peine l'eus-je vu **qu**'il s'en alla.

Translate.

...Charles XII. **ordered an assault to be made** the next morning, but he had hardly given these orders when he was informed that the whole army of the enemy was advancing against him, in consequence **of which** he was obliged to alter his resolution.

NOTES.

Ordered an assault to be made (*see* Verb, Rule VIII.); in consequence of which (*see* Pron., Rule XV.).

RULE XXXVI.

When and **on**, preceding a present participle, are rendered by **en**.

Translate.

1. Thomas Pope, on taking leave of More, could not refrain from weeping. More comforted him.... 2. When going to the scaffold, which was so weak that it seemed ready to fall, More said to the lieutenant : " I pray you, **Mr. lieutenant, see me safe up** ; as to coming down, let me shift for myself." 3. On kneeling to receive the fatal stroke, he said to the executioner : " My beard has not offended the king ; let me put it aside."

NOTES.

2. Mr., *Monsieur le*; see me safe up, put " see that I may arrive safe up " (*faites en sorte que j'arrive en haut sain et sauf*).

RULE XXXVII.

If **when** is preceded by a complete sentence, and may be suppressed without altering the sense, leave it out in French, and begin a fresh clause.

If it may be better turned into *then, and then, at that time, after which*, etc., translate it by **alors, puis, à cette époque, après quoi**, or any like expression which will be best adapted to the meaning.

> *Ex.*—I remained there until May 2, **when** I left for England, *i.e., and then* or *after which;*
> Je restai là jusqu'au deux mai, **et alors** *or* **après quoi** je partis pour l'Angleterre.
>
> He waited until last month, **when**, having completed his arrangements, he sailed for Brazil;
> Il attendit jusqu'au mois dernier; ayant *or* **alors** ayant terminé ses arrangements, il fit voile pour le Brésil.

Translate.

I.—Croissy continued in the town till the 18th of November, when, having obtained from the enemy a passport for himself and his baggage, he took his leave of the king, who still remained amidst the ruins of Stralsund.

II.—"I was then bound out to a farmer," says the disabled soldier, "where I was up both early and late; but I ate and drank well, and liked my business well enough, **till** he died, when I was obliged to provide for myself; so I was resolved to go seek my fortune."

NOTE.

Till (*see* Verb, Rule XXXIII.).

RULE XXXVIII.

Whether, coming immediately before an adjective or a noun used adjectively, and followed by " or," is generally left out.

Ex.—**Whether** rich *or* poor, we must be honest;
Riche ou pauvre, on doit être honnête.

When before a verb, and not governed by another, it is rendered by **que** with the subjunctive.

Ex.—**Whether** I die or not, keep the ring I gave you;
Que je *meure* ou non, gardez l'anneau que je vous ai donné.

Translate.

I.—He who, in the vale of obscurity, can brave adversity—who, without friends, without acquaintances, or even without hope to alleviate his misfortunes, can behave with tranquility and indifference, is truly great: whether peasant or courtier, he deserves admiration.—(Goldsmith.)

II.—**He who** is outlawed by general opinion, whether he be innocent or guilty, must undergo all the bitterness of exile, without hope, without pride, without alleviation. —(Lord Byron.)

RULE XXXIX.

While is rendered by **tandis que** when it marks *contrast* or *opposition*, and by **pendant que** when it means *during the time when*, both conjunctions governing the indicative mood. The future must be expressed whenever it is meant.

> *Ex.*—**While** you *are* there I will go to Paris, *i.e., during the time you shall be* there;
> **Pendant que** vous *serez* là j'irai à Paris.
>
> He is always well, **whilst** she is constantly unwell;
> Il est toujours bien portant, **tandis qu'**elle, elle est toujours souffrante.

Translate.

1. ...Religion is too much interested in your success not to lend you her aid. 2. While you are engaged in the field, many will repair to the sanctuary; the faithful of every name will employ that prayer which has power **with** God. 3. While you have everything to fear from the success of the enemy, you have every means of preventing that success, so that it is next to **impossible for victory not to crown** your exertions.—(R. Hall.)

NOTES.

2. With, *auprès de.*
3. Impossible for victory not to crown (*see* Verb, Rule XL.).

RULE XL.

While, immediately preceding a present participle, is generally rendered by **en** or **tout en**.

> *Ex.*—**While** *speaking* he followed all her movements with his eyes;
> **Tout en** parlant il suivait des yeux tous ses mouvements.

Translate.

1. With perseverance, the very odds and ends of time may produce results of the greatest value.   2. **Dr. Mason** Good translated **Lucretius** while riding in his carriage in the streets of London, and going his rounds among his patients.   3. Dr. Darwin composed nearly all his works in the same way.   4. Dr. Burney learnt **French** and Italian while travelling on horseback from **one musical pupil** to another.   5. Kirke White learnt Greek while walking to and from a lawyer's office, and we personally know a man of eminent position, who learnt Latin and French while going messages as an errand-boy in the streets of Manchester.—(Smiles's *Self-Help*.)

NOTES.

2. Dr. Mason (*see* Art., Rule I.).
4. French, names of languages take the definite article in French, except when preceded by "en," and after the verb "parler;" from one musical pupil, put " from one lesson of music."

ELLIPSIS AND EMPHASIS.

RULE I.

In English the conjunction **if** may be suppressed, and the verb put in the interrogative form; but in French you should express the conjunction and put the words into the usual order.

Ex.—**Had I** known it, I should have come; *i.e., "if I had known it";*
Si j'avais su cela, je serais venu.

Translate.

I.—..."Had Pope's translation been good," writes W. Cowper, " or had I thought it such, or had I not known that **it is admitted** by all whom a knowledge of the original qualifies to judge of it, to be a very **defective one**, **I had** never translated myself one line of Homer."

NOTES.
It is admitted by.. to be, (*see* Verb, Rule IV. *Rem.* and Rule XXXIX.); a very defective one, (*see* Pron., Rule XXXV.); I had translated, (*see* Verb, Rule XX.).

II.—But should Providence **determine** otherwise, should you fall in this struggle, should the nation fall, you will have the satisfaction, the purest allotted to man, of having performed your part....(R. Hall.)

NOTE.
To determine, *en décider.*

RULE II.

The *verb is often omitted* in English after such conjunctions as **if, when, because,** etc., but it should be *expressed* in French. However, it may be left out after **quoique**, *though*, unless there be a negative.

> *Ex.*—**Though younger** than her brother, she is much more advanced;
> **Quoique plus jeune** que son frère, elle est beaucoup plus avancée.
>
> **Though** *not* so strong as you, I am not afraid of you;
> **Quoique** *je ne sois pas* si fort que vous, je ne vous crains pas.

Translate.

I.—I never yet **saw** a man,
But she would **spell** him **backward**; if fair-faced,
She'd swear the gentleman should be her sister;
If black, why, nature, drawing of an antic,
Made a foul blot; if tall, a lance ill-headed;
If low, an agate very vilely cut...
(*Much Ado about Nothing.*)

NOTES.

Saw (*see* Verb, Rule XIII.); but, *i.e.* "whom she has not;" to spell backward, *repousser.*

II. Whatever **is got** by acts of absolute power **ill-obeyed**, because odious, or by contracts ill-kept, because constrained, will be narrow, feeble, uncertain, and precarious.—(E. Burke).

NOTES.

Is got (*see* Verb, Rule IV. and Rule LXXVIII.); ill-obeyed, put "*being* ill-obeyed."

III.—The most remarkable of the men who, though blind, have won themselves a name in science, is indisputably the Englishman Saunderson, who lost his sight in 1688, when one year old, in consequence of the small-pox. Despite his total blindness, he sedulously applied himself to the study of science, and taught mathematics and optics at the Oxford University with the greatest success.

IV.—A young Chinese seems to me an antediluvian man renewed. Even Englishmen, though not bred in any knowledge of such institutions, cannot but shudder at the mystic sublimity of *castes* that have flowed apart, and refused to mix, through such immemorial tracts of time.—(Th. de Quincey.)

RULE III.

So, either expressed or understood, is rendered in French by **le** or **le, la, les**.

1. By **le, la, les**, when supplying the place of a substantive which is determined.

> *Ex.*—Are you **her niece? I am**; *i.e.* "Yes, I am *so*."
> Etes-vous **sa nièce?** Oui, je **la** suis.

2. By **le**, *indeclinable*, when supplying the place of an *adjective*, a past participle, or a noun which is *not* determined.

> *Ex.*—Are you **sisters?** Yes, we are; *i.e.* "we are *so*;"
> Etes-vous **sœurs?** Oui, nous **le** sommes.

> Are you **tired?** Yes, we are; *i.e.* "we are *so*";
> Etes-vous **fatigués?** Oui, nous **le** sommes.

Le, indeclinable, is also introduced in French when some preceding verb, or a part of a sentence, might be repeated.

Ex.—He is not so poor as *you think* ; *i.e.* as you think **he is**.
Il n'est pas si pauvre que vous **le** croyez.

His arguments produced a greater effect than *he thought;*
i.e., than he thought they would have produced;
Ses arguments produisirent plus d'effet qu'il ne le pensait.

Translate.

" Sir, " said Johnson to Warton in **an argument** they had at the house of Sir Joshua Reynolds, " Sir, I am not accustomed to be contradicted." Warton replied : " It would be better, Sir, for yourself and your friends, if you were : our respect could not be increased, but our love might."

NOTE.

An argument, *une discussion.*

RULE IV.

The student should take care to render emphatically any expression which is emphasized in English.

Ex.—**You**, and **you** alone do I trust;

The literal translation:

" J'ai confiance en vous, et en vous seul,"

would not sufficiently render the stress meant to be laid on the pronoun; we should adopt such rendering as may keep it its prominent place and character, and say, for example :

C'est en vous, et en vous seul *que* j'ai confiance.

ELLIPSIS AND EMPHASIS.

As it is impossible to foresee all the cases which may present themselves, we must content ourselves with giving a few hints about some of the most usual instances, leaving with the student the care of dealing with the others.

RULE V.

You may often emphasize an expression or a sentence by placing before it **c'est, ce sont, c'était**, etc., or some other which might likewise precede it in English. For instance, in the above example you might say:

"It is you, and you alone *that* I trust."

Translate.

I.—What is that which first strikes us, and strikes us at once, in a man of education; and which, among educated men, instantly distinguishes the man of superior mind?.. Not the weight or novelty of his remarks; not any unusual interests of facts communicated by him....It is the unpremeditated and habitual *arrangement* of his words, grounded on the habit of foreseeing in every sentence the whole that he then intends to communicate.—(Coleridge).

II...."Do you wish," exclaims H. Grattan in his speech against Napoleon, "do you wish to confirm this military tyranny in the heart of Europe?...**Should you do** anything so monstrous as to leave your allies in order to confirm such a system, would not the nations exclaim: 'You have very providently watched over your interests, and very generously have you contributed to our service, and do you falter now? In vain have you stopped in your own person the flying fortunes of

Europe; in vain have you taken the eagle of Napoleon, and snatched *invincibility* from this standard, if now, when confederated Europe is ready to march, you take the lead in desertion, and preach the penitence of Buonaparte and the poverty of England.'"

NOTE.

Should you do, see Rule I.

RULE VI.

When a direct object is placed *emphatically* at the beginning of a sentence, and cannot be preceded by " it is, it was," keep it in the same place in French, only add an objective personal pronoun to the verb, so:

> *Ex.*—**The villany** you teach me, I will execute;
> Les leçons de méchanceté que vous me donnez, je **les** mettrai en pratique.

But if no stress is to be laid upon the objective, simply put it after the verb.

Translate.

I.—" The end which, I confess, I have always had in view," says G. Canning, "and which appears to me the legitimate object **of pursuit to a British statesman,** I can describe in one word: it is the interest of England."

NOTE.

Of pursuit to ... etc.; put " which a British statesman should pursue."

II.—O eloquent, just, and mighty death! whom none could advise, thou hast persuaded; what none hath dared, thou hast done; and whom all the world hath flattered, thou only hast cast out of the world and despised.
(Sir Walter Raleigh).

III.—**Positive** pleasure we cannot always obtain, and positive pain we **often** cannot remove.

NOTES.

Positive, *réel*; often (to be placed immediately after " and ").

RULE VII.

A possessive adjective, beginning a sentence, may be emphatically rendered by **à moi, à lui,** etc.

Ex.—**His** will be the shame, **yours** the glory,
A lui la honte, à **vous** la gloire.

Translate.

1..... **While** I conjure the House to pause **before it consents** to adopt the proposition of the noble lord, I cannot **help conjuring** the noble lord himself to pause before he again presses it upon the country. 2. **If,** however, **he shall persevere,** and if his perseverance shall be successful, and if the results of that success shall be such as I cannot help apprehending, his be the triumph to have precipitated those results, be mine the consolation that to the utmost of my power I have opposed them.—(G. Canning, *from his Speech on parliamentary reform*).

NOTES.

1. While (*see* Invar. Words, Rule XXXIX); before it consents (*see* Verb, Rule XXXVIII.); help conjuring, (*see* Verb, Rule XLIII.)
2. If ... he shall persevere, (*see* Verb, Rules XXIII. and XXIV.)

RULE VIII.

When two clauses are inverted, the second has generally to be modified by the addition of such words as will make it complete and emphatic.

Ex.—That he has done it alone, I cannot understand;
 ' Qu'il ait fait cela tout seul, **c'est ce que** je ne peux pas comprendre.

Where he is, and what he is doing, are questions which I cannot answer;
Où il est et ce qu'il fait, **ce sont** des questions auxquelles je ne saurais répondre.

Whether he is guilty or innocent must be left to the jury to decide;
S'il est coupable ou innocent, **c'est une question** qu'il appartient au jury de décider.

Translate.

I.—This paper, gentlemen, insists upon the necessity of emancipating the Catholics of Ireland, and that is charged as part of the libel. If they had waited another year, how much would remain for a jury to decide upon, I should be at a loss to discover.—(J. Philpot Curran.)

II.—" The chief glory of every people," says Johnson in the preface to his dictionary, " arises from its authors:

whether I shall add anything by my own writings to the reputation of English literature, must be left to time."

NOTE.

Whether, *quant à savoir si.*

III.—In a field of old Walsingham, not many months past, were digged up between forty and fifty urns, deposited in a dry and sandy soil, about a yard deep, and not far from one another; some containing two pounds of bones, with fresh impressions of their combustion.... What time the persons of these ossuaries entered the famous nations of the dead, and slept with princes and counsellors, might admit a wide solution. But who were the proprietaries of these bones, or what bodies these ashes made up, was a question above antiquarianism.

SECOND PART.

In the first twelve pieces of this part, Notes and References to Rules in Part I. are given as previously.

In the next ten pieces, **black type** refers to Rules in Part I., the numbers of which are no longer given; *italics* refer to Notes at the end of the piece.

The rest of the pieces are entirely without **notes.**

UNIVERSITY OF LONDON.

Examination of Women for Certificates of higher Proficiency (1870).

I.—OF TRANSLATION.

1. Translation is a province everybody thinketh himself qualified to undertake, but very few **are found** equal to it: the mechanic rules, the common laws, which **are to be observed**, are very seldom **obeyed**, and sometimes a translation may prove **a very bad one, where** these are most strictly regarded. 2. **Too scrupulous an** observation of rules spoileth all sorts of writings: it **maketh** them stiff and formal; it betrayeth a weak and pedantic genius, and **such** nice writers are fitter to make transcribers than translators.

3. The first qualification of a good translator is an exact understanding, an absolute mastery of the language he translateth **from** and the language he translateth **to**; we are not only required to understand our own and a foreign tongue as critics and grammarians; we must not only be masters of each separately, but we must more especially study the relation and comparison between them. 4. **In this do lie** the great art and difficulty **of translating**; and not being able to reach the full compass, the differences, the proprieties, and beauties of one language, is the foundation of all faulty rendering into another.—(H. Felton.)

NOTES.

1. Are found, *il s'en trouve* (to be placed before " very few ") : are to be observed (*see* Verb, Rule LII. and Rule IV.; obeyed, put "followed;" a very bad one, "a" to be omitted, and *see* Pron., Rule XXXV.; where, *i.e.* " in which " (*see* Pron., Rule X.)

2. Too scrupulous a (*see* Art., Rule XV.); maketh (*see* **Verb**, Rule LXXIX); such nice (*see* Art., Rule XV.)

3. From (leave it out); to, put "into."

4. In this, (*see* Pron., Rule XXIX. and Emphasis, Rule V.); do lie, (*see* Verb, Rule LIX.); of translating (*see* Invar. Words, Rule XVII.).

UNIVERSITY OF LONDON.

Second B. A. Pass Examination.—*1879. October 28.*

II:

1. Squeers, arming himself **with** his cane, **led** the way across a yard to a door in the rear of the house.

2. "There," said the schoolmaster as they **stepped** in together, "**this is** our shop, Nickleby."

3. **It was such a** crowded scene, and there were so many objects **to** attract attention, that at first Nicholas stared about him, really without **seeing** anything at all. 4. By degrees, however, the place resolved itself into a bare and dirty **room** with a couple of windows, whereof a tenth part **might** be of glass, the remainder being stopped up with **old copy-books** and paper. 5. There were a couple of **long old** desks, cut and notched and inked and damaged in **every** possible way; two or three forms, a detached desk for Squeers, and another for his assistant. 6. The ceiling was supported like that of a barn, and the walls were so stained and discoloured that **it was** impossible to tell whether they had ever been touched with paint or whitewash.

(Dickens).

NOTES.

1. With (*see* Invar. Words, Rule II.); led (*see* Verb, Rule XII.).

2. Stepped in, (*see* Verb, Rule IX.); this is (*see* Pron, Rule XXVIII., Rem.)

3. It was (*see* Pron., Rule III.); such a (*see* Art., Rule XV.); without seeing (*see* Invar. Words, Rule XVII.).
4. Room (meaning a place where people usually meet), *salle*; might (*see* Verb, Rule LXVII.); old copy-books (*see* Synopsis, Rule III.).
5. Long old desks (*see* Adj., Rule II.); in every... put "in all the manners possible."
6. It was (*see* Pron., Rule IV.).

III.—DEATH OF HENRY VIII.

1. Private orders **were given** to arrest Norfolk and Surrey, and they were **on** the same day confined to the Tower. 2. Surrey being a commoner, his trial was the more expeditious; he was condemned for high treason, and the sentence was soon after executed **upon him** (Jan. 19, 1547). 3. The innocence of the Duke of Norfolk was still, **if possible**, more apparent than **that** of his son, and his services to the crown had been greater, yet the House of Peers, without **examining** the prisoner, without trial **or** evidence, passed a bill of attainder against him, and sent it down to the commons. 4. The king was **now** approaching fast towards his end; and **fearing lest** Norfolk should escape him, he sent a message to the commons, by which he **desired them to hasten** the bill; and having given the royal assent by commission, issued orders for the execution of Norfolk on the morning of January 28, 1547. 5. But news being carried to the Tower that the king himself had expired that night, the lieutenant deferred **obeying** the warrant; and **it was not thought** advisable by the council to begin a new reign by the death of the greatest nobleman **in** the kingdom, who had been condemned by a sentence so unjust and tyrannical.

(D. Hume).

NOTES.

1. Were given (*see* Verb, Rules IV. and XII.); on (*see* Synopsis Rule XIII.).
2. Upon him (to be left out).

3. If possible (*see* Ellipsis, Rule II.); that of... (*see* Pron., Rule XXVI.); without examining (*see* Invar. Words, Rule XVII.); or (when preceded by "without," is to be translated like "nor").

4. Now (*see* Invar. Words, Rule XXI.); fearing lest (*see* Verb, Rule XXXII. and Rem.); he desired them to hasten (*see* Verb, Rule XXXIX.).

5. Deferred obeying (*see* Verb, Rule XLIII.); it was not thought (*see* Verb, Rule IV.); the greatest... in (*see* Synopsis, Rule XXII.).

IV.—THE GOAT, THE LION, AND THE FOX.

1. The goat, **according to the** Hindu tale, took shelter during a storm in the den of a lion; when he saw no chance to escape, he terrified the king of beasts **by** boasting of a celestial origin, and telling him he had been condemned **before he could** return to Heaven to eat ten elephants, ten tigers, and ten lions. 2. He had, **he said,** eaten **every** kind of animal **but** the lion; and **so saying**, he marched up to the astonished monster, who fled by a back way from his den. 3. The lion in his flight met a fox, and described to him the appearance of the goat (**an** animal **he had** never seen before), his horns, his strange beard, and above all, his **boasting** language. 4. The fox laughed, and told his majesty how **he** had been tricked. 5. They went back together, and met the goat at the entrance of the den. 6. The latter **at once** saw **his** danger, but his wits did not forsake him. 7. "**What conduct is this, you** scoundrel?" said he to the fox; "**did I not command** you to **get** ten lions, and **here** you have only brought me **one?**" 8. So saying, he advanced boldly, and the lion, again frightened by his words and actions, fled in terror, allowing the goat to return quietly to his home.

NOTES.

1. According to the, *d'après un*; by boasting (*see* Invar. Words, Rule XII.); before he could (*see* Verb, Rule XXXVIII).

2. He said (*see* Synopsis, Rule XVIII.); every, *de chaque* (*i.e., some* of each): but (*see* Invar. Words, Rule X. 2); so saying, *à ces mots*.

3. An animal (*see* Synopsis, Rule VIII.); he had seen (*see* Verb, Rule XV.); boasting, *superbe*.

4. He (relating to the *femin.* noun *majesté*), *elle*.

6. At once (*see* Invar. Words. Rule I.); his, put "the."

7. What conduct...., put " what is this conduct"; you scoundrel, (*see* Pron., Rule VII.); did I not command (*see* Verb, Rule XIII.); to get, (*see* Verb, Rule LXXVIII.); here, *voilà que*; one, (*see* Pron., Rule XXXIII.).

8. His (*see* Synopsis, Rule VII.).

V.—BUFFON'S SON.

1. Buffon's son was not nine-and-twenty when he perished on the revolutionary scaffold. 2. Having fallen into the water, **while yet a boy** of twelve years of age, **he was upbraided** with **fear**. 3. "So little afraid **was I**," replied he, " that **were I to be given** to hope I should live, like grand-papa, a hundred years, I would consent to die on the instant, if I could add one year to my father's life. No, not on the instant," said he, checking himself, " I would ask a quarter of an hour **to** enjoy the pleasure of **what I had** done."

NOTES.

2. While yet a boy, *n'étant encore qu'un enfant de;* he was upbraided with fear, put "he was upbraided with *having been afraid.*"

3. Was I (put it first); were I to be given (*see* Verb, Rule LIV., and Ellipsis, Rule I.); to (*see* Invar. Words, Rule XXXI.); what (*see* Pron., Rule XXIV.); I had done (*see* Verb, Rule XXI.)

VI.—THE BEAR.

1. The bear has no tail, and its paws are not made like the paws of a dog or cat; they bend up **as** it puts **its** foot down **to** walk, so that its feet look flat. 2. I have seen more **than** one kind of bear; some can be made tame, like **the one** I **told** you **of**, but some are hard **to** tame. 3. Some eat meat, some **do not**. All **of them** have long hair. 4. One kind has its home in the cold snow and on the ice; this bear is white; it eats fish and **will lie** in wait for a long time at a hole in the ice **for a seal to come up for air, when** he will kill the seal and eat it. 5. **Men** hunt this kind of bear for the sake of its skin, **as** the fur is long and warm; it is fond of its cubs. 6. In a bear hunt, if the dogs fly at the bear, it will take them up in its arms, and hug them **so** close **as** to kill them. 7. **It is** hard for a man to run from a bear, as **it** can get up a tree.

NOTES.

1. As, *i.e. when;* its foot (*see* Art., Rule III.); to (*see* Invar. Words, Rule XXXI.)
2. Than (*see* Invar. Words, Rule XXVI.); the one (*see* Pron. Rule XXVI.); I told you of ("to tell of," *parler de; see* Verb, Rule XIII., and Synopsis, Rule XIX.)
3. Do not (*see* Verb, Rule LXXV.); of them (leave it out).
4. Will lie (*see* Verb, Rule XIX.); for a seal to come up (*see* Verb, Rule XL.); for air, put "to breathe;" when (*see* Invar. Words, Rule XXXVII.)
5. Men (*see* Pron., Rule VIII.); as (*see* Invar. Words, Rule IV.)
6. So…as (*see* Invar. Words, Rule IX.)
7. It is (*see* Pron., Rule IV.); it, "il," would be ambiguous, so see what you must put here.

VII.—THE TWO RIVULETS.

1. The moral of the following fable will **easily** discover itself without **my explaining** it. 2. One rivulet meeting **another**, with whom it had been long united

in strictest amity, **with noisy haughtiness and disdain thus bespoke him:** 3. "**What! brother,** still in the same state! Still low and creeping! 4. Are you not ashamed when you behold **me, who,** though lately in a like condition with you, am now become a great river, and shall shortly be able to rival the Danube or the Rhine provided those friendly rains continue **which** have favoured my banks, but neglected yours?" 5. "Very fine," replied the humble rivulet, "you are now, indeed, swollen to a great extent; but, methinks you are become withal somewhat turbulent and muddy. **I** am contented **with** my low condition and my purity.— (D. Hume.)

NOTES.

1. Easily (*see* Invar. Words, Rule I.); without my explaining it (*see* Verb, Rule XLII.)
2. Another (*see* Pron., Rule XXXIII.); in, put "by a;" with noisy...etc., put "addressed him, in a loud (*bruyante*) voice, these haughty and disdainful words."
3. What (*see* Pron., Rule XXV., Rem.); brother, put "*my* brother."
4. Me, who, put "*me..., moi que,*" as the personal pronoun must be repeated both for the sake of emphasis and because "who" must come next to its antecedent; which (*see* Pron., Rule X.)
5. I (*see* Synopsis, Rule XVII. 5); contented with (*see* Invar. Words, Rule II.)

VIII.—THE COMPARISON OF WATCHES.

1. When Griselda thought that her husband **had** long enough **enjoyed** his new existence, and that there was danger **of his forgetting** the taste of sorrow, she **changed her** tone. 2. One day, **when** he had not returned home exactly at the appointed minute, she received him with a frown, **such as** would have made Mars himself recoil, if Mars **could have** beheld **such a** frown from the brow of his Venus. 3. "Dinner **has been kept waiting** for you this hour, my dear!"

" I am very sorry for it; but why **did you wait**, my dear? 4. I am really very **sorry I am** so late, but (looking at his watch) **it is** only half-past six **by me.**" " It is seven by **me.**" 5. They presented their watches to each other, **he** in an apologetical, she in a reproachful attitude. 6. " I rather think you are too fast, my dear," said the gentleman. " I am very sorry **you are** too slow, my dear," said the lady. 7. " My watch never loses a minute in the four-and-twenty hours," said he. " Nor mine a second," said she. 8. " I have **reason** to believe I am right, my love," said her husband, mildly. " Reason!" exclaimed the wife, astonished, " what reason can you **possibly** have to believe that you are right, when I tell you I am morally certain you are wrong, my love?" 9. " My only reason **for doubting** it is, that I **set** my watch **by** the sun to-day." "The sun must be wrong, then," cried the lady hastily.— (Miss Edgeworth.)

NOTES.

1. Had enjoyed (*see* Verb, Rule XVIII.); of his forgetting (*see* Verb, Rule XLII.); she changed her, *elle changea* **de.**
2. One day when (*see* Invar. Words, Rule XXXV.); such as, put "which"; could have (*see* Verb, Rule LXXIV.); such a (*see* Art., Rule XV.)
3. Has been kept waiting, put "has been waiting," and *see* Verb, Rule XVII.; why did you wait (*see* Verb, Rule XIII.)
4. I am very sorry I am (*see* Verb, Rule XXXVIII.); it is by me, put "I have."
6. I am very sorry you are (*see* Verb, Rule XXXII.)
8. Reason, put "some motives;" possibly, *bien.*
9. For doubting (*see* Invar. Words, Rule XVII.); I set (*see* Verb, Rule XIII.); by, *sur.*

IX.—LITTLE EPPIE'S MISCHIEF.

I.—1. Silas had chosen a broad slip of linen **as a means of** fastening **little Eppie** to his loom when he was busy; it made a broad belt round her waist, and was long enough to **allow of her reaching** the truckle-bed and sitting down **on it**, but not long enough **for her to attempt** any dangerous climbing. 2. One bright summer's morning the weaver had seated himself in his loom, and the noise of the weaving has began, but he had left his scissors on a ledge which Eppie's arm was long enough to reach; and now, like a small mouse watching her opportunity, she stole quietly from her corner, secured the scissors, and toddled to the bed again. 3. Having cut the linen strip in a jagged, but effectual manner, in two moments she ran out at the open door where the sunshine was inviting her, **while** poor Silas **believed her to be a better child** than usual. 4. **It was not until** he **happened to need** his scissors that the terrible fact burst upon him: Eppie had run out by herself, had, perhaps, fallen into the stone-pit.

NOTES.

1. As a means of, put "in order to;" little Eppie (*see* Art., Rule I.); allow of her reaching (*see* Verb, Rule XLII.); on it, *dessus*; for her to attempt (*see* Verb, Rule XL.)
3. While (*see* Invar. Words, Rule XXXIX.); believed (*see* Verb, Rule IX.); her to be (*see* Verb, Rule XXXIX.) ; a better child, *plus sage*.
5. It was not until (*see* Invar. Words, Rule XXIX.); he happened to need, put " he needed."

X.

II.—1. Silas, shaken by fear, rushed out, calling "Eppie!" and ran eagerly about the unenclosed space, exploring the dry cavities into which she **might have** fallen, and then **gazing with questioning dread** at the smooth surface of the water. 2. The cold drops stood on his brow. How long **had she been out?** 3. **There was one hope**, that she had crept through the stile and **got** into the fields, where he habitually **took** her to stroll. 4. But the grass was high in the meadow, and **there was no descrying** her, **if** she **were** there, except by a close search **that would be a trespass** on Mr. Osgood's crop. 5. Still, the misdemeanour **must** be committed, and poor Silas, after **peering** all round the hedgerows, traversed the grass, **beginning with perturbed vision** to see Eppie behind every group of red sorrel, and to see her **moving** always farther off **as** he **approached**. 6. The meadow was searched in vain, and he got over the stile into the next field, looking, with dying hope, towards a small pond, **which was now reduced to summer shallowness**, so as to leave a wide margin of good adhesive mud. 7. Here, however, sat Eppie, discoursing cheerfully to her **own** small boot, which she was using as a bucket **to** convey the water into a deep hoof-mark, **while** her naked foot was planted comfortably on a cushion of olive-green mud.—(G. Eliot.)

NOTES.

1. Might have fallen (*see* Verb, Rule LXXIV.); gazing with questioning dread, put "questioning with (*de*) a dismayed look."

2. Had she been out (*see* Verb, Rule XVIII.).

3. There was, put "there only remained" (*imperf.*); got (*see* Verb, Rule LXXVIII.); took (to take somebody), **mener** *quelqu'un*.

4. There was no descrying her (*see* Verb, Rule XLII., Rem.); if she were (*see* Verb, Rule XXV.); search that would be a trespass on..., put " search through (*dans*) Mr. Osgood's crop, which would make him a trespasser " (to make a trespasser, *mettre en contravention*), and *see* Pron., Rule XIV.

5. Must (*see* Verb, Rule LXIX.); after peering (*see* Verb, Rule XLVII.); beginning with perturbed vision, *croyant d'abord, dans son trouble;* see her moving (*see* Verb, Rule XLIII.); as (*see* Invar. Words, Rule VI.); he approached (*see* Verb, Rule IX.).

6. Which was now, etc., put "whose depth summer had now reduced," and *see* Pron., Rule XVIII., and Invar. Words, Rule XXI.

7. Own (to be left out); to (*see* Invar. Words, Rule XXXI.); while (*see* Invar. Words, Rule XXXIX.).

XI.—FROM THE "LETTER TO THE EARL OF CHESTERFIELD."

1. ...Seven years, my lord, have now passed **since** I waited in your outward rooms, or was repulsed from your door, **during which time** I have been pushing on my work through difficulties, of which **it is** useless to complain, and have brought it at last to the verge of publication, without **one** act of assistance, one word of encouragement, or one smile of favour. 2. **Such treatment** I did not expect, for I never **had** a patron before. 3. The shepherd of Virgil grew at last acquainted with love, and **found him a native** of the rocks.

4. Is not a patron, my lord, **one** who looks with unconcern on a man **struggling for life** in the water, and, when **he** has reached ground, encumbers him with help? 5. The notice which you have been pleased to take of my labours, **had it** been early, **had been** kind; but it has been delayed **till** I am indifferent, and cannot **enjoy it**; till I am solitary, and cannot impart it; till I am known, and do not want it. 6. I hope it is **no** very cynical asperity not to confess obligations where no benefit **has been received**, or to be unwilling that the public **should consider** me as owing **that** to a patron, **which** Providence has enabled me to do for myself.—(S. Johnson.)

NOTES.

1. Since (*see* Invar. Words, Rule XXII.); during which time (*see* Pron., Rule XV.); it is (*see* Pron., Rule IV.); one (*see* Pron., Rule XXXIV.).
2. Such treatment (*see* Art., Rule XV.); I never had (*see* Verb, Rule XIII.).
3. Found him a native of, put "found him amongst."
4. One (*see* Pron., Rule XXXIV.); struggling (*see* Verb, Rule XLIII.); for life, put "to save his life;" he (avoid ambiguity).

5. Had it been (*see* Ellipsis, Rule I.) ; had been (*see* Verb, Rule XXI.) ; till I am (*see* Verb, Rule XXXIII.) ; enjoy it (*see* Invar. Words, Rule II.).

6. Has been received, put " when I have received ;" should consider (*see* Verb, Rules XXXI. and XXVIII.) ; that...which (*see* Pron., Rule X.).

XII.—INTERVIEW WITH A MALAY.

1. ...As I had no Malay dictionary, I **addressed him in some** lines from the Iliad, considering that, of **such** languages **as** I possessed, **Greek,** in point of longitude, came geographically nearest to an Oriental **one.** 2. He worshipped me in a most devout manner, and replied in **what** I supposed **was** Malay... 3. On his departure I presented him **with** a piece of opium. 4. To him, **as an** Orientalist, I concluded that opium **must** be familiar; and the expression of his face convinced me that **it was.** 5. Nevertheless, I was struck with **some little** consternation when I saw him suddenly raise **his** hand to **his** mouth, and (**in the schoolboy phrase**) bolt the whole, divided into three pieces, at one mouthful. 6. The quantity was **enough** to kill three dragoons and their horses, and I felt some alarm for the poor creature ; but **what** could **be done** ? 7. I had given him the opium in compassion for his solitary life, on recollection that, if he had travelled on foot from London, **it must be** nearly three weeks **since** he **could have** exchanged a thought with any human being. 8. I could not violate the laws of hospitality **by having** him **surged** and drenched with **an** emetic, and thus frightening him **into a notion** that we were going to sacrifice him to some English idol. 9. No, there was clearly no help for it ; he took his leave, and **for** some days I felt anxious, but as I never **heard** of **any Malay being found dead,** I became convinced that he was used to opium, and that I **must**

have done him the service I designed, by giving him one night of respite **from** the pains of **wandering**.— (Th. de Quincey.)

NOTES.

1. I addressed him in some, put " I addressed him a few;" such ...as (*see* Pron., Rule XXXVI.) ; Greek (*see* Invar. Words, Rule XL., Note 4) ; one, put " language."
2. What (*see* Pron., Rule XXIV.) ; was, put " to be."
3. With (*see* Invar. Words, Rule II.).
4. As an (*see* Art., Rule XIV.) ; it was (*see* Verb, Rule LXXV., and Pron., Rule XXXIII.).
5. Some little, put " I was *a little* struck with consternation ;" his (*see* Pron., Rule III.) ; in the schoolboy phrase, put " according to the expression of schoolboys."
6. Enough, put " sufficient ;" what (*see* Pron., Rule XXIV.) ; could be done (*see* Verb, Rule IV.).
7. It must be, put " there must be," and *see* Verb, Rule LXVIII. ; since (*see* Invar. Words, Rule XXIII.) ; he could have (*see* Verb, Rule LXXIV.).
8. By having him surged (*see* Invar. Words, Rule XII., and Verb, Rule L.) ; an, put " some ;" into the notion, *au point de lui faire croire.*
9. For (*i.e.* during) ; I heard (*see* Verb, Rule XIII.) ; of any Malay, etc. (*see* Verb, Rule XLII.) ; I must have done (*see* Verb, Rule LXXI.) ; from, *contre ;* of wandering, *de la vie errante.*

XIII.—THE SHEPHERD'S DOG.

1. A farmer had a shepherd's dog named Gashkan, who often had dinner with *the men at* the farm. 2. When *it was* nearly *time* to call the servants, a large pot of broth was set on the hearth, and a long wooden slab was let down from the wall ; and then the dairymaid gave a loud call from the door, **which was answered by** the men in the fields. 3. But the men could pretty well tell by the shadows *on* the mountains when the time was near, and when they grew hŭngry

they **would send** Gashkan to see if dinner **were** ready.   4. The dog would push off at once, and if he saw the pot on the hearth, and the slab let down, he would run quickly back, licking **his** lips and wagging his tail; but if he saw no broth on the hearth, he returned very slowly, *with* his tail and ears drooping, and when they asked him about dinner, he would slink sadly behind his master.

NOTES.

1. The men at, put "the labourers of."
2. It was time, **il était l'heure**.
3. On, put "of."
4. With (to be left out).

XIV.—INGRATITUDE.

Blow, blow! **thou** winter wind,
Thou art not so unkind
As man's ingratitude;
Thy tooth is not so keen,
Because thou art not seen,
Although thy breath be rude.

Freeze, freeze! thou bitter sky,
Thou dost not bite so nigh
As benefits forgot:
Though thou the waters warp,
Thy sting is not so sharp
As friend remembered not.

(Shakespeare.)

XV.—FIGHTING AT SCHOOL.

1. Boys **will quarrel**, and when they quarrel will sometimes fight. 2. **Fighting** with fists is the natural and English way for English boys to settle their quarrels. 3. What substitute for it is there, or ever **was there**, among any nation under the sun ? What would you like to see take its place ? 4. Learn to box, *then*, as you learn to play cricket and football. 5. Not one of you will be the worse, but very much the better for **learning** to box **well**. 6. **Should you** never **have** to use it in earnest, there is no exercise in the world so good for the temper, and for the muscles of the back and legs. 7. As to fighting, keep out of it if you can, by all means. 8. When the time comes, if it ever **should, that** you have to say *Yes* or *No* to a challenge to fight, say *No* if you can, only **take care you make** it clear to yourselves why you say *No*. 9. It is a proof of the highest courage, **if done** *from* true Christian motives. 10. It is quite right and justifiable, if done from a simple aversion **to** physical pain and danger. 11. But don't say *No* because you fear a licking, and say or think it's because you fear God, for that's neither Christian nor honest. 12. And if you **do fight**, fight it out; and don't give in **while** you can stand and see.—(*Tom Brown's School-days.*)

NOTES.

4. Then (to be put next to " learn ").
9. From, put " for."

XVI.—FRANCE.

To kinder skies, where gentler manners reign,
I turn ; and France displays her bright domain.
Gay, sprightly land of mirth and social ease, •
Pleased with thyself, whom all the world can **please,**

How often have I led thy sportive choir,
With tuneless pipe, beside the murmuring **Loire!**
Where shading elms along the margin **grew**,
And freshen'd *from* the wave the zephyr flew;
And haply, though my harsh touch, faltering still,
But mock'd all tune, and marr'd the dancer's skill,
Yet **would** the village **praise** my wondrous power,
And dance, forgetful of the noontide hour.
Alike all ages. Dames of ancient days
Have led their children through the mirthful maze;
And the gay grandsire, skill'd in gestic lore,
Has frisk'd beneath the burden of threescore.

So blest a life these thoughtless realms display,
Thus idly busy rolls their world away;
Theirs are those arts that mind to mind endear,
For honour forms the social temper here;
Honour, that praise which real merit gains,
Or e'en imaginary worth obtains,
Here passes current; paid from hand to hand,
It shifts in splendid traffic through the land:
From courts, to camps, to cottages it strays,
And all **are taught** *an avarice of* praise;
They please, are pleased, they give **to get** esteem,
Till, seeming blest, they grow to what they seem.
(Goldsmith.)

NOTES.

From, put "by;" but, *ne faisait que* (with the *infin.*); **an** avarice of, put "to be sparing of."

XVII.—WILLIAM PITT THE YOUNGER (1759–1806):

From his Speech on the Abolition of the Slave Trade,
April 2, 1792.

1. We are living under a system of government which our own experience leads us to pronounce the best and wisest 'which *has* ever yet been framed; a system which

has become the admiration of the world. 2. From all these blessings we **must** for ever **have been** shut out, **had there been** any truth in those principles which some gentlemen have not hesitated to lay down as applicable to the case of Africa. 3. Had those principles been true, **we ourselves had** languished **to** this hour in that miserable state of ignorance, brutality, and degradation in which history proves **our ancestors to have been immersed.** 4. Had other nations adopted those principles in their conduct towards us; had other nations applied to Great Britain the reasoning which some senators of this very island **now** apply to Africa,—ages **might have passed** without **our emerging** from barbarism; 5. and we, who are enjoying the blessings of British civilisation, of British laws, and British liberty, might at this hour have been little superior, *either* in morals, in knowledge, or refinement, to the rude inhabitants of the coast of Guinea.

NOTE.

5. Either...or, *soit...soit.*

XVIII.—NICHOLAS NICKLEBY AND SMIKE.

1. The poor soul was poring hard over a tattered book, with *the* traces of recent tears still upon his face, **vainly** endeavouring to master some task which a child of nine years old, possessed of ordinary powers, **could have** conquered with ease, but which, to the addled brain of the crushed boy of nineteen, was a sealed and hopeless mystery...Nicholas laid **his** hand on **his** shoulder.

2. "I can't do it," said the dejected creature, **looking up** with **bitter disappointment** in every feature.

"Do not try," replied Nicholas.

3. The boy shook his head, and closing the book with a sigh, looked vacantly round, and laid his head upon his arm. He was weeping.

4. "**Do not**, for God's sake," said Nicholas, *in an* agitated voice; "I cannot bear to **see you**."

5. "They are more hard with me than ever," sobbed the boy.

"I know it," rejoined Nicholas. "**They are**."

6. "But for you," said the outcast, "I should die. They **would** kill me, they **would**; I know they would."

7. "*You will do better*, poor fellow," replied Nicholas, shaking his head mournfully, "**when I am** gone."

8. "Gone!" cried the other, looking intently in his face.

9. "Softly," rejoined Nicholas. "Yes."

"Are you going?" demanded the boy, *in an earnest whisper*.

10. "I cannot say," replied Nicholas, "I was speaking more to my own thoughts, than to you."

11. "Tell me," said the boy, imploringly, "Oh, **do tell** me? **will** you go—will you?"

12. "I shall be driven to that at last!" said Nicholas. "The world is before me after all..."

13. "Should I ever meet you there?" demanded the boy, speaking with **unusual volubility**.

"Yes," replied Nicholas, willing to soothe him.

14. "No, no!" said the other, clasping him by the hand, "**should I**—should I—tell me that again. Say I should be sure to find you."

15. " You **would**," replied Nicholas, with the same humane intention, " and I would help and aid you, and not bring fresh sorrow on you as I have **done** here."— (Charles Dickens.)

NOTES.

1. The, put " some."
4. In a voice, the French say " *of* a voice."
7. You will do better, put " all will go better."
9. In an earnest whisper, *à voix basse et d'un ton suppliant.*

XIX.—HAMLET'S SOLILOQUY ON LIFE AND DEATH.

To be, or not to be, that is the question:
Whether 'tis nobler *in the mind,* to suffer
The stings and arrows of outrageous fortune,
Or to take arms against a sea of troubles,
And **by** opposing end them?—To die,—to sleep—
No more; and, by **a** sleep, to say we end
The heart-ache, and the thousand natural *shocks*
That flesh is heir to,—'tis a consummation
Devoutly **to be wished.** To die—to sleep;—
To sleep! perchance to dream: ay, there's the rub;
For in that sleep of death what dreams **may come**,
When we have shuffled off this mortal coil,
Must give us pause.—There's the respect
That makes *calamity of so long life:*
For who **would** bear the whips and scorns of time,
Th' oppressor's wrong, the proud man's contumely,
The pangs of despised love, the law's delay,
The insolence of office, and the spurns
That patient merit of th' unworthy takes,
When **he himself might** his quietus make
With a bare bodkin? Who would fardels bear,

To groan and sweat *under a weary life,*
But that the dread of something after death,
The undiscover'd country, **from whose bourn**
No traveller returns, puzzles the will,
And makes us rather bear **those** ills we have,
Than fly *to* others that we know not **of ?**...
(Shakespeare.)

NOTES.

Whether 'tis, put " is it ;" in the mind, put "for the soul ;" must, put " this is what must ;" makes calamity of so long life, put " makes calamity last so long ; " under a weary life, put " under the weight of a weary life ; " to, put " towards."

XX.—FROM "THE SCHOOL FOR SCANDAL."

The Old Husband and the Young Wife.

I.—*Sir Peter:* Well, then, let our future contest be, who shall be **most** obliging.

Lady Teazle: I assure you, Sir Peter, good nature becomes you. You look now as **you did** before we were married, when you used to walk with me under the elms, and tell me stories of **what** a gallant you were in your youth, and chuck me under the chin, and ask me if I thought I **could** love an old fellow, who would deny me nothing, didn't you?

Sir Peter: Yes, yes, and you were so kind and attentive—

Lady Teazle: Ah, **so I was**, and **would** always **take** your part when my acquaintance used to abuse you, and turn you into ridicule.

Sir Peter: Indeed!

Lady Teazle: Ay, and when my cousin Sophy has called you a stiff, peevish old bachelor, and laughed at me **for thinking** of marrying **one** who might be my father, I have always defended you, and said, I didn't think you so ugly by all means.

Sir Peter: Thank you.

Lady Teazle: And I **dared** say you'd make *a very good sort of a* husband.

Sir Peter: And you prophesied right; and we shall now be the happiest couple...

Lady Teazle: And never differ again ?

Sir Peter: No, never.

NOTE.

A very good sort of a, *une très bonne pâte* **de.**

XXI.

II.—*Sir Peter*: Indeed, my dear Lady Teazle, you must watch your temper very seriously; for in all our little quarrels, my dear, if you recollect, my love, you always **began** first.

Lady Teazle: I beg your pardon, my dear Sir Peter; indeed, you **always gave** the provocation.

Sir Peter: Now, see, my angel—take care—**contradicting** is not the way to keep friends.

Lady Teazle: Then don't you begin it, my love.

Sir Peter: There, now, you—you are going on. You don't perceive, my love, that you are just doing the very thing which **you know always** makes me angry.

Lady Teazle: Nay, you know, if you **will** be angry without any reason, my dear...

Sir Peter: There! now you want to quarrel again.

Lady Teazle: No, I'm sure **I don't**: but if you will be so peevish...

Sir Peter: There, now! who begins first?

Lady Teazle: Why, you, to be sure. I said nothing; but **there's no bearing** your temper.

Sir Peter: No, no, madam; the fault's in your own temper.

Lady Teazle: Ay, you are just what my cousin Sophy said you would be.

Sir Peter: Your cousin Sophy is a forward, impertinent gipsy.

Lady Teazle: You are a great bear, I'm sure, to abuse my relatives.

Sir Peter: Now may all the plagues of marriage be doubled on me if ever I try to be friends with you any more!

Lady Teazle: So much the better.

XXII.—THE BOY AND THE CAKE.

1. My **good old** aunt, who never **parted** from me **at** the end of a holiday without **stuffing** a sweetmeat, or some nice thing, into my pocket, **had dismissed** me one evening with a smoking plumcake, **fresh** from the oven. 2. On my way to school a **grey-headed old** beggar saluted me. 3. I had no pence **to** console him **with**, and, in the vanity of self-denial, I made him

a present of the whole cake. 4. I walked on a little, buoyed up, as one is on such occasions, with a sweet soothing of self-satisfaction; but **before I had got** to the end of London Bridge, my better feelings returned, and I burst into tears, thinking **how ungrateful I had been** to my good aunt, to **go and give** her good gift away to a stranger, that I had never seen before, and who **might** be a bad man for aught I knew. 5. And then I thought of the pleasure my aunt would be taking in thinking that I—**I myself**, and *not* another —would eat her nice cake—and **what** should I say to her the next time I **saw** her. How naughty I **was** to part with her pretty present. 6. And the odour of that spicy cake came back upon my recollection, and the pleasure and the curiosity I had taken **in** seeing her make it, and her joy when she sent it to the oven, and how disappointed she would feel that I had never had a bit of it in my mouth at last—and I blamed my impertinent spirit of almsgiving, and, above all, I wished never to see the face again of that insidious, good-for-nothing, old grey-headed impostor.—(Charles Lamb.)

NOTE.

5. Not (when *no* verb follows), *non pas.*

XXIII.—THE IMPOSTOR AND THE MANDARIN.

An Emperor of China had devoted himself to the study of alchemy. An impostor brought him an elixir, declaring that if he would drink it, he would become immortal. A Mandarin, who was present, having in vain tried to undeceive him, took the cup and drank the liquor. The Emperor, enraged at his presumption, condemned him to death. "Sire," answered the Mandarin, "if this liquor can bestow immortality, you cannot put me to death; if not, what harm have I done?" This speech appeased the Emperor, who admired and praised the wisdom of his minister.

XXIV.—FRENCH, ENGLISH, AND GERMAN.

A Frenchman, an Englishman, and a German were commissioned, it is said, to give the world the benefit of their views on that interesting animal, the Camel. Away goes the Frenchman to the *Jardin des Plantes*, spends an hour there in rapid investigation, returns, and writes a *feuilleton*, in which there is no phrase the Academy can blame, but also no phrase which adds to the general knowledge. He is perfectly satisfied, however, and says: "*Le voilà, le chameau!*"—The Englishman packs up his tea-caddy and a magazine of comforts; pitches his tent in the East; remains there two years studying the Camel in its habits; and returns with a thick volume of facts, arranged without order, expounded without philosophy, but serving as valuable materials for all who come after him.—The German, despising the frivolity of the Frenchman, and the unphilosophic matter-of-factness of the Englishman, retires to his study, there *to construct the Idea of a Camel from out of the depths of his Moral Consciousness.* And he is still at it.—(G. H. Lewes, *Life and Works of Goethe*).

XXV.—THE LOVE OF OUR COUNTRY.

Whence does this love of our country, this universal passion proceed? Why does the eye ever dwell with fondness upon the scenes of infant life? Why do we breathe with greater joy the breath of our youth? Why are not other soils as grateful, and other heavens as gay? Why does the soul of man ever cling to that earth where it first knew pleasure and pain, and under the rough discipline of the passions was roused to the dignity of moral life? Is it only that our country contains our kindred and our friends? And is it nothing but a name for our social affections? It cannot be this; the most friendless of human beings has a country which he admires and extols, and which he would, in the same circumstances, prefer to all others under heaven. Tempt him with the fairest face of nature, place him by living waters under the shadowy trees of Lebanon, open to his view all the gorgeous allurements of the climates of the sun,—he will love the rocks and deserts of his childhood better than all these, and thou canst not bribe his soul to forget the land of his nativity; he will sit down and weep by the waters of Babylon when he remembers thee, o Sion!—(Sydney Smith).

XXVI.—THE DEAD WARRIOR.

Home they brought her warrior dead:
    She nor swooned nor uttered cry.
All her maidens, watching, said:
    "She must weep or she will die."

Then they praised him, soft and low,
    Called him worthy to be loved,
Truest friend and noblest foe;
    Yet she neither spoke nor moved.

Stole a maiden from her place,
    Lightly to the warrior stept,
Took the face-cloth from the face;
    Yet she neither moved nor wept.

Rose a nurse of ninety years,
Set his child upon her knee;
Like summer-tempest came her tears.
" Sweet my child, I live for thee!"
(Tennyson).

XXVII. THE PEDLAR AND THE MONKEYS.

An Indian pedlar was passing through a great forest. About noon, the heat became so intense that the poor man resolved to rest. He lay down under a tree whose great branches completely protected him from the sun, opened the box he had been carrying on his back, took from it a cotton cap, which he put on his head, and fell asleep. On awaking, he was surprised to see his box had been emptied, and that all the cotton caps it contained had disappeared. "Bless me!" he cried out, raising his eyes. And lo! he saw the branches of the tree filled with monkeys, each of whom had one of his caps on his head. It was a funny sight; but the pedlar scarcely felt inclined to laugh. At last an idea struck him. He got up, took off his cap, turned it round three times in the air, and carefully replaced it in the box. He then went and lay down behind the bushes, and, stretched on the ground, awaited the end. The monkeys immediately came down from the tree; and one after another put his cap back into the box, after turning it round three times, exactly as he had seen the man do.

XXVIII.—A CLEVER TERRIER.

Terriers are a clever race of dogs, and there are a great many kinds of them. They are good watch-dogs, and can be taught all manner of tricks. In short, they are bright, active, clever fellows. I was told a very funny story of a terrier by his master. This gentleman made a great pet of his dog, and made him welcome in any room of his house, except his business room. There Pepper (that was the name of the dog) was never allowed to enter, however he might whine and scratch. One day Pepper's master was writing in this room, when three taps came at the door. " Come in !" he cried. No one came in, but " tap, tap, tap," sounded again. " Come in !" he cried, louder. The door did not open, but there was " tap, tap, tap," a third time. Out of patience, the gentleman flung the door open, and in walked Mr. Pepper. He had observed that people who got in there did not whine and scratch, but gave three taps ; so he did the same with his tail.

XXIX.—DEATH OF CHARLES II.

Towards the close of the year 1684 he was prevented, by a slight attack of what was supposed to be the gout, from rambling as usual... It was not supposed, however, that his constitution was seriously impaired. On the evening of Sunday, the first of February, 1685, the king had complained that he did not feel quite well. He had no appetite for his supper : his rest that night was broken ; but on the following morning he rose, as usual, early. Scarcely had he risen from his bed when his attendants perceived that his utterance was indistinct, and that his thoughts seemed to be wandering. Several men of rank had, as usual, assembled to see their sovereign shaved and dressed. He made an effort to converse with them in his usual gay style ; but his ghastly look surprised and alarmed them. . Soon his face grew black; his eyes turned in his head ; he uttered a cry, staggered, and fell into the hands of Thomas, Lord Bruce, son of the Earl of Ailesbury. A physician who had charge of the royal retorts and crucibles happened to be present. He had no lancet, but he opened a vein with a penknife. The blood flowed freely, but the king remaining still insensible, he was borne to his bed.—(Macaulay.)

XXX.—HOME FOR THE HOLIDAYS.

Home for the holidays, here we go;
Bless me! the train is exceedingly slow!
Pray, Mr. Engineer, get up your steam,
And let us be off, with a puff and a scream!
We have two long hours to travel, you say;
Come, Mr. Engineer, gallop away!
Two hours more! why, the sun will be down
Before we reach dear old London town!
And then what a number of fathers, and mothers,
And uncles, and aunts, and sisters, and brothers,
Will be there to meet us—oh! do make haste,
For I'm sure, Mr. Guard, we have no time to waste!
Thank goodness, we shan't have to study and stammer
Over Latin, and sums, and that nasty French grammar;
Lectures, and classes, and lessons are done,
And now we'll have nothing but frolic and fun.
Home for the holidays, here we go!
But this Fast Train is really exceedingly slow.

We shall have sport when Christmas comes,
When " snap-dragon " burns our fingers and thumbs:
We'll hang mistletoe over our dear little cousins,
And pull them beneath it and kiss them by dozens:
We shall have games at " blind-man's buff,"
And noise and laughter, and romping enough:
We'll crown the plum-pudding with bunches of bay,
And roast all the chestnuts that come in our way;
And when Twelfth Night falls, we'll have such a cake,
That as we stand round it the table shall quake.

We'll draw " King and Queen " and be happy together,
And dance old " Sir Roger " with hearts like a feather.
Home for the holidays, here we go !
But this Fast Train is really exceedingly slow.

(Eliza Cook.)

XXXI.—DRYDEN AND POPE.

In acquired knowledge, the superiority must be allowed to Dryden, whose education was more scholastic, and who, before he became an author, had been allowed more time for study, with better means of information. His mind has a larger range, and he collects his images and illustrations from a more extensive circumference of science. Dryden knew more of man in his general nature, and Pope in his local manners. The notions of Dryden were formed by comprehensive speculation, and those of Pope by minute attention. There is more dignity in the knowledge of Dryden, and more certainty in that of Pope.

Poetry was not the sole praise of either, for both excelled likewise in prose ; but Pope did not borrow his prose from his predecessor. The style of Dryden is capricious and varied; that of Pope is cautious and uniform. Dryden observes the motions of his own mind ; Pope constrains his mind to his own rules of composition. Dryden is sometimes vehement and rapid ; Pope is always smooth, uniform, and gentle. Dryden's page is a natural field rising into inequalities, and diversified by the varied exuberance of abundant vegetation ; Pope's is a velvet lawn, shaven by the scythe and levelled by the roller.—(S. Johnson : *Lives of the Poets.*)

XXXII.—FROM "ALEXANDER'S FEAST."

. . . .
Now strike the golden lyre again :
A louder yet, and yet a louder strain.
Break his bands of sleep asunder,
And rouse him, like a rattling peal of thunder.
    Hark, hark ! the horrid sound
        Has rais'd up his head !
        As awak'd from the dead,
    And amaz'd, he stares around.
Revenge ! revenge ! Timotheus cries ;
        See the Furies arise :
        See the snakes that they rear,
        How they hiss in their hair,
And the sparkles that flash from their eyes.
    Behold a ghastly band,
    Each a torch in his hand !
Those are Grecian ghosts, that in battle were slain,
        And unburied remain
        Inglorious on the plain :
        Give the vengeance due
        To the valiant crew !
Behold how they toss their torches on high,
    How they point to the Persian abodes,
And glittering temples of their hostile gods !
The princes applaud, with a furious joy ;
And the king seiz'd a flambeau with zeal to destroy ;
        Thais led the way,
        To light him to his prey,
And, like another Helen, fir'd another Troy.
. . . .
                          (Dryden.)

XXXIII.—THE BATTLE OF IVRY.

Hurrah! the foes are moving. Hark to the mingled din
Of fife, and steed, and trump, and drum, and roaring
culverin.
The fiery duke is pricking fast across Saint André's
plain,
With all the hireling chivalry of Guelders and Almayne.
Now by the lips of those ye love, fair gentlemen of
France,
Charge for the golden lilies!—upon them with the
lance!
A thousand spurs are striking deep, a thousand spears
in rest,
A thousand knights are pressing close behind the snow-
white crest;
And in they burst, and on they rushed, while, like a
guiding star,
Amidst the thickest carnage blazed the helmet of
Navarre.

Now, God be praised, the day is ours. Mayenne hath
turned his rein.
D'Aumale hath cried for quarter. The Flemish count
is slain.
Their ranks are breaking like thin clouds before a Biscay
gale;
The field is heaped with bleeding steeds, and flags, and
cloven mail.
And then we thought on vengeance, and, all along our
van,
"Remember Saint Bartholomew!" was passed from
man to man.
But out spake gentle Henry, "No Frenchman is my foe:
"Down, down, with every foreigner, but let your
"brethren go!"
Oh! was there ever such a knight, in friendship or
in war,
As our sovereign lord, King Henry, the soldier of
Navarre? (Macaulay.)

XXXIV.—MADAME DE SÉVIGNÉ TO Mʳ DE POMPONE.

I have a pretty little story to tell; it is very true and will amuse you. The king has lately become quite a poet, and frequently makes verses. The other day he composed a little madrigal, with which, however, he was not very well satisfied. The next time he saw Marshal de Gramont, he said to him: "Marshal, read this madrigal, and tell me if you ever saw anything so stupid. Since it is known that I am an amateur of poetry, I am continually annoyed by such productions." The marshal, after reading it, said to the king: "Your Majesty judges correctly of everything; it is, indeed, the most ridiculous madrigal that I ever read." The king laughed heartily, and said: "Is not the composer a great ass?" "Sire," replied the marshal, "it is impossible to call him anything else." "Well," said the king, "I am delighted to hear you speak so frankly; I am the composer." "Good God! Sire, permit me to read it again, I perused it hastily." "No, no, marshal, first impressions are always the most natural."

The king enjoyed the joke, and everybody pitied the poor old courtier. For my part, I am apt to reflect upon things, and I wish the king would do the same; he might judge from this incident how seldom he hears the truth.

XXXV.—FROM ANTONY'S ORATION.

If you have tears, prepare to shed them now.
You all do know this mantle; I remember
The first time Cæsar ever put it on:
'Twas on a summer's evening, in his tent,
That day he overcame the Nervii.
Look! in this place ran Cassius' dagger through;

See what a rent the envious Casca made!
Through this the well-beloved Brutus stabb'd;
And as he plucked his cursed steel away,
Mark how the blood of Cæsar follow'd it,
As rushing out of doors, to be resolved
If Brutus so unkindly knock'd, or no;
For Brutus, as you know, was Cæsar's angel.
Judge, oh, ye gods! how dearly Cæsar loved him.
This, this was the unkindest cut of all.
For when the noble Cæsar saw him stab,
Ingratitude, more strong than traitor's arms,
Quite vanquished him; then burst his mighty heart!
And, in his mantle muffling up his face,
Even at the base of Pompey's statue,
Which all the while ran blood, great Cæsar fell.
Oh! what a fall was there, my countrymen!
Then I, and you, and all of us, fell down,
Whilst bloody treason flourished over us.

* * * * * * * *

(Shakespeare.)

XXXVI.—GULLIVER AND THE DWARF.

I should have lived happy enough in that country, if my littleness had not exposed me to several ridiculous and troublesome accidents, some of which I shall venture to relate. Glumdalclitch often carried me into the gardens of the court in my smaller box, and would sometimes take me out of it, and hold me in her hand, or set me down to walk. I remember, before the dwarf left the queen, he followed us one day into those gardens, and my nurse having set me down, he and I being close together, near some dwarf apple-trees, I must needs show my wit by a silly allusion between him and the trees, whereupon the malicious rogue, watching his opportunity when I was walking under one of them, shook it directly over my head, by which a dozen apples, each of them near as large as a Bristol barrel, came tumbling about my ears; one of them hit me on the back as I chanced to stoop, and knocked me down flat on my face. But I received no other hurt, and the dwarf was pardoned at my desire, because I had given the provocation.—(Swift.)

XXXVII.—THE HARE AND THE TORTOISE.

(Compare " Le Lièvre et la Tortue," in Lafontaine's Fables, Book VI., Fab. 10.)

A forward hare, of swiftness vain,
The genius of the neighbouring plain,
Would oft deride the drudging crowd—
For geniuses are ever proud.
He'd boast his flight, 'twere vain to follow,
For dog and horse he'd beat them hollow;
Nay, if he put forth all his strength,
Outstrip his brethren half a length.
A tortoise heard his vain oration,
And vented thus his indignation:
" O puss! it bodes thee dire disgrace
When I defy thee to the race.
Come, 'tis a match; nay, no denial,
I lay my shell upon the trial."
'Twas "done," and "done," "all fair," "a bet,"
Judges prepared, and distance set.
The scampering hare outstripped the wind;
The creeping tortoise lagged behind,
And scarce had passed a single pole,
When puss had almost reached the goal.
" Friend tortoise," quoth the jeering hare,
" Your burden's more than you can bear;
To help your speed it were as well
That I should ease you of your shell;
Jog on a little faster, prithee,
I'll take a nap and then be with thee."

The tortoise heard his taunting jeer,
But still resolved to persevere,
On to the goal securely crept,
While puss, unknowing, soundly slept.
The bets were won, the hare awoke,
When thus the victor tortoise spoke:
"Puss, though I own thy quicker parts,
Things are not always done by starts;
You may deride my awkward pace,
But slow and steady wins the race!"—(Lloyd.)

XXXVIII.—THE SHIPWRECK.

'Twas twilight, and the sunless day went down
    Over the waste of waters; like a veil,
Which, if withdrawn, would but disclose the frown
    Of one whose hate is mask'd but to assail.
Thus to their hopeless eye the night was shown,
    And grimly darkled o'er the faces pale,
And the dim, desolate deep: twelve days had Fear
    Been their familiar, and now Death was here.

. . . .

Then rose from sea to sky the wild farewell—
    Then shriek'd the timid, and stood still the brave,—
Then some leap'd overboard with dreadful yell,
    As eager to anticipate their grave;
And the sea yawn'd around her like a hell,
    And down she suck'd with her the whirling wave,
Like one who grapples with his enemy,
And strives to strangle him before he die.

And first one universal shriek there rush'd,
    Louder than the loud Ocean, like a crash
Of echoing thunder; and then all was hush'd,
    Save the wild wind, and the remorseless dash

Of billow's; but at intervals there gush'd,
  Accompanied with a convulsive splash,
A solitary shriek, the bubbling cry
Of some strong swimmer in his agony.

(Lord **Byron**).

XXXIX.—THE VICAR OF WAKEFIELD AND HIS WIFE.

I was ever of opinion that the honest man, who married and brought up a large family, did more service than he who continued single, and only talked of population. From this motive, I had scarce taken orders a year before I began to think seriously of matrimony, and chose my wife as she did her wedding-gown,—not for a fine glossy surface, but such qualities as would wear well. To do her justice, she was a good-natured, notable woman, and as for her education, there were few country ladies who could show more. She could read any English book without much spelling; but for pickling, preserving, and cookery, none could excel her. She prided herself also upon being an excellent contriver in housekeeping, though I could never find that we grew richer with all her contrivances. However, we loved each other tenderly, and our fondness increased as we grew old. There was in fact nothing that could make us angry with the world or each other. We had an elegant house, situate in a fine country, and a good neighbourhood. The year was spent in moral or rural amusements, in visiting our rich neighbours, and relieving such as were poor. We had no revolutions to fear, nor fatigues to undergo; all our adventures were by the fireside, and all our migrations from the blue bed to the brown.—(Goldsmith).

XL.—OF FRIENDSHIP.

The second fruit of friendship is healthful and sovereign for the understanding, as the first is for the affections; for friendship maketh indeed a fair day in the affections from storm and tempests, but it maketh day-light in the understanding, out of darkness and confusion of thoughts; neither is this to be understood only of faithful counsel, which a man receiveth from his friend; but, before you come to that, certain it is, that whosoever hath his mind fraught with many thoughts, his wits and understanding do clarify and break up, in the communicating and discoursing with another; he tosseth his thoughts more easily; he marshalleth them more orderly; he seeth how they looked when turned into words; finally, he waxeth wiser than himself; and that more by an hour's discourse than by a day's meditation. It was well said by Themistocles to the king of Persia, "That speech was like cloth of arras, opened and put abroad," whereby the imagery doth appear in figure; whereas in thoughts they lie but as in packs. Neither is this second fruit of friendship, in opening the understanding, restrained only to such friends as are able to give a man counsel (they indeed are best), but even without that a man learneth of himself, and bringeth his own thoughts to light, and whetteth his wits as against a stone, which itself cuts not. In a word, a man were better relate himself to a statue or picture, than to suffer his thoughts to pass in smother.

(Bacon).

XLI.—ROBINSON CRUSOE'S FIRST ALARM:

It happened one day, about noon, going towards my boat, I was exceedingly surprised with the print of a man's naked foot on the shore, which was very plain to be seen in the sand. I stood like one thunderstruck, or as if I had seen an apparition. I listened, I looked around me, but I could hear nothing, nor see anything. I went up to a rising ground to look farther; I went up the shore and down the shore, but it was all one, I could see no other impression but that one. I went to it again to see if there was any more, and to observe if it might not be my fancy; but there was no room for that, for there was exactly the very print of a foot, toes, heel, and every part of a foot; how it came thither I knew not, nor could in the least imagine. But after innumerable fluttering thoughts, like a man perfectly confused and out of myself, I came home to my fortification, not feeling, as we say, the ground as I went on; but terrified to the last degree, looking behind me at every two or three steps, mistaking every bush and tree, and fancying every stump at a distance to be a man. Nor is it possible to describe how many various shapes my affrighted imagination represented things to me in; how many wild ideas were found every moment in my fancy, and what strange, unaccountable whimsies came into my thoughts by the way...I had no sleep that night; the farther I was from the occasion of my fright, the greater my apprehensions were, which is something contrary to the nature of such things, and especially to the usual practice of all creatures in fear. But I was so embarrassed with my own frightful ideas of the thing, that I formed nothing but dismal imaginations to myself, even though I was now a great way off it.—(De Foe.)

XLII.—PLEASURES OF A WINTER EVENING.

Now stir the fire, and close the shutters fast,
Let fall the curtains, wheel the sofa round,
And while the bubbling and loud-hissing urn
Throws up a steamy column, and the cups,
That cheer but not inebriate, wait on each,

So let us welcome peaceful evening in.
Not such his evening who, with shining face,
Sweats in the crowded theatre, and, squeezed
And bored with elbow-points through both his sides,
Outscolds the ranting actor on the stage :
Nor his, who patient stands till his feet throb,
And his head thumps, to feed upon the breath
Of patriots, bursting with heroic rage,
Or placemen, all tranquillity and smiles.
This folio of four pages, happy work!
Which not e'en critics criticise ; that holds
Inquisitive attention, while I read,
Fast bound in chains of silence, which the fair,
Though eloquent themselves, yet fear to break ;
What is it, but a map of busy life,
Its fluctuations, and its vast concerns ?
Here runs the mountainous and craggy ridge,
That tempts ambition. On the summit see
The seals of office glitter in his eyes ;
He climbs, he pants, he grasps them ! At his heels,
Close at his heels, a demagogue ascends,
And with a dexterous jerk soon twists him down,
And wins them, but to lose them in his turn.

. . . .
(Cowper.)

UNIVERSITY OF LONDON.

Examination of Women for Certificates of higher Proficiency (1870).

XLIII.—DIRGE AT SEA.

Sleep ! we give thee to the wave,
Red with life-blood of the brave :
Thou shalt find a noble grave :
    Fare thee well !

Sleep! thy billowy field is won,
Proudly may the funeral gun,
'Midst the hush at set of sun,
    Boom thy knell!

Lonely, lonely is thy bed;
Never there may flower be shed,
Marble reared, or brother's head
    Bowed to weep.

Yet thy record on the sea,
Borne through battle high and free,
Long the red-cross flag shall be;
    Sleep! oh, sleep!

(F. Hemans.)

UNIVERSITY OF LONDON.

General Examination for Women, May, 1876.

XLIV.

(*a*) Gibbon, the historian, was one day attending the trial of Warren Hastings in Westminster Hall, and Sheridan, having perceived him there, took occasion to mention "the luminous author of 'The Decline and Fall.'" After he had finished, one of his friends reproached him with flattering Gibbon. "Why, what did I say of him?" asked Sheridan. "You called him the luminous author." "Luminous! O, I meant *vo*luminous."

(*b*) A Yorkshire nobleman, who was fond of boasting of his Norman descent, said to one of his tenants, who, he thought, was not addressing him with proper respect: "Do you know, fellow, that my ancestors came over with William the Conqueror?" "And, perhaps," retorted the sturdy Saxon, "they found mine here when they comed."

UNIVERSITY OF LONDON.

First B.A. Examination for Honours, August 14, 1879.

XLV.—NIAGARA IN WINTER.

As I stood gazing on the sun, and the rainbow, and the glittering spray, and the sparkling snow, and as the constant roar of the cataract had become to me, through its even monotony of sonorous continuity, quite soft and subdued, the very oddest, the very absurdest, the most incongruous thing it is possible to conceive, happened. I thought I had worked myself up to the proper state of rapture. The sun had worked marvels in me., I was absorbed. I was wonderstruck. I was delighted. Here was the grand sight—the show of shows—the spectacle that, from the most unimpressionable, extorts the exclamation of wonder. I was invoking Phœbus Apollo—I was crying "*Evoe!*" or "*Mehercle!*"—when an abominably ludicrous thing happened.

It was in this wise. Mr. Sol Davis is a thrifty man, and keeps live stock. From the rear of his premises there came gravely and consequentially waddling towards me, a certain domestic bird. This bird, it may be, flattered himself that his plumage was white; but, contrasted with the virgin snow over which he sacrilegiously waddled, he had a dirty, tawny hue. And the varlet thought, no doubt, that he had red legs. Red! These were like unto the worn-out jacket of an untidy militia-man. His bill was unbearable. He was the ugliest biped I ever set eyes upon; and yet I dare say Mr. Sol Davis thought him in the plumpest of conditions, and intended to send him presently into the States, with a view to the Christmas market. There, the truth must out. He was a goose, and this beast of a bird waddled to the brink of Table Rock, and stood beside me, gazing out upon Niagara.

It would be a mean and paltry thing, I knew, for a strong man to kick a goose over a precipice. It would have been a cruel and dishonest thing to steal Mr. Sol Davis's property, or wring its neck. Yet something must be done, I felt. Why didn't he fly away? Why didn't he waddle back? No; there he remained, ruminating, and occasionally gobbling to himself. Perhaps he was indulging in aspirations that the sage and onion crop had given out, and that he would not be roasted until next Thanksgiving Day. I told him savagely to get out of that. He turned his bill and his eye upwards to me, stood on one leg, and hissed slightly, as though to say: "Have I not as much right here as you, brother? What do *you* think of the Falls?"

UNIVERSITY OF LONDON.

Second B.A. Pass Examination, October 28, 1879.

EXAMINERS:

REV. P. H. E. BRETTE, B.D., AND PROF. CASSAL, L.L.D.

XLVI.—CHARLES DICKENS'S READINGS.

(*a*) Dickens's habits as a speaker differed from those of most orators. He gave no thought to the composition of the speech he was to make till the day before he was to deliver it. Whether the effort was to be a long or short one, he never wrote down a word of what he was going to say; but when the proper time arrived for him to consider his subject, he took a walk into the country, and the thing was done. When he returned he was all ready for his task. He liked to talk about the audiences that came to hear him read, and he gave the palm to his Parisian one, saying it was the quickest to catch his meaning. Although he said many were always present in the room in Paris who did not fully understand English, yet the French eye is so quick to detect expression that it never failed instantly to understand what he meant by a look or an act. "Thus, for instance," he said, "when I was impersonating Steerforth in *David Copperfield*, and gave that peculiar grip of the hand to Emily's lover, the French audience burst into cheers and rounds of applause." He considered the storm scene in *David Copperfield* one of the most effective of his readings. The character of *Jack Hopkins* in *Bob Sawyer's Party* he took great delight in representing.—(J. T. Field.)

XLVII.—SELF-MADE MEN.

(*b*) We sometimes wonder if the successful man is altogether to be envied. We should imagine his happiest days must be those in which he is working successfully—not those in which he has gained his fortune and need work no longer. The early days of extreme struggle and penury are, of course, very trying; but we should think the opposite extreme equally disagreeable. While he is managing a prosperous business his time is full and his mind occupied; but when he "retires," what a blank must his existence become. It is hard to learn to be idle after long years of unremitting toil. The stories of the old tallow-chandler, who always visited his establishment on "melting-days," long after he had left the firm; of the retired grocer, who found life hang so heavily on his hands that he fitted up his back room with a counter and scales, and employed himself with weighing out tea for imaginary customers, may be apocryphal, but they have at least an air of probability.

What can a man whose whole life has been spent in hard work do with himself in idle hours? People born to riches are accustomed to have leisure, and know how to fill up their time with amusement, if not with work. Literature, art, society, country sports, shooting, fishing, riding—all these things make up the daily occupation of the man who inherits rank or wealth; and after his fashion he works as hard as his poorer brethren. But this art of enjoying holidays, so to speak, needs to be acquired in youth. If a man has worked behind the counter nearly all his life, with scant leisure for improving a defective education, he cannot at fifty or sixty develop a sudden passion for literature—a sudden love of art. A taste for outdoor exercises cannot be acquired in middle age. Society presents few charms to those who are admitted to it too late. We may ridicule the mistakes committed by the *nouveau riche* in the attempt to live in accordance with his newly-attained position; but he is rather to be pitied than sneered at.—(*Globe.*)

UNIVERSITY OF LONDON.

Second B.A. Examination for Honours, 1879.

XLVIII.—JAMES WATT.

(*a*) Watt has been called the great *Improver* of the steam-engine, but, in truth, as to all that is admirable in its structure or vast in its utility, he should rather be described as its *Inventor*. It was by his invention that its action was so regulated as to make it capable of being applied to the finest and most delicate manufactures, and its power so increased as to set weight and solidity at defiance. By his admirable contrivance, it has become a thing stupendous alike for its force and its flexibility—for the prodigious power that it can exert, and the ease, the precision, and ductility with which that power can be varied, distributed and applied. The trunk of an elephant, that can pick up a pin and rend an oak, is as nothing to it. It can engrave a seal, and crush masses of obdurate metal before it, draw out, without breaking, a thread as fine as gossamer, and lift a ship of war like a bubble in the air. It can embroider muslin and forge anchors—cut steel into ribands, and impel loaded vessels against the fury of the winds and waves.—(Jeffrey.)

XLIX.—THE RAGGED SCHOOLS.

(b) I am listening here in Rome,
    England's strong......

But these others, children small,
    Spilt like blots about the city,
Quay, and street, and palace wall,
    Take them up into your pity.

In the alleys, in the squares,
    Begging, lying little rebels;
In the noisy thoroughfares
    Straggling on with piteous trebles.

Patient children—think what pain
    Makes a young child patient—ponder!
Wrong too commonly to strain
    After right, or wish, or wonder.

Wicked children, with peaked chins,
  And old foreheads! There are many
With no pleasures except sins,
  Gambling with a stolen penny.

Sickly children, that whine low
  To themselves and not their mothers,
From mere habit; never so
  Hoping help or care from others.

Healthy children, with those blue
  English eyes; fresh from their Maker,
Fierce and ravenous, staring through
  At the brown loaves of the baker.

I am listening here in Rome,
  And the Romans are confessing,
"English children pass in bloom,
  All the prettiest made for blessing."

. . . . . .

O, my sisters! children small,
  Blue-eyed, wailing through the city;
Our own babes cry in them all,
  Let us take them into pity!

(Mrs. E. Browning.)

UNIVERSITY OF LONDON, 1879.

Second D. Lit. Examination.

L.—WHAT A BOOK REALLY IS.

(*a*) A book is essentially not a talked thing, but a written thing; and written, not with the view of mere communication, but of permanence. The book of talk is printed only because its author cannot speak to thousands of people at once; if he could, he would; the volume is mere *multiplication* of his voice. You cannot talk to your friend in India; if you could, you would; you write instead; that is mere *conveyance* of voice. But a book is written, not to multiply the voice merely, not to carry it merely, but to preserve it. The author has something to say which he perceives to be true and useful, or helpfully beautiful. So far as he knows, no one has yet said it; so far as he knows, no one else can say it. He is bound to say it, clearly and melodiously if he may; clearly at all events. In the sum of his life, he finds it to be the thing, or group of things, manifest to him;—this the piece of true knowledge, or sight, which his share of sunshine and earth has permitted him to seize. He would fain set it down for ever, engrave it on rock, if he could, saying: " This is the best of me; for the rest, I ate, and drank, and slept, loved, and hated, like another; my life was as the vapour, and is not; but this I saw and knew: this, if anything is mine, is worth your memory." That is his *writing*; it is, in his small human way, and with whatever degree of true inspiration is in him, his inscription or scripture. That is a book.—(Ruskin.)

LI.—THE GLADIATOR'S DEATH.

(*b*) I see before me the gladiator lie:
    He leans upon his hand; his manly brow
    Consents to death, but conquers agony,
    And his droop'd head sinks gradually low.
    And through his side the last drops, ebbing slow
    From the gash, fall heavy, one by one,
    Like the first of a thunder shower; and now
    The arena swims around him—he is gone;
Ere ceased the inhuman shout which hail'd the
    wretch who won.

He heard it, but he heeded not—his eyes
Were with his heart, and that was far away;
He reck'd not of the life he lost nor prize,
But where his rude hut by the Danube lay,
There were his young barbarians all at play,
There was their Dacian mother—he, their sire,
Butcher'd to make a Roman holiday—
All this rush'd with his blood—shall he expire,
And unavenged? Arise, ye Goths, and glut your ire!

(Byron.)

THE ROYAL MILITARY COLLEGE.

November and December, 1877.

LII.

For a while Wallace contented himself by improving the discipline and raising the spirits of his men by trivial skirmishes and attempts on inconsiderable places, in which he was so successful as to acquire a renown which rapidly increased his army; but it was still far inferior to the host with which Surrey, whom Edward had left as governor of Scotland, overtook him at Stirling. At that time the Forth was spanned by a bridge so narrow as scarcely to admit more than two persons abreast: behind this bridge Wallace stationed his army, and Surrey, contrary to his own judgment, was persuaded by the unskillful impetuosity of Cressingham to cross it to attack the enemy; but only a small portion of his army had reached the other side of the river when it was attacked and overpowered by Wallace; the bridge broke under the weight of the squadrons pressing across it to help their comrades; thousands were drowned in the river, thousands were slain by the Scots, who gave no quarter, and Surrey fled, almost unaccompanied, to England to announce his own defeat and the loss of the kingdom entrusted to him.

ROYAL MILITARY ACADEMY, WOOLWICH, AND ROYAL MILITARY COLLEGE, SANDHURST.

July, 1879.

LIII.

I spent several years in gaol, until there came to that part of the kingdom a good man, who had full powers to free from servitude all such prisoners as had stout limbs and sinews. In other words, a recruiting officer changed my destination, and instead of handling a wheelbarrow in the public service, it became my nobler duty, as a member of a free corps, to fight in the public cause. Determined to be a soldier in earnest, I put myself forward on all occasions; I was the first in every attack, and when we were compelled to retreat, I used my legs to such good purpose that the enemy could never overtake me. For a time I got on very well; I received a command in a troop of horse, with hope of still further promotion; but one day, when I was sent on a foraging expedition, I captured oxen, sheep, goats, and poultry, and not only emptied granaries and barns, but also every drawer, strong box, or closet, whether in houses or in churches. As ill luck would have it, the owners took it into their heads to complain, and certain officers charged me with pillaging. I was brought to a court-martial, and finally degraded to the ranks.

THE ROYAL MILITARY ACADEMY,

Nov. and Dec. 1879, *and the Royal Military College, Sandhurst.*

LIV.

It was dark before we reached Rangazava, a small town by the seaside, where we remained for the night. One room, about thirty or thirty-five feet square, served the purposes of sitting-room, sleeping-room, and kitchen. A fire was kindled between some stones fixed on a heap of sand, the edges of which were kept up by pieces of wood. A large, shallow, round, earthen pot was then put on the fire to boil rice in, and a piece of meat, which we had brought with us, was fixed by the side of the fire to roast. As soon as the rice was cooked, the kettle was put on, and by the time it boiled everything had been made ready. I was amused to see the trouble and interest with which my friend (a stout chief more than six feet high) overlooked and directed the cooking of the evening meal. After supper, the chief gave me a clean mat; and, after taking off my shoes and using my bag for a pillow, I lay down to rest, and slept quietly till daybreak.

ROYAL MILITARY COLLEGE, SANDHURST.
July 8, 1880.

LV.

On September the tenth, at three o'clock a.m., the vanguard was under arms, and proceeded in the direction of the enemy, followed by the rest of the army within an hour. Suddenly a strong force of Turcoman cavalry appeared on the right-hand side and attacked the rear. The Cossacks sent against them gave way before the furious assault of the Turcomans, who surrounded the train and threw themselves upon the escort, which, by some mismanagement, did not come up to the prescribed number. The Russians give their losses in this primary encounter as seven dead, attributing to the enemy a loss of thirty men. But as the enemy succeeded in getting into the train, and could only be dislodged by artillery fire, it is evident that the Turcomans used their swords to some purpose. Indeed, it is admitted that, but for the presence of mind displayed by General B......., commander of the infantry in the main force, the whole train would have been lost before the beginning of the battle. The aspect of the fierce horsemen of the Steppe at the moment of charging was truly grand. Pistol in hand, and sword between teeth, they came on at a tremendous gallop, and in a moment were engaged in a hand-to-hand conflict with the Cossacks, who gave way before the shock.

CIVIL SERVICE OF INDIA.

Open Competition of 1879.

LVI.

The barometer points to wet.
He is wrong and his sister is right.
It is hotter here than in the open air.
Nothing was any good.
With his friend it was not the same thing.
There can be no question of going to-morrow.
You are all abroad in your reasoning.
Adversity has its uses.

LVII.

In the midst of my labours and my changes of place I had the happiness of being able to cultivate my mind in intimacy with a young man of merit whom Providence bestowed on me for companion and friend. His fondness for the natural sciences had made him join our expedition, and he behaved himself on it as a good soldier; but it was easy to see that political sympathy played only a secondary part in his resolution. He had no desire for promotion, no aptitude for strategical studies. His herbal and his observations in zoology occupied him a great deal more than the success of the war and the triumph of liberty. He fought too well, when the opportunity came, ever to merit the reproach of lukewarmness; but up to the very eve of the combat, and from the day after it, he [seemed unaware that there was a question of aught but a scientific excursion in the savannahs of the new world. His portmanteau was always filled, not with money and clothes, but with specimens of natural history; and whilst we, as we lay on the grass, were attentive to the slightest noises which might reveal to us the enemy's approach, he was absorbed in the analysis of a plant or an insect. He was an admirable young man, pure as an angel, disinterested as a stoic, patient as a savant, and playful and affectionate along with it all. When a surprise placed us in danger, he had no cares and exclamations but for the precious pebbles and invaluable blades of grass which he carried behind his saddle; and yet, when one of us was wounded, he tended him with incomparable kindness and zeal.

OPEN COMPETITION

For Appointments as Student Interpreter at Constantinople.
1879.

LVIII.—LAST YEARS OF GEORGE III.

All the world knows the story of his malady; all history presents no sadder figure than that of the old man, blind and deprived of reason, wandering through the rooms of his palace, addressing imaginary parliaments, reviewing fancied troops, holding ghostly courts. I have seen his picture, as it was taken at this time, hanging in the apartment of his daughter, the Landgravine of Hesse-Hombourg, amidst books and Windsor furniture, and a hundred fond reminiscences of her English home. The poor old father is represented in a purple gown, his snowy beard falling over his breast, the star of his famous order still idly shining on it. He was not only sightless, he became utterly deaf. All light, all reason, all sound of human voices, all the pleasures of this world of God, were taken from him. Some slight lucid moments he had; in one of which the queen, desiring to see him, entered the room, and found him singing a hymn, and accompanying himself at the harpsichord. When he had finished, he knelt down and prayed aloud for her, and then for his family, and then for the nation, concluding with a prayer for himself that it might please God to avert his heavy calamity from him, but if not, to give him resignation to submit. He then burst into tears, and his reason again fled. What preacher need moralize on this story? What words, save the simplest, are requisite to tell it? It is too terrible for tears.—(Thackeray: *The Four Georges.*)

HOME CIVIL SERVICE EXAMINATIONS.

Clerkships (Class I.).—October, 1879.

LIX.

The houses of the city were full of dying women and children, the streets with old men gasping out their last breath. The bodies remained unburied, for either the emaciated relatives had not strength for the melancholy duty, or in the uncertainty of their own lives neglected every office of kindness or charity. Some, indeed, died in the act of burying their friends; others crept into the cemeteries, lay down on a bier, and expired. There was no sorrow, no wailing; they had not strength to moan; they sate with dry eyes and mouths drawn up into a kind of bitter smile. Those who were more hardy looked with envy on those who had already breathed their last. Many died, says the historian, with their eyes steadily fixed on the Temple. There was a deep and heavy silence over the whole city, broken only by the robbers as they forced open houses to plunder the dead, and in licentious sport dragged away the last decent covering from their bodies; they would even try the edge of their swords on the dead.

LX.

It is very hard that because you do not get my letters, you will not let me receive yours. I have not had a line from you these five weeks. Of your honours and glories fame has told me; and for aught I know, you may be a field-marshal by this time, and despise such a poor cottager as me. Take notice, I shall disclaim you in my turn, if you are sent on a command against Dantzic, or to usurp a new district in Poland. I have seen no armies, kings, or empresses, nor are they what I want to hear of. I like to hear you are well and diverted. For my part, I wish you were returned to your plough. Your Sabine farm is in high beauty. I have lain there twice within this week, going to and from a visit to G. Selwyn, near Gloucester—a tour as much to my taste as yours to you. For fortified town I have seen ruined castles. What can I tell you more? Nothing. Everybody's head but mine is full of elections. I had the satisfaction at Gloucester, where G. Selwyn is canvassing, of reflecting on my own wisdom.

AGRÉGATION DE LA LANGUE ANGLAISE.

Concours de 1872. Composition du 14 août.

LXI.—A WINTER EVENING IN THE COUNTRY.

Come evening, once again, season of peace;
Return, sweet evening, and continue long!
Methinks I see thee in the streaky west,
With matron-step slow moving, while the night
Treads on thy sweeping train, one hand employed
In letting fall the curtain of repose
On bird and beast, the other charged for man
With sweet oblivion of the cares of day.;
Not sumptuously adorned, nor needing aid,
Like darkly-featured night, of clustering gems.
A star or two, just twinkling on thy brow,
Suffices thee, safe that the moon is thine
No less than hers, not borne indeed on high
With ostentatious pageantry, but set
With modest grandeur in the purple zone,
Resplendent less, but of an ampler round.

Come then, and thou shalt find thy votary calm,
Or make me so. Composure is thy gift;
And whether I devote thy gentle hours
To books, to music, or the poet's toil;
To weaving nets for bird-alluring fruit;
Or twining silken threads round ivory reels,
When they command whom man was born to please:
I slight thee not, but make thee welcome still.
Just when our drawing-room begins to blaze
With lights, by clear reflection multiplied,
Our pleasures too begin. But me perhaps
The glowing heart may satisfy a while
With faint illumination, that uplifts
The shadows to the ceiling, there by fits
Dancing uncouthly to the quivering flame.
Not undelightful is an hour to me
So spent in parlour twilight; such a gloom
Suits well the thoughtful or unthinking mind,
The mind contemplative, with some new theme
Pregnant, or indisposed alike to all.

Thus oft, reclined at ease, I lose an hour
At evening, till at length the freezing blast,
That sweeps the bolted shutter, summons home
The recollected thoughts; and snapping short
The glassy threads with which the fancy weaves
Her brittle toils, restores me to myself.
How calm is my recess; and how the frost,
Raging abroad, and the rough wind, endear
The silence and the warmth enjoyed within!
I saw the wood, and fields at close of day
A variegated show; the meadows green,
Though faded, and the lands, where lately waved
The golden harvest, of a mellow brown,
Upturned at present by the forceful share.
To morrow brings a change, a total change:
Fast falls a fleecy shower; the downy flakes
Descending, and with never ceasing lapse
Softly alighting upon all below,
Assimilate all objects. Earth receives

Gladly the thickening mantle ; and the green
And tender blade, that feared the chilling blast,
Escapes unhurt beneath so warm a veil.

(Cowper).

AGRÉGATION DE LA LANGUE ANGLAISE.

Paris, août 1879.

LXII.—ELEGY TO THE MEMORY OF AN UNFORTUNATE LADY.

What beck'ning ghost, along the moonlight shade
Invites my steps, and points to yonder glade ?
'Tis she ! but why that bleeding bosom gor'd,
Why dimly gleams the visionary sword ?
Oh, ever beauteous, ever friendly ! tell,
Is it, in heaven, a crime to love too well ?
To bear too tender, or too firm a heart,
To act a lover's or a Roman part ?
Is there no bright reversion in the sky,
For those who greatly think, or bravely die ?

Why bade ye else, ye Pow'rs ! her soul aspire
Above the vulgar flight of low desire ?
Ambition first sprung from your blest abodes ;
The glorious fault of angels and of gods ;
Thence to their images on earth it flows,
And in the breast of kings and heroes glows.
Most souls, 'tis true, but peep out once an age,
Dull sullen pris'ners in the body's cage :
Dim lights of life, that burn a length of years
Useless, unseen, as lamps in sepulchres ;
Like eastern kings a lazy state they keep,
And close confin'd to their own palace, sleep.

From these, perhaps (ere nature bade her die),
Fate snatch'd her early to the pitying sky.
As into air the purer spirits flow,
And separate from their kindred dregs below,
So flew the soul to its congenial place,
Nor left one virtue to redeem her race.

But thou, false guardian of a charge too good,
Thou, mean deserter of thy brother's blood!
See on these ruby lips the trembling breath,
These cheeks now fading at the blast of death:
Cold is that breast which warm'd the world before,
And those love-darting eyes must roll no more.
Thus, if eternal justice rules the ball,
Thus shall your wives, and thus your children fall.
(Pope.)

Hachette's Catalogue Raisonné
OF NEW
FRENCH EDUCATIONAL COURSE.

THE study of modern languages has, during the last few years, entered upon a new stage of development in English Schools, and been thoroughly revolutionised by the progress of modern science. The natural consequence of this movement was at once to supersede the time-honoured grammars of Hamel, Lévizac, Wanostrocht, &c.; even Noël and Chapsal had to relinquish their claims, and a general demand sprang up for new educational works, in connection with the teaching, more particularly, of French. It is for the purpose of meeting this desideratum that Messrs. HACHETTE have issued the series of works, the list of which is appended, and which, taking the pupils from the nursery, lead them gradually on till they are qualified to compete for Scholarships and Exhibitions at the Universities.

The complete Educational Catalogue may be had gratis on application.

HACHETTE'S
ILLUSTRATED FRENCH PRIMER;
OR THE CHILD'S FIRST FRENCH LESSONS.
Edited by HENRI BUÉ, B.-ès-L.,
French Master at Merchant Taylors' School, London.
The easiest Introduction to the Study of French, with numerous Wood Engravings.
NEW AND CHEAPER EDITION.
1 vol. small 8vo. cloth. Price 1s. 6d.

"There is scarcely a page without a cleverly-executed engraving, and a child could certainly learn French from no better devised or more interesting manual."—*Literary Churchman.*

GRAMMARS AND EXERCISE BOOKS.
EARLY FRENCH LESSONS. By HENRY BUÉ, B.-ès-L., French Master at Merchant Taylors' School, London. New edition, 64 pages, cloth, price 8d.

The compiler of this little book has had in view to teach the young beginner as many French words as possible in the least tedious manner. He has found by experience that what children dislike most to learn are lists of words, however useful and well chosen, and that they very soon get weary of disconnected sentences, but commit to memory most readily a short nursery rhyme, anecdote, or fable. Hence the selection he has made.

THE FIRST FRENCH BOOK.
By HENRI BUÉ, B.-ès-L.,
French Master at Merchant Taylors' School, London.

1 Vol. 176 Pages. Cloth, price 10d. Ninth Edition.

This small book, drawn up according to the requirements of the first year will prove of the most valuable assistance to all beginners.

Adopted by the School Board for London, etc.

It contains Grammar, Exercises, Conversation and Vocabulary. Every lesson is followed by a short dialogue for conversational practices The volume comprises the whole Accidence. The rules are stated in the clearest possible manner. A chapter on the Philology of the language, and some for reading and translation, a complete index, and two complete Vocabularies, follow the grammatical portion. Its moderate price and its completeness will make it one of the best books for use in our Middle-Class and National Schools and other large establishments.

THE SECOND FRENCH BOOK.

1 Vol. 208 Pages. Third edition. Cloth, price 1s.

KEY TO THE SAME. For Teachers only. (*In preparation.*)

OPINIONS OF THE PRESS.

One of "Her Majesty's Inspectors of Schools" writes: "Thanks for your admirable *First French Book*, which seems to me remarkably well adapted, in respect of both scope and arrangement, for school use. It ought to be, and I think will be, largely adopted."

"This is a book, small as regards size and price, but containing in quantity at least matter which would furnish forth far larger and more pretentious volumes. M. Bué's method and treatment are excellent; to any person unacquainted with French, but wishing to study that language, or to any teacher wishing to form classes for its study, we can cordially recommend his work. Books for use in school or class are often compiled by others than teachers, and the result is not always satisfactory. M. Bué is a teacher himself, and his lessons show that he understands the difficulties his brethren may labour under, and the best means by which they can be surmounted. We are glad to learn that the volume under notice has been adopted by the London School Board."—*The Irish Teachers' Journal.* Feb. 2nd, 1878.

"This little book is a model both of cheapness and of completeness. In 176 pages it gives beginners the principal rules of the French accidence, thus enabling them to practise conversation after a very few lessons. M. Bué commences by a list of easy and useful words to be learned by heart; the elementary grammar comes next, each chapter being followed by a vocabulary and two exercises. The reading lessons which terminate the volume are amusing anecdotes of graduated difficulty, and the vocabularies are so compiled as to preclude the necessity of a separate dictionary. The pupil has thus in a very small duodecimo all the help he requires towards a quick and easy mastery of the elements of the French language."—*School Board Chronicle.*

"M. Bué's 'First French Book' is much to be commended. The lessons are very gradual, and the rules are explained with a simplicity that must greatly help both teacher and pupil. At the end of each lesson a short vocabulary, a model exercise, and a conversation are given. At the end of the verbs is a 'short chapter for the inquisitive,' which is well worth getting up, even by more advanced pupils. The chief merit of elementary books of this kind lies in their arrangement, and in this respect we have seen no better book than M. Bué's."—*School Guardian,* Nov. 10th, 1877.

"A handy little volume, which may serve with advantage as an introduction to the study of more elaborate works."—*The Pictorial World,* Oct. 13, 1877.

"This is one of the best first-books to French that has ever been published. The difficulties of the language are presented in a series of exercises and lessons, through which the student is led before he realises that he has really had genuine difficulties presented to him. The vocabularies contained in the book have been selected very skilfully. A 'short chapter for the inquisitive' is excellent. There is a French-English vocabulary containing nearly 1,500 words in most frequent use."—*The Weekly Times,* Oct. 14, 1877.

"This is a very excellent little work, and will be welcomed both in schools and for private teaching. It bears the impress of an experienced teacher; and is marked with great care in pointing out the peculiarities of the language in construction, idiom, and pronunciation. The printing also deserves a word of notice, the variations in termination, &c., to which it is desired to call attention, being given in excellent bold type—so that the utmost use is made of the eye—probably the most powerful of all senses in assisting the memory, especially in the case of young people. There is no doubt that it will quite fulfil the author's wish, modestly expressed in the preface, of becoming 'a useful and handy primer.'"—*The London and China Express,* Oct. 12, 1877.

"A great deal more of the information needed by a beginner than much larger works often contain, will be found in this little pocket grammar and exercise book. Only an experienced teacher could so well anticipate the preliminary difficulties and remove them from the path of a young linguist as M. Bué has done in his primer."—*Public Opinion,* Nov. 10, 1877.

PRACTICAL AND THEORETICAL

FRENCH CLASS BOOKS.

By PAUL BAUME.

These particularly modern Works, which have been unanimously praised by the Press, and well received by the educational world, are especially adapted to preparing for Public Examinations. "*Ni trop ni trop peu*" has been the Author's motto, and the marked favour with which his various works have been received is a sufficient proof that he carried out his motto to the satisfaction of Instructors and Principals of Schools and Colleges throughout the United Kingdom.

PAUL BAUME'S

Practical French Grammar
and Exercises,

FOR THE USE OF BEGINNERS AND GENERAL CLASSES.

Eighth Edition, Price 3s. 6d.

*** The chief features of the Practical French Grammar are :—

1stly. Each page of practice faces a page of theory.
2dly. No dictionary is required.
3dly. It is constructed on the progressive system, each page of practice being as it were an examination paper on every previous subject.
4thly. The Rules, 142 in number, are short, and such as can be easily explained to young pupils.

N.B.—Especial attention is directed to pages 6 and 7 of the Practical French Grammar, in which the system of teaching and manner of using the books are fully explained.

Key

To Exercises in Practical French Grammar,
WITH HINTS TO TEACHERS AND ANNOTATIONS.

Price 2s. 6d.

PAUL BAUME'S
French Syntax & Exercises,
FOR THE USE OF ADVANCED STUDENTS.
Second Edition, Price 4s.

₊ The chief features of the French Syntax are :—
1stly. Theory and practice facing each other.
2dly. The comprehensive nature of the practical pages, each containing a vocabulary of idiomatic, familiar, and colloquial expressions; quotations from French classics, illustrating the rules opposite; and, lastly, familiar English to be turned into French.

N.B.—The French Syntax is intended to prepare for the higher class of public examinations, and should be used by those students only who are well acquainted with the accidence of the French language, and know the irregular verbs. The system and advantages of the French Syntax are fully explained in the preface.

Key
To the Translations and Exercises in French Syntax,
FOR THE USE OF TEACHERS AND SELF-TAUGHT STUDENTS.
Price 2s. 6d.

"The appearance of a seventh edition of M. Baum's well-known grammar speaks for itself. It possesses distinctly a praiseworthy character of its own, marked chiefly by a just prominence given to 'practice,' a clear direct style of exposition, and a refreshing freedom from technicalities. It extends to 250 pages, is amply furnished with carefully graduated exercises, bestows due attention on the irregularities of the verb, and contains many well-selected lists of nouns .... Altogether this grammar is an admirable work of the kind, essentially designed for use, devoid of pedantic phraseology, systematic, and therefore simple. It may also be commended on the score of cheapness and of beautiful typography."—*Educational News.*

"The attractiveness of Syntax is fully given effect to by M. Baume, who illustrates the idiomatic peculiarities of Gallic construction in 1000 racy colloquialisms. The rules, which form the basis of his work, are simple and comprehensive, and their operation is unmistakably exhibited in 100 reading, parsing, and translating lessons. Some 40 of its 154 pages are taken up with preliminary rules of accidence and construction, a list of irregular verbs, &c., so as to obviate the necessity of referring to preliminary books, and to give to his present work a character of completeness. Its more extensive use in the schools would certainly be productive of excellent fruits."—*Educational News.*

PAUL BAUME'S
FRENCH MANUAL
OF
GRAMMAR, CONVERSATION, AND LITERATURE.

Second Edition, Price 3s.

₊ This new work is on a totally different plan from the ordinary run of Readers and Conversation Books, from which grammatical knowledge is generally excluded. The Manual is divided into 80 lessons. Each lesson, which may be prepared in part or wholly, according to the ability of the pupil, contains three divisions:—

1stly. A set of examination questions and answers on grammar.
2dly. A familiar conversation of a modern type on a given subject.
3dly. A biographical sketch of and quotation from a noted French writer, with hints for the translation of difficult expressions, historical notes, &c.

The whole Book thus forms an extensive examination paper on grammar, with 461 questions and answers systematically and progressively arranged; a set of 80 familiar conversations on given subjects; and a Reader, or elementary course of literature, containing 80 biographical sketches of and quotations from the best French prose writers and poets, in chronological order.

This French Manual is intended to be a useful as well as a necessary adjunct to any French grammar that may be in the hands of pupils.

"In preparing his Manual, M. Baume, not content merely to string together a number of chance extracts, has succeeded, by means of a chronological series of classical quotations, in tracing the development of French literary style. The excerpts are of the most diversified character, and include specimens from the writings of eighty authors, ranging from Rabelais to Hugo and Taine. A novel and excellent feature is the introduction of brief biographic sketches of the various writers."—*Educational News.*

"Together, these three works form an almost ideal series, yet each may be employed independently, or in conjunction with other class-books. They are all capitally got up, and may be safely recommended for private as well as for class use. M. Baume has issued a Key to the exercises contained in his work on Syntax, and a Key to the exercises in the Practical French Grammar."—*Educational News.*

BRACHET'S
PUBLIC SCHOOL ELEMENTARY FRENCH GRAMMAR.
With Exercises. By A. BRACHET, Lauréat de l'Académie Française, and adapted for English Schools by the Rev. P. H. E. BRETTE, B.D., and GUSTAVE MASSON, B.A., *Officiers d'Académie; Past and Present Examiners in the University of London.* Tenth Edition.

PART I.—ACCIDENCE, With Examination Questions and Exercises, Cloth, 176 pages, small 8vo. With a complete French-English and English-French Vocabulary. Price 1s. 6d.

PART II.—SYNTAX. With Examination Questions and Exercises, and a complete French-English and English-French Vocabulary. Price 1s. 6d.

KEY TO THE EXERCISES. For Teachers only. Price 1s. 6d.

A SUPPLEMENTARY SERIES OF EXERCISES.
Vol. I.—ACCIDENCE. With a Supplement to Grammar and a Vocabulary to the Exercises. Cloth, price 1s.

VOL. II.—SYNTAX. (*In preparation.*

KEY TO THE SAME. For Teachers only. (*In preparation.*)

OPINIONS OF THE PRESS.

"A good school-book. The type is as clear as the arrangement."—*Athenæum*, Jan. 6, 1877.

"We are not astonished to hear that it has met with the most flattering reception."—*School Board Chronicle*, March 10, 1877.

"We have no hesitation in stating our opinion that no more useful or practical introduction to the French language has been published than this."—*Public Opinion*, March 24, 1877.

"England is fortunate in the services of a small knot of French masters like MM. Masson and Brette, who have, alike by their teaching and their school-books, done much for the scientific study of the language and literature of France. After successfully introducing into English form the 'Public School French Grammar,' in which M. Littré's researches are happily applied by M. Brachet so as to show the relation of modern French to Latin, MM. Brette and Masson here translate and adapt the Petite or Elementary French Grammar. That has at once proved as popular as the more elaborate treatise."—*Edinburgh Daily Review*, March 20, 1877.

"Of this excellent school series we have before us the 'Public School Elementary French Grammar'—(1) Accidence, and (2) Syntax. Brachet's work is simply beyond comparison with any other of its class; and its scientific character is not sacrificed in the very judicious adaptation which has made it available for English students.—*There is no better elementary French Grammar, whether for boys or for girls.*"—*Hereford Times*, April 11, 1877.

"Messrs. HACHETTE issue some valuable contributions to their series of French Educational works. M. Auguste Brachet is well known as one of the most scientific and learned of French philologists and grammarians, and the practical utility of his 'Elementary French Grammar' is proved by the fact that the translation of it by the Rev. P. H. Brette, head master of the French School at Christ's Hospital, and Mr. G. Masson, assistant master at Harrow, has already reached a second edition."—*The Scotsman*, April 10, 1877.

Specimen Page from the
PUBLIC SCHOOL ELEMENTARY FRENCH GRAMMAR.

PRELIMINARY REMARKS
ON THE HISTORY AND GEOGRAPHY OF THE
FRENCH LANGUAGE.

Geography.—The French language extends over the whole of France, with the exception of one single province, Brittany, where, out of a population of 1,800,000, one million of individuals speak a language known by the name of **Bas-Breton**, and which is Celtic in its origin. To this important exception three small groups can be further added: the department of the North, where 200,000 inhabitants out of 1,200,000 speak the **Flemish language**, an offshoot from the German; the department of Lower-Pyrenees, where 120,000 persons speak the **Basque**, a very ancient idiom, the origin of which is unknown; finally, the department of Eastern Pyrenees (formerly the province of Roussillon), where 130,000 inhabitants speak the **Catalonian** language, derived from the Latin.

If the domains of the French language do not correspond exactly with the present territory of France, they include, on the other hand, several important districts outside the limits of that country, which represent an aggregate of a little more than 3,600,000 inhabitants, distributed as follows:—Belgium, 1,600,000; Germany, 1,000,000; French Switzerland, 400,000; finally, the Channel Islands, 60,000.

To these numbers we must add, out of Europe, the English colonies of Canada and Mauritius, which have retained the use of the French language, to say nothing of the French settlements (Algeria, Guiana, Senegal, etc.); we find thus 1,500,000 inhabitants more to be placed to the account of the French linguistic wealth.

With reference to the language, France is divided into two regions, **North** and **South**, the limits of which can be marked by tracing on the map a line extending from La Rochelle to Grenoble

North of this line all cultivated people speak French; the peasants understand French, but make use of *patois* closely connected with it. These *patois* are four in number: 1. The **Norman**, spoken in the western district; 2. The **Picard**, in the northwestern; 3. The **Lorrain**, in the eastern; 4. The **Burgundian**,

IRREGULAR AND DEFECTIVE VERBS.

Taire (= to keep silent, to conceal).

Prim. Tenses. Taire, taisant, tû, je tais, je tus.
See *plaire. Conjugated with the auxiliary* **avoir**.

Se taire (= to hold one's tongue), being a reflexive verb, is conjugated with *être* in its compound tenses.

Traire (= to milk).

Prim. Tenses. Traire, trayant, trait, je trais, no *Past. Def.*

Ind. Pres.	Je trais, tu trais, il trait, nous trayons, vous trayez, ils traient.
Imperf.	Je trayais, etc., nous trayions, etc.
Fut.	Je trairai, etc., nous trairons, etc.
Cond. Pres.	Je trairais, etc., nous trairions, etc.
Imper.	Trais, trayons, trayez.
Subj. Pres.	Que je traie, etc., que nous trayions, que vous trayiez, qu'ils traient.
Infin.	Traire.
Part.	Trayant, trait, traite.

This verb has neither *Past Def.*, nor *Imperf. Subj.*
Conjugated with the auxiliary **avoir**.

Vaincre (= to conquer).

Prim. Tenses. Vaincre, vainquant, vaincu, je vaincs, je vainquis.

Ind. Pres.	Je vaincs, tu vaincs, il vainc, nous vainquons, vous vainquez, ils vainquent.
Imperf.	Je vainquais, etc., nous vainquions, etc.
Past Def.	Je vainquis, etc., nous vainquîmes, etc.
Fut.	Je vaincrai, etc., nous vaincrons, etc.
Cond. Pres.	Je vaincrais, etc., nous vaincrions, etc.
Imper.	Vaincs, vainquons, vainquez.
Subj. Pres.	Que je vainque, etc., que nous vainquions, etc.
Imperf.	Que je vainquisse, etc., que nous vainquissions, etc.
Infin.	Vaincre.
Part.	Vainquant, vaincu, vaincue.

Conjugated with the auxiliary **avoir**.

Vivre (= to live).

Prim. Tenses. Vivre, vivant, vécu, je vis, je vécus.

Ind. Pres.	Je vis, tu vis, il vit, nous vivons, vous vivez, ils vivent.
Imperf.	Je vivais, etc., nous vivions, etc.
Past Def.	Je vécus, etc., nous vécûmes, etc.
Fut.	Je vivrai, etc., nous vivrons, etc.

THE PUBLIC SCHOOL FRENCH GRAMMAR.

Giving the latest Results of Modern Philology. (New edition.) 1 vol. small 8vo. 336 pages. Cloth. Price 2s. 6d. By A. BRACHET, Lauréat de l'Institut de France, and adapted for English Schools by the Rev. P. H. E. BRETTE, B.D., and GUSTAVE MASSON, B.A.

EXERCISES. ACCIDENCE.—PART I. Price 1s. 6d.
——————— SYNTAX.—PART II. (*In preparation.*)

KEY TO THE EXERCISES OF ACCIDENCE, by E. JANAU. For Teachers only, cloth, 1s. 6d
KEY TO THE EXERCISES OF SYNTAX, by E. JANAU. (In preparation.)

The present work cannot fail to be generally adopted for pupils who, having already a sufficient knowledge of Greek and Latin, are able to begin the study of French through the medium of comparative grammar.

Departing from the old routine of putting before children a mere series of rules of an apparently arbitrary character, and which can neither be explained or justified, M. BRACHET shows that historical philology accounts for every grammatical fact, whether rule or exception, and that even linguistic *bizarreries*, as we would deem them, have their *raison d'être*, if we only trace up modern French to its origins.

OPINIONS.

"The best grammar of the French language that has been published in England."—PROFESSOR ATTWELL.

"St. Luke's Middle Class School, Torquay.
" I have much pleasure in being able to compliment you on the publication of such an excellent work. The historical portion of the work is clearly brought out, and contains much valuable information. To all those accustomed to the preparation of our higher Examinations, such information is of the greatest importance, and I am sure it will be fully appreciated. The Transition from the Latin to the French of the present day is so clearly shown, that it reads more like a pleasing story than an exposition of grammar. The author has a happy knack of putting his details in a most interesting form; and he has certainly succeeded in proving that French Grammar is not so repulsive as some of the old cut-and-dried books make it. . . .—F. GARSIDE, M.A., *Head-Master*."

"Uppingham School.
" C'est bien certainement l'ouvrage le plus complet et le plus sérieux de ce genre écrit en anglais.—DR. L. PARROT."

"University College, Aberystwyth.
" The French Grammar seems to me thoroughly to justify its title, and to be one well fitted to be adopted in our Public Schools. It seems to be particularly valuable for its rational explanations derived from historical philology of irregularites which have hitherto had to be accounted for very imperfectly and unsatisfactorily. The explanation too, given of the endings of the future, etc., is admirable.—H. N. GRIMLEY.

" The editors have doubtless sufficient reason for pinning their faith to M. Brachet's theory, although if we are not mistaken, his conclusions as to the small part played by the ancient dialects of Gaul in the formation of the French language are by no means unchallenged by etymologists of the present day. Any doubt on this point does not, however, prevent us from expressing our pleasure at the appearance of a book which, while retaining much of the suggestiveness of M. Brachet's work, is put into a form more suitable for our schools. We would give emphatic approval to the chapters upon the formation of substantives, adjectives, and auxiliary verbs, in which the origin of each termination is clearly explained."—*Academy*, Sept. 9, 1876.

" *The last and most scientific French grammar we know has just been published by Hachette & Co.* It is entitled 'The Public School French Grammar,' by A. Brachet, adapted for English use by Dr. Brette and M. Gustave Masson. The Etymology and the Syntax are specially good, and the entire volume is admirable."—*The Freeman*.

"'The Public School French Grammar' is a work of a very different stamp. We will not say that it is the ideal French Grammar, because, as we have already hinted, we do not believe in such a thing; but it is as good as any that we have seen. It is based on the researches of M. Brachet, that is of M. Littré, and aims at giving a rational account of the formation of inflexions and growth of forms in modern French by the help of their analogues in Latin."—*Athenæum*, August 19, 1876

THE PHILOLOGY OF THE FRENCH LANGUAGE.

By A. L. MEISSNER, Ph.D.,
Professor of Modern Languages in the Queen's University in Ireland.

New and cheaper edition of the Author's Palæstra Gallica. With an Appendix of Specimens of Old French, from the 9th to the 15th Century, and a set of Examination Questions.
1 vol., small 8vo. cloth. Price 3s.

"On ne peut que donner des éloges à la manière dont l'auteur a compris et exécuté son travail."—GASTON PARIS, *Revue Critique.*

"Nous voyons avec satisfaction l'Histoire et la Grammaire scientifique de notre langue désormais représentées dans la littérature scolaire de l'Angleterre par ce recommendable manuel."—H. GAIDOZ, *Revue de l'Instruction Publique.*

"The Professor of Modern Languages in the Queen's University presents in this text-book the groundwork of his lectures in Queen's College, Belfast; and a good solid foundation it is, on which both lecturers and students may build with safety. Of course it is not, nor is it intended to be, light reading. The author's object is not to exhibit the results of modern philology in an attractive form for popular readers, but rather to supply materials of thought and suggestive hints to those who wish to acquire a philological knowledge of the French language in its successive stages.... Beginning with a brief but excellent account of the origin of modern French—including an accurate survey of the several characteristic distinctions between the Romance languages and the parent Latin, and a description of the three dialects of the Langue d'Oïl—he proceeds to set forth under the head of "Phonology" the various changes of letters which have taken place in passing from one period to another. The remainder of the work is devoted to "Morphology," or an account of the formation of words by the modification or addition of syllables or the composition of words. The forms assumed by verbs at different periods of the language are clearly and fully set forth. By way of illustration the etymology of many words is explained—of some more than once, because they happen to be instances of more than one general principle—which is no bad thing, and is far better than giving derivations in an isolated way without pointing out the law to which they conform."—*Athenæum.*

"A well-written and thoughtful treatise on the history and philology of the French language, scholarly in its tone and treatment, and full of valuable information on many of the most interesting points of comparative grammar. Though primarily intended for advanced students following a course of college lectures or preparing for some of the higher competitive examinations, it may be used with great advantage in the upper forms of our public schools."—*Educational Times.*

"This book supplies a want which has long been felt. The French language is at present learned too much as a mere matter of rote, and the pupil knows nothing of the formation and history of the language. Dr. Meissner's work supplies this information in a satisfactory manner. It is scholarly, accurate, and thorough. It is a work which ought to be used in all schools where Latin is taught, and it will be read with much interest and much profit alike by those who teach French and those who teach Latin. The book has only to be known to come into extensive use."—*Museum.*

PERINI, N.

ONE HUNDRED QUESTIONS AND EXERCISES ON THE GRAMMAR OF THE FRENCH LANGUAGE. Second edition. Price 2s.

The above work, now in the hands of all candidates preparing for examinations, contains all the most important questions on the Grammar of the French Language. Each question is followed by a blank, for the answer thereto.

QUERIES ON THE PHILOLOGY OF THE FRENCH LANGUAGE.
Price 1s. 6d. A sequel to the above work.

ROULIER, A.

SYNOPSIS OF FRENCH GRAMMAR. 48 pages, small 8vo. Cloth Price 6d.

a

FRENCH COMPOSITION.

The First Book of French Composition.
Materials for Translating English into French, for Elementary Classes.
By A. ROULIER,
Fellow Univ. Gallic.
1 vol., small 8vo, cloth. Third edition, entirely revised. Price 1s. 6d.
Adopted by the School Board for London.

This work is designed for beginners, and may be put into the hands of any person knowing the elementary rules concerning substantives, articles, and adjectives, and the conjugation of regular verbs.

The Second Book of French Composition.
By A. ROULIER.
1 vol., small 8vo., cloth, 278 pages. Price 3s.

The Children's Own Book of French Composition.
A Series of Easy Exercises on Idiomatic Construction, adapted for the use of Young People.
By EMILE D'AUQUIER.
With a Preface by JULES BUÉ, M.A., &c. Price 1s. 6d.
Can be used in Conjunction with the "Children's Own French Book."
1 vol., small 8vo., cloth. 200 pages.

OPINIONS OF THE PRESS.

"It seems a good idea, and might produce satisfactory results if carefully worked out."—*Educational Times*, July 1st.

"The process of instruction resembles that by which an English child would learn to speak French on being transferred very early to a French home."—*School Board Chronicle*, June 16th.

"The learner will find this a very useful companion in his early French studies."—*The Schoolmaster*, June 30th.

Half-Hours of French Translation;
OR,
Extracts from the best English Authors to be rendered into French; and also passages translated from contemporary French Writers to be retranslated. Arranged progressively, with idiomatic notes.
By ALPHONSE MARIETTE, M.A.
Professor and Examiner of the French Language and Literature at King's College, London.
New Edition. 1 vol., small 8vo., 392 pages cloth, price 4s. 6d.
KEY TO THE SAME.
1 vol. small 8vo, 300 pages. Cloth, price 6s.

LE VERBE.

A complete Treatise on French Conjugation.

COMPREHENDING

1st.—The Auxiliary and Regular Verbs.

2nd.—The Passive, Reflective, Neuter, and Impersonal Verb

3rd.—The Irregular and Peculiar Verbs.

4th.—The Defective Verbs.

By EMILE WENDLING, B.A.,

Lecturer and Examiner at Durham University.

Third Edition, revised, improved, and considerably enlarged.

Cloth, price 1s. 6d.

To the first edition which appeared last year, many additions and improvements have been made, such as a chapter on verbs conjugated negatively, interrogatively, and interrogatively negatively, and an excellent chapter on the formation of tenses. The book may safely be recommended to those who study French, to be gone through systematically; those who are already conversant with that language will find it a very useful book of reference.—*Eastern Morning News*, April 26th, 1875.

Vous avez mis devant l'élève d'une manière complète et claire les difficultés de nos verbes irréguliers. Je pense que votre livre sera un puissant aide pour le maître avec des élèves de peu de dispositions.—Ch. Delhavé, Manchester Grammar School.

Vous avez rendu les règles claires et simples, c'est-à-dire que vous avez atteint le but que doit se proposer tout grammairien.—B. Buisson, Charterhouse.

Je viens de parcourir vos tableaux. Je les trouve très-clairs et admirablement imprimés.—Alfred G. Havet.

Le traité sur les verbes est fort clair et très-complet. La forme adoptée permet de trouver sans difficulté le renseignement qu'on veut chercher et rien n'est omis de ce qu'il importe de savoir.—Th. Karcher.

JULLIEN, B., Docteur ès Lettres, etc.,

MANUEL DE LA CONJUGAISON DES VERBES.

1 vol., small 8vo, Cart.   Price 1s

FRENCH VERB COPY BOOKS.

PERINI, N.
FIVE AND TWENTY EXERCISES on two hundred French Verbs. Paper covers, price 6d.

The above work is intended to meet a want long felt in English schools. The plan of the book is very simple, and yet it goes thoroughly into the subject. It possesses, moreover, the great advantage of entirely relieving the teacher of the tiresome and laborious task of setting verbs to conjugate.

A KEY to the above work sold to teachers only. Price 1s.

PINOT DE MOIRA.
FRENCH VERB COPY-BOOK. 24 pages in Paper Wrapper. Third edition. Price 8d.

That this little work has gone within a very short time through two editions is, perhaps, the best recommendation for its usefulness.

ROULIER, A,
French Master at Charterhouse School.

HACHETTE'S FRENCH PARSING AND DERIVATION PAPER. Price per dozen sheets (24 forms) 1s.

Hachette's Modern Dialogues.
FAMILIAR AND PROGRESSIVE.
At 1s. 6d. per Volume.

ENGLISH AND FRENCH DIALOGUES. By RICHARD and QUÉTIN, with Dialogues on Railway and Steamboat Travelling, and a Comparative Table of Monies and Measures. New edition, carefully revised by the Rev. P. H. ERNEST BRETTE, B.D., Head-Master of the French School, Christ's Hospital, London; and GUSTAVE MASSON, B.A., Assistant Master of Harrow School, Examiners in the University of London.

"Messrs. Brette and Masson have issued a carefully-revised edition of Richard and Quétin's familiar and progressive English and French Dialogues. In its improved shape the little work cannot fail to prove extremely useful." *School Board Chronicle,* July 1, 1871. *(Adopted by the School Board for London.)*

ENGLISH AND GERMAN. New edition, Revised, Corrected, and Augmented. With a Comparative Table of the New Monies and Measures. By RICHARD and KAUB.

(Adopted by the School Board for London.)

ENGLISH AND SPANISH. By RICHARD and LARAN. New edition Revised, Corrected, and Augmented.

NEW WORD BOOKS.

Price 6d. per Volume.

ENGLISH AND FRENCH. By RICHARD and QUÉTIN. Cloth, 96 pages.

ENGLISH AND GERMAN. By RICHARD and KAUB. Cloth, 80 pages

A NEW ETYMOLOGICAL FRENCH WORD BOOK,
English and French,
together with the Derivations of the French Words.

Edited by V. KASTNER, M.A., Officier d'Académie.

[*In preparation.*]

OUTLINES OF FRENCH LITERATURE
Leading Facts and Typical Characters.
A SHORT GUIDE TO FRENCH LITERATURE.
With Two Chronological Tables, an Index, &c.
Cloth, price 1s. 6d.

The *Outlines* are intended to meet the wants of two classes of Students namely, those who have not yet formed an intimate acquaintance with French Literature, and those who, in view of an Examination, wish to take a brief survey of the ground over which they have travelled.

Beginners will have their attention arrested by those authors and literary events with which everyone should be familiar, *whilst the table of suggested readings, at the end of the volume, contains a list of the typical masterpieces best calculated to serve as a foundation for more extended studies.*

" Mr. Gustave Masson's ' Outlines of French Literature ' contains a great amount of information in very small space. His book is trustworthy, and is capable of being very useful as an introduction to the study of French literature.—*Scotsman.*

" Primers and *résumés* are now so completely the order of the day that M. Masson's 'Outlines' will no doubt be welcomed as a matter of course. The present little work does not aim at anything beyond a syllabus which pupils may develop at leisure, and which can likewise be used as a memento by students who wish to take in without difficulty the leading facts and typical characters in the history of French intellectual life. The chronological table which follows the 'Outlines' contains every date of importance, and the list of suggested readings given from the programme issued by the authority of the Minister of Public Instruction in Paris, will prove of much service to all those who, having little spare time at their disposal, want to be directed at once to the best authors and the most noteworthy productions. M. Masson's volume is, so far as we are aware, the first attempt of the kind, and its elementary character commends it specially to the notice of School Board teachers."—*School Board Chronicle.*

CLASS-BOOK OF COMPARATIVE IDIOMS.

ENGLISH PART. By JULES BUÉ, Honorary M.A., of Oxford; Taylorian Teacher of French, Oxford; Examiner in the Oxford Local Examinations from 1858; and W. COLLETT SANDARS, Taylorian Exhibitioner, Oxford. New Edition. 1 vol., small 8vo. cloth, 2s.

FRENCH PART. Exercices sur les Formes Idiomatiques Comparées. New Edition. Cloth, 2s.

GERMAN PART. By Dr. Th. Wehe and A. Lennheim. Cloth, price 2s.

"A great improvement upon the old-fashioned conversation books which have tried the patience of generations of students. The idiomatic expressions in which the French and English languages abound are freely introduced into the dialogues, and the student has thus the opportunity of becoming easily acquainted with the principal points of difference between the two tongues."—*Public Opinion.*

"As a means for perfecting one's acquaintance with the idiomatic peculiarities both of English and French, and the difference of construction between them, the above volumes are the very best that could possibly be contrived. The rules are so simply stated that a mere child will easily comprehend them, and by fixing them, no less than the idioms themselves, in the memory, become thoroughly au fait as to conversation."—*Bell's Weekly Messenger.*

"The 'Class-Book of Comparative Idioms' recently issued by Messrs. Hachette, is intended to supersede the ordinary dialogues which are so extensively used in schools at the present day. The French phrases and their English equivalents being printed in separate volumes, the reader will be able to employ with great advantage the materials thus placed within his reach, either for *viva voce* instruction or as subjects for written translations; and particular care has been taken to exclude obsolete, unusual, or slang expressions."—*Saturday Review.*

CLASS-BOOK OF FRENCH CORRESPONDENCE.

VOL. I.—COMMERCIAL CORRESPONDENCE. By A. RAGON, French Master at the City of London College.

PART I.—General forms; Circulars; Offers of Service; Letters of Introduction, and Letters of Credit. Price 2s.

PART II. (*In preparation*).

DURING FOUR *successive* Years the pupils of Mons. Ragon, from the City of London College, have obtained the FIRST FRENCH PRIZES (of £5) from the Society of Arts; and this year his pupils had, out of the 125 Certificates given by the Society for French, 56 awarded to them, with the first and second prizes, and also the first prize to Ladies, and none but his pupils had the 7 first-class Commercial Certificates that were granted. In these Examinations the Members of upwards of 180 Institutions in all parts of the Kingdom compete.

Vol. II.—GENERAL CORRESPONDENCE. By H. J. V. DE CANDOLE, Ph.D., M.A., French Master at Clifton College. 1 vol., small 8vo., cloth. Price 2s.

CHOICE READINGS
FROM FRENCH HISTORY.
Edited, with Notes, Indices, Glossary, &c.
By GUSTAVE MASSON.

The following series of extracts will be found to differ considerably from the usual compilation of the *morceaux choisis*. The object of the Editor has been to reprint and annotate several pieces which may answer the purpose, not only of illustrating the progress of French litterature, but also of bringing out in strong relief certain episodes and characters in the political annals of our neighbours on the other side of the Channel. It is hoped that the "readings" thus taken from the pages of authors who could say of the events they describe: *quorum pars magna fui*, may be useful both from the historical and the literary point of view. Students will be able to follow almost step by step the development of the language, and, at the same time, to form a correct estimate of the brilliant gallery of memoirs and autobiographies which have contributed so much to the glory of France.

The most accurate texts are invariably used, and copious notes, indices, and glossaries explain every detail, historical or philological, requiring elucidation.

Part I.—FROM RONCEVAUX TO MONTLHÉRY (778—1465).
1 vol. small 8vo, with a Map. Cloth, 2s. 6d.
Indispensable to all Students preparing for the higher Examinations.

Part II.—FROM FORNOVO TO ROCROY (1495—1643).
[*In preparation.*]

Part III.—FROM LENS TO WATERLOO (1648—1815).
[*In preparation.*]

LIST OF WORKS WHICH HAVE SUPPLIED EXTRACTS FOR PART I.

La Chanson de Roland (edit. GAUTIER).—**La Chanson d'Antioche** (edit. PAULIN PARIS).—**Poëme de la Croisade contre les Albigeois** (edit. G. MEYER).—**Villehardouin** (edit. DE WAILLY).—**Aucassin et Nicolette**—**Joinville** (edit. DE WAILLY).—**Froissart** (edit. LUCE).—**Commines** (edit. DUPONT).—**Gringore** (edit. DAFFIS).—**Guillaume de Tyr.**—**Cousinot.**—**Le Ménestrel de Reims.**—**Mathieu d'Escouchy.**—**Lefèvre de Saint Rémy.**—**Chronique de Duguesclin.**

"M. GUSTAVE MASSON has been well advised in drawing up a short volume of selections from old French history to serve at once as a reading book and a historical manual. It is to be hoped that the little book may be widely used, for its intrinsic merit is great, and the delusion (almost as prevalent in France as in England) that old French is an unreadable jargon cannot be too soon removed. The selections are made very judiciously, and for the most part from the best extst."—(*Saturday Review.*)

"The CHOICE READINGS, by M. GUSTAVE MASSON, is a book we can recommend with unusual pleasure. It consists of specimens of French literature, historical rather than imaginative, extending from the eleventh century to the end of the fifteenth, and including the famous 'Chanson de Roland,' the 'Roman de Rou,' by Wace, extracts from Froissart, and other *pièces historiques*, which would seldom fall in the way of an ordinary reader. Senior pupils, male or female, will thus be able to study the progressive modifications in the French language, at the same time that they learn something of French history. We have seldom seen a book of which, in its class, we approve so highly."—(*Literary Churchman.*)

"M. Masson's 'Choice Readings from French History, from Roncevaux to Montlhéry' (Hachette), is a scholarly book. Beginning with that stock quotation, the oath of Louis the Germanic, it goes on to the song of Roland, and cites from the Roman de Rou the destruction of Mantes by William the Conqueror. There are extracts from the Chronicle of Ernoul; from Froissart, of course; from De Montreuil's Chronicle of Joan of Arc, the last extract being Villon's ballad-epitaph on himself and those who were to be hanged along with him. The notes are full, and the glossary is a treasure of old French. The map shows the state of the country at the accession of the Valois. Altogether the book is one of the best we ever saw of the kind."—(*Graphic*).

"Illustrates mediæval literature in a very interesting way."—(*Daily Chronicle*).

FRENCH POETRY FOR ENGLISH SCHOOLS.

La Lyre des Enfants.
FRENCH NURSERY RHYMES, POEMS, ROUNDS, AND RIDDLES,
For Schools and Families.
With Explanatory Notes by C. B.
The entire contents of the Volume are not only easy but amusing.
1 vol. small 8vo. cloth. Price 1s.

Class-Book of French Poetry for the Young.
By PAUL BARBIER,
One of the French Masters at the Manchester Grammar School.
One vol. small 8vo. cloth. Price 1s.

In selecting these pieces of French Poetry for the use of Children between seven and twelve years of age, I have ever had in view the purity and simplicity of the language. Notes have been thought to be superfluous. Those using the book will notice how careful I have been not to sacrifice art for the purpose of suiting the class of children for whom the book is intended. Most of the pieces, whether narratives, fables, or subjective effusions, contain moral lessons inculcating in the learner principles of honesty, probity, truth, or gratitude towards God.

Recueil de Poésies pour les Jeunes Filles.
PAR MME. DE WITT
(*née* GUIZOT).
1 vol. small 8vo. 320 pages. Price 2s.

J'ai eu entre les mains plusieurs choix de poésies destinés aux jeunes filles; aucun ne m'a jamais pleinement satisfaite. Comme les recueils du même genre composés pour les colléges, ceux-là visent uniquement à faire connaître aux jeunes personnes la littérature classique de notre langue, classiques de tous les siècles et de tous les genres, il est vrai, mais dans le choix desquels on n'a pas tenu assez compte des goûts particuliers, des tendances et des besoins d'imagination de la jeunesse. On veut orner sa mémoire, on ne cherche pas à éveiller le sentiment du beau, et à diriger dans la bonne voie ce noble désir de l'admiration si profondément empreint dans les âmes bien nées.

C'est là précisément ce que j'ai tenté de faire dans le volume que j'offre ici aux mères et aux filles.

Graduated French Readers.

THE ELEMENTARY FRENCH READER. A collection of short interesting and instructive stories for beginners, adapted for use in Middle-Class Schools, &c., with a complete French-English Vocabulary. Edited by ELPHÉGE JANAU, French Master at Blackheath Proprietary School. New Edition. Price 8d.

At the request of several leading members of the Scholastic Profession, I have undertaken to compile an Elementary French Reader, suitable, on account of its price and contents, to Middle-Class and other Schools. The matter contained in this book will afford ample scope for the teacher to exercise his pupils in conversation and elementary translation, while the bold type chosen will make it more pleasant to read.

The Vocabulary gives every word in the text, the plural of nouns and adjectives (when formed otherwise than by the addition of *s*), and the feminine of all adjectives, thus avoiding the use of a dictionary. For purposes of reference, I have added a list of regular and irregular verbs.

I trust this little volume will answer the purpose I had in view when compiling it, and meet with the approbation of Teachers.

(*Adopted by the School Board for London.*)

THE INFANTS' OWN FRENCH BOOK. Very short Stories adapted for quite Young Children, and printed in large type. With a complete French-English Vocabulary. Edited by E. JANAU. Small 8vo., cloth, price 1s.

HACHETTE'S CHILDREN'S OWN FRENCH BOOK. A Selection of amusing and instructive Stories in Prose, adapted to the use of very young people. Edited by the Rev. P. H. E. BRETTE, B.D., and GUSTAVE MASSON, B.A., of Harrow. Fifteenth edition. 1 vol., small 8vo. 216 pages, cloth 1s. 6d.

(*Adopted by the School Board for London.*)

HACHETTE'S FIRST FRENCH READER. Adapted to the use of young people. Sixty-sixth Thousand. 1 vol., small 8vo., 400 pages, cloth 2s. Edited by the Rev. P. H. E. BRETTE, B.D., and GUSTAVE MASSON, B.A., of Harrow.

"One of the most popular educational works in this country."—*Weekly Review.* (*Adopted by the School Board for London.*)

HACHETTE'S SECOND FRENCH READER. Edited by HENRY TARVER, of Eton College. New Edition. 1 vol. small 8vo. cloth, price 1s. 6d. (*Adopted by the School Board for London.*)

HACHETTE'S THIRD FRENCH READER. By B. BUISSON, M.A., First French Master at Charterhouse. 1 vol. small 8vo. cloth, 2s.

The four first Readers are supplemented by a Vocabulary; the two last by Elucidatory Notes.

SERIES OF MODERN FRENCH AUTHORS.

Vol. I.—EDMOND ABOUT. Edited by the Rev. P. H. E. Brette, B.D., of Christ's Hospital, and Gustave Masson, B.A., of Harrow. New edition. 1 vol. small 8vo. cloth, 2s.

"The present collection is the best and most amusing ever published in England."—*Bristol Times.*

"The result is a book which we would at once put in the hands of our daughter, and bid her study it thoroughly."—*Weekly Review.*

"There can be no hesitation in earnestly recommending the immediate adoption of this book in every collegiate institution and public school throughout the country."—*Bell's Weekly Messenger.*

"The work can hardly be too highly commended for its interest, instructiveness, and cheapness."—*Athenæum.*

Vol. II.—PAUL LACOMBE. Petite Histoire du Peuple Français. With Grammatical and Explanatory Notes by Jules Bué. Honorary M.A., Oxford. 1 vol. small 8vo. New edition. Price 2s.

Vol. III.—TÖPFFER. Edited by the Rev. P. H. E. Brette, B.D., and Gustave Masson, B.A., of Harrow. Contents: Histoire de Charles; Histoire de Jules. 1 vol. small 8vo. 112 pages, cloth, 1s.

Vol. IV.—MAD. DE WITT, née GUIZOT.—DERRIÈRE LES HAIES. One of the most interesting of the well-known "Historical Pictures," Mme. de Witt relates in this story the Vendean War, 1793-1794. Edited by Paul de Bussy, B.-ès-L. New edition. Price 2s.

Vol. V.—VILLEMAIN.—LASCARIS, OU LES GRECS DU XVe SIÈCLE Nouvelle Historique, with a Biographical Sketch of the Author, and a Selection of Poems on Greece. Edited by A. Dupuis, B.A. Price 1s. 6d.

Vol. VI.—ALFRED DE MUSSET. Edited by Gustave Masson, B.A. Cloth, price 2s.

Vol. VII.—PONSARD.—LE LION AMOUREUX. Edited by H. J. V. de Candole, M.A., Ph.D. of Clifton College. Cloth, price 2s.

Vol. VIII.—GUIZOT. Guillaume le Conquérant ou l'Angleterre sous les Normands. (1027-1087.) Edited by A. J. Dubourg, Principal French Master in Liverpool College. Cloth, price 2s.

VOL. IX.—GUIZOT. Alfred le Grand ou l'Angleterre sous les Anglo-Saxons. By H. LALLEMAND, B-ès-Sc., Owens' College. Cloth, price 2s. 6d.

VOL. X.—CHATEAUBRIAND. Les Aventures du dernier Abencerage. By A. ROULIER, B.A., Charterhouse. Cloth, price 1s.

VOL. XI.—SCRIBE, EUGÈNE.—BERTRAND ET RATON, OU L'ART de Conspirer. Comédie en 5 actes et en prose. Edited with Grammatical, Philological, and Explanatory Notes, by JULES BUÉ, Hon. M.A. of Oxford, Taylorian Teacher of French, Oxford; Examiner in the Oxford Local Examinations, etc. Cloth, price 1s. 6d.

VOL. XII.—BONNECHOSE, ÉMILE DE.—LAZARE HOCHE. Seventh Edition. Edited, with Grammatical and Explanatory Notes, and an Index of the Historical and Geographical Names, by HENRI BUÉ, B.-ès-L. Cloth, price 2s.

VOL. XIII.—PRESSENSÉ, MAD. E. DE.—ROSA. Edited, with Grammatical and Explanatory Notes, by GUSTAVE MASSON, B.A., Officier d'Académie, etc. Cloth, price 2s.

VOL. XIV.—MÉRIMÉE, PROSPER.—COLOMBA. Edited, with Grammatical and Explanatory Notes, by the Rev. P. H. E. BRETTE, B.D., Examiner in the University of London. Cloth, price 2s.

VOL. XV.—XAVIER DE MAISTRE.—UN VOYAGE AUTOUR DE ma Chambre. With Grammatical and Explanatory Notes for the use of Schools, by JULES BUÉ, Hon. M.A. of Oxford, Taylorian Teacher of French, Oxford; Examiner in the Oxford Local Examinations, etc. Cloth, price 1s.

VOL. XVI.—D'AUBIGNÉ.—HISTOIRE DE BAYART. Numerous Illustrations and a Map. Edited, with Grammatical and Explanatory Notes, for the use of Schools, by JULES BUÉ, Hon. M.A. of Oxford, Taylorian Teacher of French, Oxford, etc. Cloth, price 2s.

VOL. XVII.—SAINTINE.—PICCIOLA. Edited, with Grammatical and Explanatory Notes, by PAUL BAUME, Professor of the French Language and Literature, formerly of the Royal Military College, Sandhurst, Graduate, etc. Book I. Cloth, price 1s. 6d.

VOL. XVIII.—Do., do., Book II., edited by the same. Cloth, price 1s. 6d. Or VOLS. XVII. and XVIII., *bound in One Volume*. Price 2s. 6d.

[*Other Volumes in preparation.*]

HACHETTE'S FRENCH CLASSICS,

AND

"CHEFS-D'ŒUVRE DU THÉATRE FRANÇAIS."

UNDER the above title Messrs. Hachette issue a series of the best French plays, belonging to the classical and also to the modern or *romantique* schools. Each dramatic work is carefully annotated, and preceded by a critical and biographical introduction. The list will ultimately include not only the acknowledged master-pieces of Molière, Corneille, and Racine, but choice specimens from the writings of Beaumarchais, Piron, Regnard, Voltaire, Marivaux, &c., &c.

The volumes will be edited by some of the most eminent French Masters in this country.

Price per Volume, 6d.; in cloth, 1s.

SERIES I.

BRUEYS.

L'AVOCAT PATELIN. Edited by GUSTAVE MASSON, B.A., of Harrow The appendix to this volume contains several long extracts from the mediæval "Farce de Maistre Pathelin," and will thus prove useful to the students of old French literature.

CORNEILLE.

LE CID. By JULES BUÉ, M.A., of Oxford.
CINNA. By HENRY TARVER, of Eton.
HORACE. By the Rev. P. H. E. BRETTE, B.D., of Christ's Hospital.
POLYEUCTE. By GUSTAVE MASSON, B.A., of Harrow.
LE MENTEUR. By B. BUISSON, M.A., Charterhouse.
LA SUITE DU MENTEUR. By A. DUPUIS, B.A., King's College School.

MOLIERE.

L'AVARE. By GUSTAVE MASSON, B.A., of Harrow.
LE BOURGEOIS GENTILHOMME. By FRANCIS TARVER, M.A., of Eton.
LES FEMMES SAVANTES. By A. ROCHE, Director of the "Educational Institute" in London.
LES FOURBERIES DE SCAPIN. By H. J. V. DE CANDOLE, M.A. Ph.D., of Clifton College.
LE MALADE IMAGINAIRE. By A. E. RAGON, City of London College.
LE MEDECIN MALGRE LUI. By H. LALLEMAND, B.-ès-Sc., of Owens' College, Manchester.
LE MISANTHROPE. By the Rev. P. H. E. BRETTE, B.D.
LES PRECIEUSES RIDICULES. By A. DUPUIS, B.A.
TARTUFFE. By JULES BUÉ, M.A., of Oxford.

MUSSET, ALFRED DE.

ON NE SAURAIT PENSER A TOUT. By GUSTAVE MASSON, B.A. of Harrow.
IL FAUT QU'UNE PORTE SOIT OUVERTE OU FERMÉE. By GUSTAVE MASSON, B.A., of Harrow.

RACINE.

ANDROMAQUE. By Henry Tarver, of Eton.
ATHALIE. By the Rev. P. H. E. Brette, B.D., of Christ's Hospital.
BRITANNICUS. By Gustave Masson, B.A., of Harrow.
ESTHER. By A. Roche, Esq.
IPHIGENIE. By Jules Bué, M.A., of Oxford.
PHÈDRE. By Henri Bué, B.-ès-Sc., of Merchant Taylors' School, London.
LES PLAIDEURS. By Francis Tarver, M.A., of Eton.

VOLTAIRE.

MEROPE. By Charles Delhavé, B.-ès-L.
ZAÏRE. By Paul de Bussy, B.-ès-L.

SERIES II.

CORNEILLE.

LE CID. Translated into English Blank Verse by Walter Nokes. 1 vol. small 8vo., bound 3s. 6d.
HORACE. Translated into English Blank Verse by Walter Nokes. 1 vol. small 8vo. Paper wrapper, 2s. 6d., bound 3s. 6d.

LA FONTAINE.

FABLES. With Grammatical, Explanatory, and Etymological Notes, by Francis Tarver, M.A., Oxon; French Master at Eton College. New edition. 1 vol. small 8vo., 450 pages, cloth, 2s.

THEODORE LECLERCQ.

PROVERBES DRAMATIQUES.
L'HUMORISTE; ou, Comme on fait son lit on se couche. LA JOURNÉE DIFFICILE; ou, Aide-toi, le ciel t'aidera. With English Notes by H. J. Browne, French Master at St. Charles's College, Bayswater. Cloth, price 1s.
Excellently adapted for private theatricals.
"Plus d'un proverbe de M. Théodore Leclercq n'est qu'un caractère de la Bruyère développé, étendu, mis en action. L'HUMORISTE, par exemple, est un petit chef-d'œuvre de ce genre."—*Sainte-Beuve.*

PIRON.

LA METROMANIE. By Francis Tarver, M.A., of Eton. Price 1s., cloth, 1s. 6d.
A celebrated critic has said of this piece: "Piron semble avoir écrit LA MÉTROMANIE devant quelque image de Molière, les yeux fixés sur les traits du contemplateur, interrogeant sur l'art de créer un caractère."

PONSARD.

LE LION AMOUREUX. Edited by H. J. V. de Candole, M.A., Ph.D. (Vol. VII. of Modern Readers.) Price 1s. 6d., cloth 2s.

SCRIBE, E.

BERTRAND ET RATON ou l'Art de conspirer. Edited by Jules Bué, Hon. M.A. of Oxford; Taylorian Teacher of French, Oxford, &c. Cloth, price 1s. 6d.

VOLTAIRE.

HISTOIRE DE CHARLES XII. Edited by Gustave Masson, B.A. of Harrow, with a Map of Central Europe. 1 vol. small 8vo., price, 2s

VOLTAIRE.

SIÈCLE DE LOUIS XIV. Chapitres I — XIII. Edition Classique accompagnée d'une Carte de la France à la mort de Louis XIV, et d'une Notice sur le Siècle de Louis XIV, et de Notes par A. GARNIER; with Grammatical and Explanatory English Notes, and an Index of Historical and Geographical Names by VICTOR OGER. New Edition. 1 vol., small 8vo. 280 pages. Price 2s.

SIÈCLE DE LOUIS XIV. Chapitres XIV—XXIV. Edition Classique accompagnée de deux Cartes. Edited, with Grammatical and Explanatory Notes, and an Index of Historical and Geographical Names, by V. KASTNER, M.A. Cloth. Price 2s.

OPINIONS OF THE PRESS.

" Messrs. Hachette are rendering a service to education by publishing this excellent series of French Classics. . . . . We cannot doubt that the series will meet with a hearty welcome from both teachers and pupils, and give an impulse to the study of the best French writers in this country."—*Athenæum.*

" We have not met with works of the class executed with equal care, system, and intelligence."—*Sunday Times.*

" The names of the editors are a sufficient guarantee of the excellence of these volumes."—*Weekly Review.*

" We call attention to each of these publications for the purpose of showing how admirably they are adapted for the improvement of our young men and women in the acquirement of the French language."—*Bell's Weekly Messenger.*

" Cette collection mérite réellement de trouver dans le public anglais un grand nombre de lecteurs."—*Revue Anglo-Française.*

" These gentlemen have all done their work as might be expected from their acquirements and professional experience."—*The Times,* February 25, 1873.

" To all who are interested in the study of French we heartily commend a series of School Books published by Hachette & Co., and edited by Rev. P. H. E. Brette, B.D., by Gustave Masson, B.A., by A. Roche, and F. Tarver, and others. The volumes published are all classic. The texts are most carefully edited, with grammatical and explanatory notes. There are plays of Molière, Racine, and Corneille, and some capital extracts from Edmond About, which are rich in modern idioms. For cheapness, practicalness, and trustworthiness the volumes cannot be too highly commended."—*The Freeman.*

" Mr. Charles Delhavé, of Manchester, has produced an excellent edition of Voltaire's 'Mérope,' which has been published by Messrs. Hachette in their valuable French Educational Series. Mr. Delhavé's notes give the English rendering of every passage which is likely to puzzle readers who are not thorough masters of the French language, while the model style of the original renders the little volume an invaluable school book."—*The Warrington Examiner,* April 29, 1876.

Ouvrages reçus en Dépôt.
LE THÉATRE FRANÇAIS DU XIXE SIECLE.

Publié par une société d'éminents professeurs de la littérature française en Angleterre.

Price per Vol. 9d.; in Cloth, 1s.; or each Series bound in One Vol., 3s. 6d.

SÉRIE I.

1. **Hugo**, *Hernani*, by GUSTAVE MASSON, B.A., Harrow School, Examiner in the University of London.
2. **Scribe**, *Le Verre d'Eau*, by JULES BUÉ, M.A., Taylorian Teacher of French, Oxford.
3. **Delavigne**, *Les Enfants d'Edouard*, by FRANCIS TARVER, M.A., Eton College.
4. **Bouilly**, *l'Abbé De l'Epée*, by V. KASTNER, M.A., Queen's College and Charterhouse School.

SÉRIE II.

5. **Mélesville et Duveyrier**, *Michel Perrin*, by GUSTAVE MASSON, B.A., Harrow School.
6. **Sandeau**, *Mademoiselle de la Seiglière*, by H. J. V. DE CANDOLE, M.A., Ph.D., French Lecturer, University College, Bristol, and of Clifton College.
7. **Scribe**, *Le Diplomate*, by A. RAGON, City of London College.
8. **Dumas**, *Les Demoiselles de Saint-Cyr*, by FRANCIS TARVER, M.A., Eton College.

SÉRIE III.

9. **Lebrun**, *Marie Stuart*, by H. LALLEMAND, B.-ès-Sc., French Lecturer, Owen's College, Manchester.
10. **Labiche et Jolly**, *La Grammaire*, Comédie-Vaudeville, by G. PETILLEAU.
11. **Girardin (Mme. de)**, *la Joie fait Peur*, par L. J. V. GÉRARD, Esq., Leicester.
12. **Scribe**, *Valérie*, by A. ROULIER, B.A., Bedford College and Charterhouse School.

SÉRIE IV.

13. **Coppée**, *Le Luthier de Crémone*. Comédie, by Professor A. MARIETTE, M.A.
14. **Coppée**, *Le Trésor*. Comédie, by Professor A. MARIETTE, M.A.
15. **De Banville**, Th., *Gringoire*, Comédie, by HENRI BUÉ, B.-ès-L.
16. *In preparation.*

OTHER VOLUMES IN PREPARATION.

THE THÉATRE FRANÇAIS DU XIXe SIÈCLE will comprise the *chefs-d'œuvre* of AUGIER, BOUILLY, COPPÉE, DE BANVILLE, DELAVIGNE, DUMAS, VICTOR HUGO, LEBRUN, SANDEAU, SARDOU, SCRIBE, and others, carefully edited, and correctly and elegantly printed.

In no form can the French language as now spoken, its spirit and idioms, be studied to greater advantage than in the masterpieces of the contemporary French Drama. This fact almost every intelligent French teacher acknowledges.

The study of well-selected plays has the great advantage of bringing under the notice of the pupil a constant succession of well chosen idiomatic phrases. The pupil cannot help retaining a great number of such phrases, and acquires thus the gift of French Conversation much more rapidly than by reading extracts of stories.

Each play is preceded by a short critical notice, and accompanied by such notes as are indispensable, and a careful rendering of the most difficult expressions. Professors and Teachers may add such explanations as they consider desirable.

"The present series is strictly limited to the French dramatic literature of the nineteenth century, and the specimens now before us contrast very favourably with a similar series published in Germany. The notes are of a more ambitious character, though strictly limited to what is absolutely necessary; the material execution is infinitely superior, and the whole series will, no doubt, occupy a select and permanent position in the library of every student of modern French literature. . . . One of the chief advantages of the new recueil is that it accustoms the reader to colloquial French, and familiarises him with the idiomatic phrases and constructions now in use."—*School Board Chronicle.*

"Nearly all these plays, it will be seen, are by leaders of the revolt against the classic drama, and they embody in themselves sufficient explanation of the success of that revolt. Each play is given in the form of a handy little volume, and is carefully edited with notes. The series deserves the attention of students of the French language and literature."—*Scotsman.*

"Cheapness and good print are not the only attractive features of this edition; it has a preface, giving a short and clear sketch of the plot of the play, and notes explaining the various idioms, which prove such stumbling-blocks in the way of beginners."—*The Navy.*

XAVIER DE MAISTRE.
La Jeune Sibérienne; Le Lépreux de la Cité d'Aoste.

With a biographical sketch of the author, and grammatical and explanatory notes suitable for students preparing for Examination. By V. KASTNER, M.A., Officier d'Académie; Professor of French Literature in Queen's College, and one of the French Masters at the Charterhouse.

1 vol. 150 pages. Cloth, 1s. 6d.

SOUVESTRE, E.
Le Philosophe sous les Toits.
JOURNAL D'UN HOMME HEUREUX.

With Explanatory notes by JULES BUÉ, Hon. M.A. Oxford; Taylorian Teacher of French, Oxford; Examiner in the Oxford Local Examinations from 1858, etc.

1 vol. 232 pages. Cloth, price 1s. 6d.

MADAME E. DE PRESSENSÉ.
Rosa.

With grammatical and explanatory notes by GUSTAVE MASSON, B.A., Officier d'Académie; Assistant Master and Librarian, Harrow School; French Examiner at Charterhouse.

1 vol. 300 pages. Cloth, price 2s.

The difficulty of finding in the French language a really unexceptionable children's book is still often remarked; but Madame De Pressensé has, we believe, solved the problem. "Rosa" is a gem of its kind, and it is not too much to say that it would be impossible to select a volume combining a healthier religious and unsectarian tone with greater literary merit.

THE NEW GERMAN SERIES.

The attention of the Heads of Colleges and Schools is respectfully directed to this new Series of German School Books, which has been projected with a view to supply thoroughly reliable text-books edited by German scholars of the highest reputation, and at a price which will bring them within the reach of all. The Series comprises now :—

VOL. I.
The Illustrated German Primer.
Being the Easiest Introduction to the Study of German for all Beginners. Price 1s.

VOL. II.
The Children's Own German Book.
A Selection of Amusing and Instructive Stories in Prose. Edited by Dr. A. L. MEISSNER, Professor of Modern Languages in the Queen's University in Ireland. Small post 8vo, cloth, 1s. 6d. New Edition.

"We have not the slightest hesitation in saying that this is one of the very best educational works of the class to which it belongs, that has ever been published. It is a short and easy reading book, most cleverly adapted both for young and old beginners, consisting of most excellent German selections, yet so adapted as to be suited to pupils of the simplest comprehension. The first chapters contain subjects and words that are in everyday use, and the anecdotes those with which every English child being well acquainted, would consequently take double interest in discovering in a foreign tongue. The Vocabulary is very complete, and free from all perplexing abbreviations of grammatical definitions. There is one point of the utmost importance connected with this 'German Book' which gives it amost especial value, and should not by any means be overlooked, that its selections, from the first to the last page, are so cleverly made as to insure a most easy and comprehensive means of learning words and phrases that are prevalent in conversation ; so that, so soon as their meaning and use are ascertained, both young and old will find the gift of speaking in German facilitated to an extent that has never yet been obtained. We can therefore recommend the use of this book most warmly."—*Bell's Weekly Messenger*.

VOL. III.
The First German Reader.
A Selection of Episodes from German History, etc., etc. Edited by Dr. A. L. MEISSNER. Small post 8vo, cloth, 1s. 6d.

" The volume contains various extracts, arranged, as much as possible, progressively according to their difficulty. The first part contains a series of episodes from German history; the second, short stories and legends. This volume, moreover, has the especial advantage that whilst it instructs beginners by giving them an insight into the language, it cannot fail also to make them wish to become further acquainted with German literature."—*Bell's Weekly Messenger.*

VOL. IV.
The Second German Reader.
A Selection of Episodes from German Life, etc. Edited by Dr. A. L. MEISSNER. Small post 8vo, cloth, 1s. 6d.

Buchheim's Deutsche Prosa.

Two Volumes, sold separately.

VOL. V.

Schiller's Prosa.

Containing Selections from the Prose Works of Schiller, with Notes for English Students. By Dr. BUCHHEIM, Professor of the German Language and Literature, King's College, London. Small post 8vo, cloth, 2s. 6d.

VOL. VI.

Goethe's Prosa.

Containing Selections from the Prose Works of Goethe, with Notes for English Students. By Dr. BUCHHEIM. Small post 8vo, cloth, 2s. 6d.

VOL. VII.

Bué's Class-Book of Comparative Idioms.

German Part. Edited by Professor R. LENNHEIM, late German Master to H.R.H. the Prince Imperial; and Dr. Th. WEHE, Principal German Master in Dulwich College, and late Lecturer of German at King's College. Cloth, price 2s.

VOL. VIII.

Richard and Kaub's New English and German Dialogues.

New Edition, Revised and Corrected. With a Comparative Table of the new German Moneys, Weights, and Measures. Cloth, 32mo, Price 1s. 6d. *Adopted by the School Board for London.*

VOL. IX.

Richard and Kaub's New English and German Word Book.

Cloth, 32mo, 80 pages, price 6d.

VOL. X.

The First German Book.

GRAMMAR, CONVERSATION AND TRANSLATION.

With a List of useful Words to be committed to memory, and Two Vocabularies. By A. LEOPOLD BECKER, Foreign Language Master, Blundell's School, Tiverton. Cloth, 196 pages. Price 1s.

OPINIONS OF THE PRESS.

"It is not often that so perfectly satisfactory a first book as this comes in our way. Though it is strictly confined to the essential elements of the language, these are so clearly stated and so admirably arranged that, provided the lessons are, as the author requires, "thoroughly mastered," a good practical knowledge may be acquired. The classification of the nouns and verbs is at once theoretically correct and practically easy. The brief chapter explaining the philology of German and English, and that on the interchange of letters in the two languages, will be found interesting and useful. This neat little volume is printed in clear, bold type, and may be had for the moderate price of one shilling."—*The Athenæum*, October 9, 1880.

"'The First German Book' seems to combine simplicity with clearness in an admirable degree."—*Daily Chronicle*, October 9, 1880.

"This neat little volume is strictly confined to teaching the elements of the German Language, and will prove useful alike to pupils in middle-class schools and to the self-student, who will value it as a useful and acceptable pocket companion. The various lessons appear to have been prepared with as much simplicity as possible, the aim of the author being to ensure the success of the learner by easy and agreeable stages."—*The Exeter and Plymouth Gazette.*

"Mr. Becker is good on separable and inseparable prefixes; and we are glad that he gives a long vocabulary of words to be learnt by heart (which, by the way, he prints in English as well as in German character); the best German scholar we ever knew had laid his foundation by regularly learning sixty or eighty words a day."—*The Graphic.*

From C. S. BERE, M.A. (Oxford).

"The book is admirably constructed. It is gradual and simple, and does not overwhelm the young student at the outset of his study, with the many variations and exceptions with which each step is beset, but most of which need not be learnt till a fair acquaintance with a language has been attained. . . . The sentences for translation, in this book, are bright, natural, and not too numerous. . . . The short conversations (sometimes varied by the introduction of proverbs and familiar sayings) are also in natural language. They are such as are likely to take place, and not imaginary ones, which no one ever dreamt of using.

"A good *Vocabulary* is added, and the book itself is very handy and easily used. Altogether we do not know a more attractive book for the study of a language difficult indeed of mastery, but inexhaustible in its treasures."—*The Blundellian*, October, 1880.

J. S. Levin, Steam Printing Works, 2, Mark Lane Square, E.C.

www.ingramcontent.com/pod-product-compliance
Lightning Source LLC
Chambersburg PA
CBHW030756230426
43667CB00007B/990